North Pole
Spitzbergen
Nova Zembla
North Cape
Arctic Circle
Gulf of Obe
Lena R.
OKHOTSK SEA
L. Baikal
Jesso I.
Niphon I.
Sea of Aral
TURKESTAN
Black S.
MEDITERRANEAN SEA
PRUSSIA
AUSTRIA
TUNIS
TRIPOLI
Isthmus of Suez
Tropic of Cancer
SAHARA OR GREAT DESERT
EGYPT
PERSIA
AFGHAN-ISTAN
BELOO-CHISTAN
Persian Gulf
Himalaya Mts
HINDOSTAN
Hoang Ho
Yang tse Kiang R.
Formosa
Ladrone Islands
Luzon I.
PHILIPPINE ISLANDS
CHINA SEA
BAY OF BENGAL
ARABIAN SEA
NUBIA
SENEGAM-BIA
Kong Mts
L. Tchad
UPR GUINEA
Mt Cameroons
GULF OF GUINEA
Strait of Bab el Mandeb
Socotra
C. Guardafui
C. Comorin
Ceylon
Mindanao
Caroline Is
Albert Nyanza L.
Victoria Nyanza L.
Equator
Longitude East from Greenwich
C. Lopez
Ascension I.
L. Tanganyika
L. Dilolo
L. Nyassa
Zambezi R.
INDIAN
Equatorial Current
Java
Borneo
New Ireland
New Britain
New Guinea
Gulf of Carpentaria
St Helena
L. Ngami
Bourbon
Mauritius
Tropic of Capricorn
North West Cape
AUSTRALIA
Orange R.
CAPE COLONY
Cape of Good Hope
C. Leeuwin
Kerguelen I.
Van Diemens Land or Tasmania
Bass Strait
Antarctic Circle
Enderby's Land
ANTARCTIC CONTINENT
ANTARCTIC OCEAN
South Pole
South Frigid Zone

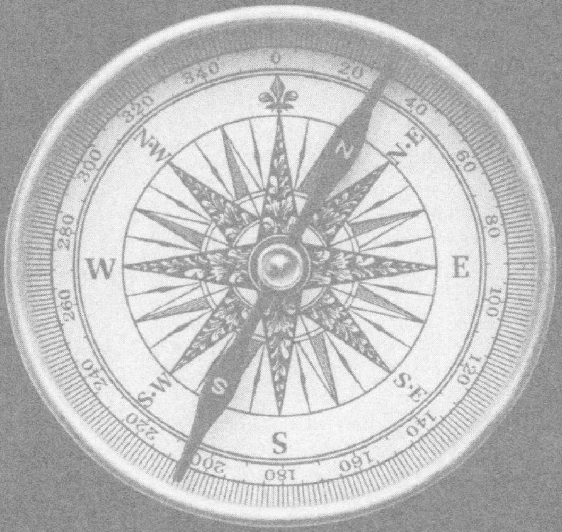
0
20
40
N.E
60
80
E
100
120
S.E
140
160
180
S
200
220
S.W
240
260
W
280
300
N.W
320
340

TREASURES OF

WORLD HISTORY

To our children and grandchildren

THIS IS A WELBECK BOOK

First published in 2020 by Welbeck
an imprint of Welbeck Non-Fiction Limited,
part of the Welbeck Publishing Group
20 Mortimer Street
London
W1T 3JW

Printed in Dubai

A CIP catalogue for this book is available from the British Library

ISBN: 978 0 233 00604 8

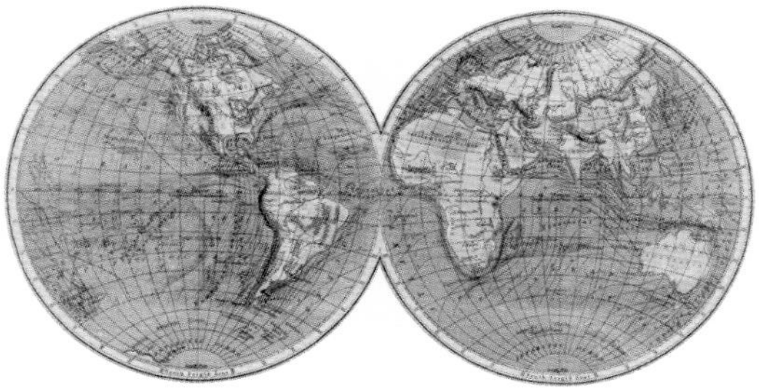

TREASURES OF

WORLD HISTORY

THE STORY OF CIVILIZATION
TOLD THROUGH ITS
50 MOST IMPORTANT DOCUMENTS

PETER SNOW
& ANN MACMILLAN

FOREWORD BY
DAN SNOW

WELBECK

Contents

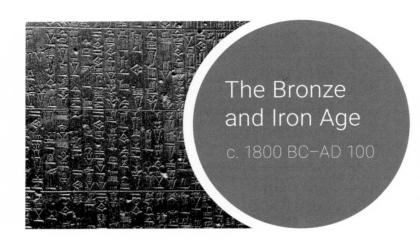

The Bronze and Iron Age

c. 1800 BC–AD 100

Medieval and Early Modern Period

c. 600–1648

The Age of Revolution

1776–1893

The 20th Century and Beyond

1903–present

Foreword by Dan Snow

Nothing beats the original. We can summon up anything now. The entire output of five millennia of human intellectual and creative endeavour is on your screen in an instant. That makes the original documents even more special. They are far more than their transcript, more than just an assemblage of words. They are a product of people, artists and thinkers, they belong to a certain time and place.

Their history and context are illuminated through their physical character. The odd juxtaposition of rough rock and polished intricacy of the Rosetta Stone, the delicacy of the Dead Sea Scrolls, the organized, channelled rage of the Declaration of Independence – even plans for the Beatles' legendary tour of North America scrawled on the back of an envelope are all treasures. Not just for their content, but for their form.

Their value is immensely increased by hindsight, by the knowledge of what these documents, stories, speeches and arguments drove people to do. We are the only animal on the planet that will lay down its life for an idea. A plan, a religion, an appeal made by someone we will never meet, who may well be long dead. We can be persuaded to donate money or vote for policies that will adversely affect us by words, poetry and music. The treasures selected in the following pages have inspired, overwhelmed, illuminated, mobilized ever since they were first written, carved or set in print. They have helped to construct the invisible infrastructure of laws, convention, ethics and belief that encase us. They have provided some understanding of the universe that, by an as yet undiscovered mystery, we find ourselves inhabiting. The impact of some has faded, but others retain their allure. The Declaration of Independence, for example, has never lost its centrality as the well-spring of the American republic and Mary Wollstonecraft's assertion of women's equality is, if anything, more influential than at any time since it was published.

It is strange and wonderful to see your childhood laid out in book form. The two distinguished authors who have selected these treasures are mum and dad to me. They are sharing the books, maps, stories and music that mean the most to them and unsurprisingly therefore they are very familiar to me. We listened to Beethoven's Fifth Symphony on car journeys to and from sites of historical interest. We knew the Gettysburg Address, the words of Nelson Mandela and the diary of Anne Frank intimately. These treasures are universal, but they are also particular, woven into the stories of families and communities. Each is given meaning by the hopes and customs of the reader. They belong to all of humanity, but also to ourselves, every single one of us.

November 2019

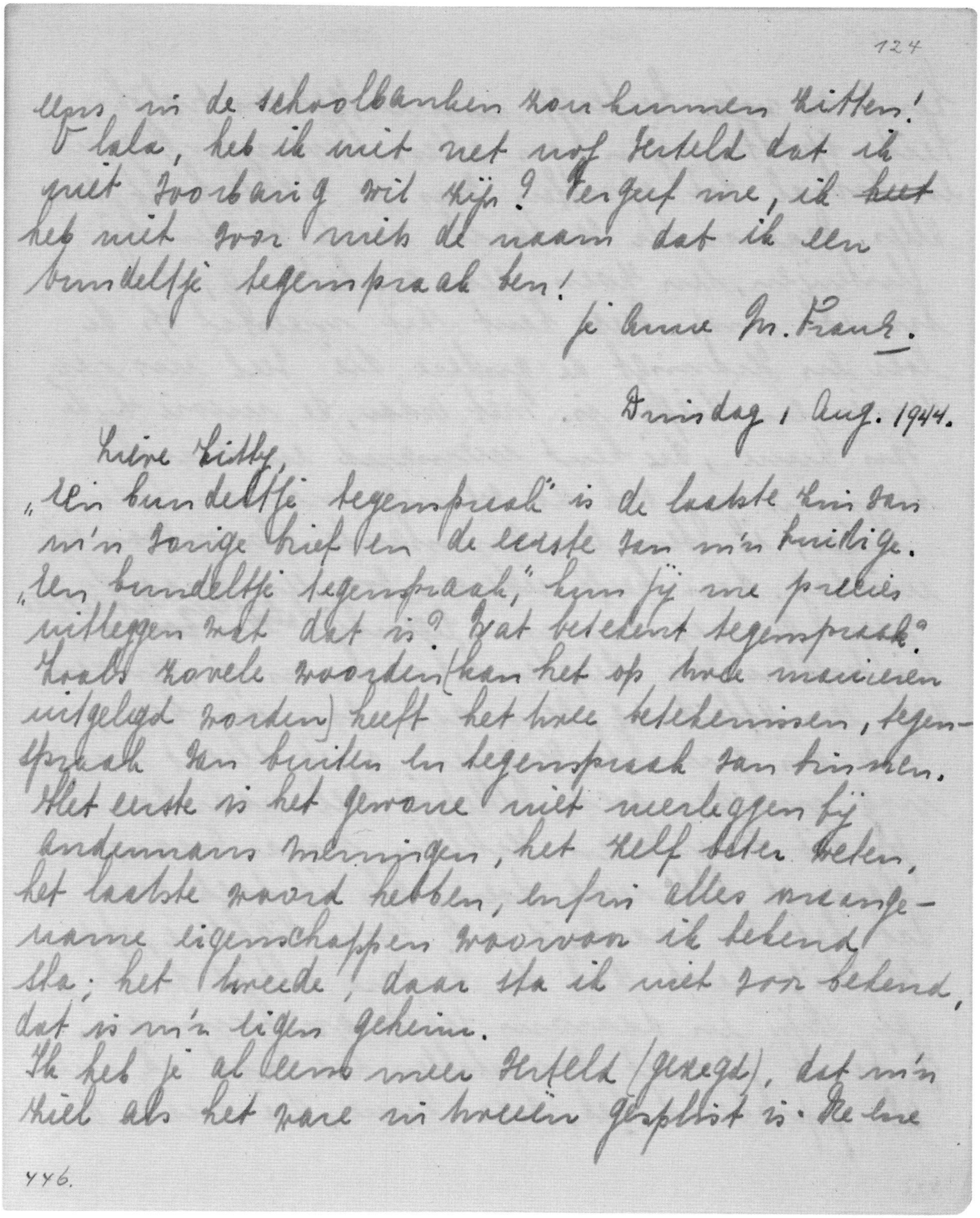

124

eens, in de schoolbanken zou kunnen zitten!
O lala, heb ik niet net nog verteld dat ik niet voorbarig wil zijn? Vergeef me, ik ~~heet~~ heb niet voor niets de naam dat ik een bundeltje tegenspraak ben!

je Anne M. Frank.

Dinsdag 1 Aug. 1944.

Lieve Kitty,

„Een bundeltje tegenspraak" is de laatste zin van m'n vorige brief en de eerste van m'n huidige. „Een bundeltje tegenspraak," kun jij me precies uitleggen wat dat is? Wat betekent tegenspraak? Zoals zovele woorden (kan het op twee manieren uitgelegd worden) heeft het twee betekenissen, tegenspraak van buiten en tegenspraak van binnen. Het eerste is het gewone niet neerleggen bij andermans meningen, het zelf beter weten, het laatste woord hebben, enfin alles onaangename eigenschappen waarvan ik bekend sta; het tweede, daar sta ik niet voor bekend, dat is m'n eigen geheim.
Ik heb je al eens meer verteld (gezegd), dat m'n ziel als het ware in tweeën gesplitst is. De ene

446.

A page from the diary of Anne Frank dated 1 August 1944 (see p. 170).

NORTH PACIFIC OCEAN
NORTH ATLANTIC OCEAN
ARCTIC OCEAN
NORTH AMERICA
CANADA
UNITED STATES
ALASKA
GULF OF ALASKA
BERING SEA
Aleutian Islands
BEAUFORT SEA
Queen Elizabeth Islands
BAFFIN BAY
Baffin Island
Greenland
GREENLAND SEA
NORWEGIAN SEA
ICELAND
Reykjavík
LABRADOR SEA
Nuuk
HUDSON BAY
NORTHWEST TERRITORIES
NUNAVUT
Yellowknife
Whitehorse
Juneau
Fairbanks
Anchorage
Edmonton
Winnipeg
Regina
Minneapolis
Chicago
Ottawa
Montreal
Toronto
New York
Washington, DC
Halifax
Hebron
Newfoundland
Bermuda
Azores
San Francisco
Portland
Seattle
Boise
Denver
Vancouver
EAST SIBERIAN SEA
LAPTEV SEA
KARA SEA
BARENTS SEA
Svalbard
Novaya Zemlya
SEA OF OKHOTSK
Kuril Islands
Hokkaido
Honshu
JAPAN
Vladivostok
RUSSIA
SIBERIA
Noril'sk
Salekhard
Arkhangelsk
Vorkuta
Moscow
Yekaterinburg
Omsk
Tomsk
Novosibirsk
Bratsk
Irkutsk
Chita
Qiqihar
Harbin
Changchun
Beijing
Hohhot
Ulaanbaatar
MONGOLIA
GOBI
ASIA
CHINA
KAZAKHSTAN
Astana
Karaganda
Almaty
Urumqi
UZBEKISTAN
TURKMENISTAN
KYRGYZSTAN
TAJIKISTAN
AFGHANISTAN
IRAN
EUROPE
UNITED KINGDOM
IRELAND
London
NORWAY
SWEDEN
FINLAND
DENMARK
FRANCE
Bordeaux
PORTUGAL
Lisbon
SPAIN
GIBRALTAR
Rabat
MOROCCO
ALGERIA
LIBYA
Tripoli
Rome
UKRAINE
TURKEY

Introduction

The success of *Treasures of British History* written by Peter and our son Dan has inspired us to widen our horizons. Our lifetime experience as journalists makes us relish the challenge of selecting and researching the 50 documents which best illustrate global history. This time our canvas is the whole world. We began with around 200 texts and had lively arguments about how to trim the list down. In the end we agreed on a broad sweep across 4,000 years and all five continents.

We start in ancient Babylon with a law-giver's decrees and end with today's very latest revelations about the immensity of the universe. Many of our discoveries come from Europe and North America but we also embrace countries as far apart as China, South Africa and Australia.

Some of these documents changed the course of history, such as Britain's Magna Carta, the Tennis Court Oath which sparked the French Revolution, and the American Declaration of Independence. The visionary notes and sketches of Leonardo da Vinci and the collected works in Shakespeare's First Folio are milestones in art and literature. We celebrate leaps in technology with the ingenuity of Brunel's marine engineering and Berners Lee's World Wide Web. Einstein's Theory of Relativity and the discovery of the structure of DNA are examples of explosive breakthroughs in science. Equally revolutionary are Mary Wollstonecraft's bold demand for women's rights and the 270 metre (885 foot) long petition which led to New Zealand becoming the first country to give women the vote. For us, two landmarks crucial to the history of war and peace, are the Treaty of Westphalia which set the standard for ending conflicts and a map of D-Day, the largest amphibious invasion ever. To rule out no field of human expression we include the briskly pencilled poem that inspired the US national anthem, the original rules of English football and the names of cities scrawled on an envelope that led to a record-breaking Beatles tour.

Some of our documents could have been lost forever. The touching inscription on Tutankhamun's chalice and the scattered pages of Anne Frank's diary survive only by chance. Others narrowly missed being published. Both Copernicus and Darwin had to overcome their fear of offending Christian beliefs.

Writing this book made us question what constitutes a document. For Peter, the lines of the graph of Neil Armstrong's heartbeat as he landed on the moon were more striking than the rather dry lines of Apollo 11's official report. Ann insisted on including an artist's sketch of Coco Chanel's pioneering fashions.

What you see here are very much our personal choices. You, our readers, may disagree and we hope that will lead you to think of what your selection would be. After all, human civilization is so rich in treasures that there are countless documents which could fill this book. It is a constant source of astonishment to us that our world contains such an abundance.

Peter Snow and Ann MacMillan,
December 2019

The Bronze and Iron Age

c. 1800 BC–AD 100

1

Hammurabi's Code

As one of the earliest examples of a complete written legal system, Hammurabi's Code is a key part of the framework of civilization. It contains 282 edicts of the Babylonian King Hammurabi, who ruled Mesopotamia. These laws were carved on a stele around 1750 BC, perhaps one of the earliest examples of something "written in stone", unable to be altered. Hammurabi's Code covers everything from trade, workers' pay and property to marriage, adultery and inheritance. It set legal precedents such as "innocent until proven guilty" which still survive today.

RIGHT The laws of Hammurabi are inscribed on a stone block or "stele" 2.25 metres (7 feet 4 inches) high. Discovered by French archaeologists digging in Iran in 1901, it is now on display at the Louvre Museum in Paris.

OPPOSITE The 282 laws are written in cuneiform script in Akkadian, a Babylonian language. Law 196 states that "if a man put out the eye of another man, his eye shall be put out." It is the earliest example of "lex talonis", the law of retaliation.

When members of a French archaeological expedition in 1901 dug up three pieces of black stone in the ancient city of Susa in Persia (modern-day Iran), they could hardly have imagined that they had unearthed one of the world's oldest and most important treasures. Now in the Louvre Museum in Paris, the broken stone plaque or "stele" of Hammurabi, king of ancient Babylon from 1792 to 1750 BC, resembles a giant finger pointing to the sky. Made of diorite, it is 2.25 metres (7 feet 4 inches) high and surmounted by an engraving of Hammurabi with Shamash, the ancient Mesopotamian god of the sun, justice, morality and truth. Sixteen columns of cuneiform (wedge-shaped) script are carved onto the front, 28 columns on the back. The code is written in Akkadian, the everyday language of the Babylonian Empire, so that it could be widely read and understood.

King Hammurabi was a great warrior who expanded Babylon from a city state to include the whole of Mesopotamia along the fertile Euphrates and Tigris river valleys. He insisted that people of different cultures in the territories he conquered lived together in peace. In the stele's text, Hammurabi calls himself "the protecting king", who wrote down laws so that "the strong might not injure the weak, in order to protect the widows and orphans ... to settle all disputes and heal all injuries". He states that his laws aim "to bring about the rule of righteousness in the land, to destroy the wicked and the evil-doers ... and to enlighten the land, to further the well-being of man". There are 282 laws in all, mainly to do with business, property and family. They had a profound effect on Hammurabi's subjects and throughout history.

The code includes one of the earliest examples of an accused person being considered innocent until proven guilty. There is a ground-breaking provision for people in a

Map showing the Babylonian territory upon Hammurabi's ascension in c.1792 BC and upon his death in c.1750 BC

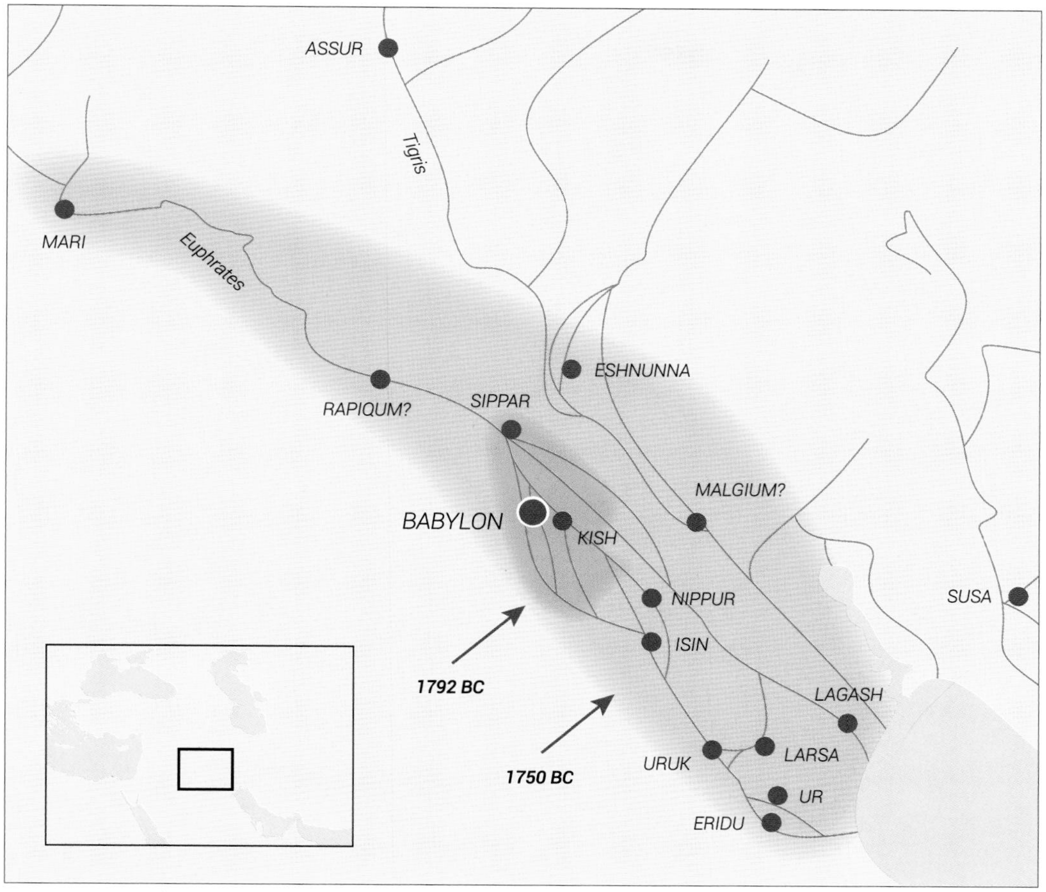

dispute to appear before a judge, with witnesses to back their claims. Minimum wages are set: for example field labourers and herdsmen are entitled to "eight gur [1 gur = 303 litres] of corn per year", while an ox-driver or sailor received just six. The laws mention three social classes: "man"; "freed man"; and "slave". Doctors are paid according to the class of their patients. Law 221 reads: "If a physician heals the broken bone or diseased soft part of a man, the patient shall pay the physician five shekels." Law 223 says: "If he were a slave his owner shall pay the physician two shekels." The code also lists punishments, many of them brutal. If a son hits his father, his hand is to be cut off. If a son rejects his adoptive parents, his tongue must be cut out. A wet nurse whose charge dies while she feeds another baby would have her breast removed. Incest between mother and son leads to both being burned to death (while a father committing incest with his daughter is simply exiled). Twenty-eight crimes, including adultery, robbery, perjury and witchcraft, carry the death sentence.

Most importantly, the code contains early examples of "lex talionis", the law of retribution – the familiar "eye for an eye" principle of the Old Testament. Law 196 states: "If a man put out the eye of another man, his eye shall be put out." The severity of punishments again varies according to the social class of the offender. Under Law 199, for example, "If he put out the eye of a man's slave ... he shall pay half of its [the slave's] value."

Historians believe that invading forces seized the stele bearing Hammurabi's Code from the Babylonian city of Sippar in the twelfth century BC and carried it to Susa, where it somehow survived the centuries. When it was discovered in AD 1901, it was believed to be the oldest written list of laws in the world. Since then, evidence of earlier codes dating back to the twenty-first century BC have come to light, but they are not nearly as comprehensive as Hammurabi's Code. His laws clearly continued to have an influence: fragments of them have been found on fifth-century BC clay tablets in the Middle East, 1,300 years after the reign of Hammurabi. However illiberal many of his laws may sound to us, they remain the earliest comprehensive code of rules in human history. Today Hammurabi's image appears alongside those of other historic lawgivers in the chamber of the US House of Representatives in the US Congress, the US Supreme Court and in law courts around the world.

OPPOSITE An engraving at the top of the stele shows Hammurabi (standing) receiving the laws from Shamash, the ancient Mesopotamian god of the sun, justice, morality and truth. In the text on the stele Hammurabi declares that his laws aim "to bring about the rule of righteousness in the land."

2

Tutankhamun's Wishing Cup

This treasure was the first object British archaeologist Howard Carter spotted when he opened the famous tomb of Tutankhamun in the Valley of the Kings in 1922. The cup, promising the young king eternal life, bears the inscription: "May your spirit live, may you spend millions of years, you who love Thebes, sitting with your face to the north wind, your eyes beholding happiness." The tomb dates from c.1330 BC and was arguably the greatest archaeological discovery of all time.

The British archaeologist Howard Carter was a rather shy man, but he was as persistent and obsessive as a terrier. He'd been scouring Egypt for treasures from the past since the 1890s, and by 1922 he was exploring the Valley of the Kings, that haunting place we've both – like many others – been captivated by on our travels in Upper Egypt. Up to that time, Carter and all other archaeologists had found every royal tomb empty. But there was one Egyptian pharaoh whose tomb no one had yet found – the short-lived boy-king Tutankhamun, who died towards the end of the fourteenth century BC. Carter's determination to find it was as strong as ever, but his wealthy financial backer, Lord Carnarvon, was losing his patience; if the tomb was not found after one more season, he told Carter, then funding would be revoked.

One day, a little boy carrying water for Carter's team accidentally discovered a stone step beside the entrance to the vast empty tomb of Ramses VI. It was the morning of 4 November 1922. With mounting excitement, Carter had his team clear what turned out to be 16 steps leading down to a doorway. It was marked with the cartouche, or signature, of Tutankhamun, and beyond it was a passage that led to another door. Carter described in his

OPPOSITE The first room – the Antechamber – exactly as the British archaeologist Howard Carter saw it when he opened the tomb. It is stashed with furniture and other items to accompany Tutankhamun into the next life.

OPPOSITE ABOVE The alabaster Wishing Cup in the shape of a lotus flower. The king's titles are in the square, and circling the top is the inscription wishing Tutankhamun eternal life.

diary the immense excitement that followed when he and Lord Carnarvon entered the tomb on 26 November: "Feverishly we cleared away the remaining last scraps of rubbish until we had only the clean sealed doorway before us. We made a tiny breach in the top left-hand corner to see what was beyond."

With the help of a candle, Carter peered through the hole he had made.

Lord Carnarvon said to me: "Can you see anything?" I replied to him: "Yes, it is wonderful." I then with precaution made the hole sufficiently large for both of us to see. With the light of an electric torch as well as an additional candle we looked in. Our sensations and astonishment are difficult to describe as the better light revealed to us the marvellous collection of treasures. Our sensations were bewildering and full of strange emotion.

What they were seeing were the fabulously rich contents of a royal tomb that had remained hidden for nearly 3,400 years. It was their first glimpse of more than 5,500 items – some of them made of gold and adorned with jewellery. They had been packed into four small rooms surrounding Tutankhamun's mummified body to provide him with all he would need in the next world, where it was believed he would live for ever. One of the very first objects that Carter came upon was the elegant alabaster Wishing Cup, whose brief inscription wishing the king an afterlife of "millions of years" seems to us to give the clearest meaning to this magnificent burial.

The climax of Carter's discovery was Tutankhamun himself. Four shrines – one inside the other – covered the sarcophagus, which itself contained three coffins packed within each other. The final coffin, made of solid gold, contained the mummy of the king, his head wrapped in bejewelled bandages and resting inside the most stunning and now world-famous gold mask.

You can see all these treasures from 2020 onwards, just as Carter and Carnarvon saw them, in the new Grand Egyptian Museum at

Giza near Cairo. We spent a whole day in the old Cairo Museum enraptured not just by the unimaginable opulence of the tomb's contents but also by the quality of the workmanship. This period of Egyptian history, towards the end of the eighteenth dynasty, which lasted from around 1550 to 1290 BC, represented the flowering of ancient Egyptian art, much of it embodied in the Tutankhamun treasure.

Tutankhamun's life and death also mark one of the most dramatic moments in Egypt's history. Some of the details are still debatable, but it seems he was the son of Amenophis IV, whose unique contribution to Egyptian history was that he condensed the great pantheon of Egyptian gods to just one, the sun-god Aten, and built himself a new capital called Akhetaten, now known as Amarna – a ruin on the east bank of the Nile. Tutankhamun inherited the throne at the age of nine or ten, married his half-sister and, plagued by malaria and other disabilities, died after a reign of only nine years. He began life under what the Egyptian priestly establishment saw as his father's heresy of believing in just one god, and he was persuaded to return to the old orthodoxy and to move the capital back to Thebes. Even though Tutankhamun's short reign was not marked by any act of great distinction, his burial has assured him everlasting fame.

OPPOSITE The gold mask that crowned the king's mummified body weighs 10 kg (22 lb) and is made of gold inlaid with precious stones. The eyes are quartz, the pupils obsidian. Carter described it as "placid but beautiful".

RIGHT Howard Carter opens the door of the second of the four golden shrines that protected the king's body.

3

The *I Ching*

The *I Ching*, also known as the Book of Changes, is one of the oldest and best-known Chinese books and is still consulted widely today. Scholars believe that it came into being as a divination manual more than 3,000 years ago and was used to predict the future. Over successive centuries, scholars, poets, philosophers and kings added their thoughts to this book of wisdom. Although open to various interpretations, it is viewed as an essential guide to the universe and has had a major impact on Eastern thought.

RIGHT Bamboo strips covered in ancient Chinese text dating back to 300 BC. They form the earliest known version of the I Ching*, a divination manual used to predict the future.*

OPPOSITE The Chinese philosopher Confucius, surrounded by followers, consults the I Ching*. He reportedly replaced the binding of his copy three times because he used it so much.*

In 1994, an extraordinary manuscript turned up in a Hong Kong antiques market. It had been looted by grave-robbers from a burial site in the ancient state of Chu (eighth to third century BC) in central China. Consisting of 58 bamboo strips covered in ancient Chinese script, the manuscript is now in the Shanghai Museum. It is the oldest known version of the *I Ching*, dating from around 300 BC, but archaeological discoveries confirm that the text's origins go back long before that.

The *I Ching*'s early history is shrouded in mystery. Legend suggests it was created by the first mythical emperor of China, Fu Xi, who was half man, half serpent. The more solid evidence of oracle bones (the inscribed shoulder bones of oxen or turtle shells) indicates that it originated with diviners who answered individuals' questions about the future. The questions ranged from family and business matters to the best time to plant a crop. The diviner carved the questions on the bones or shells, heated them until cracks appeared, and then worked out the answers from the pattern of the cracks. A solid crack or line (yang) meant "yes", a broken one (yin) meant "no". As time passed, this simple divination system became more sophisticated. A single line was replaced by a trigram (three lines stacked on top of each other). There were eight possible combinations of broken and unbroken lines in a trigram, so eight possible answers to each question.

It is thought that the *I Ching* was further refined around 1050 BC, when Emperor Wen, founder of the Zhou dynasty, changed the three-line trigrams to six-line hexagrams. This increased the number of possible outcomes – combinations of solid and broken lines – to 64. Advice was written to accompany each

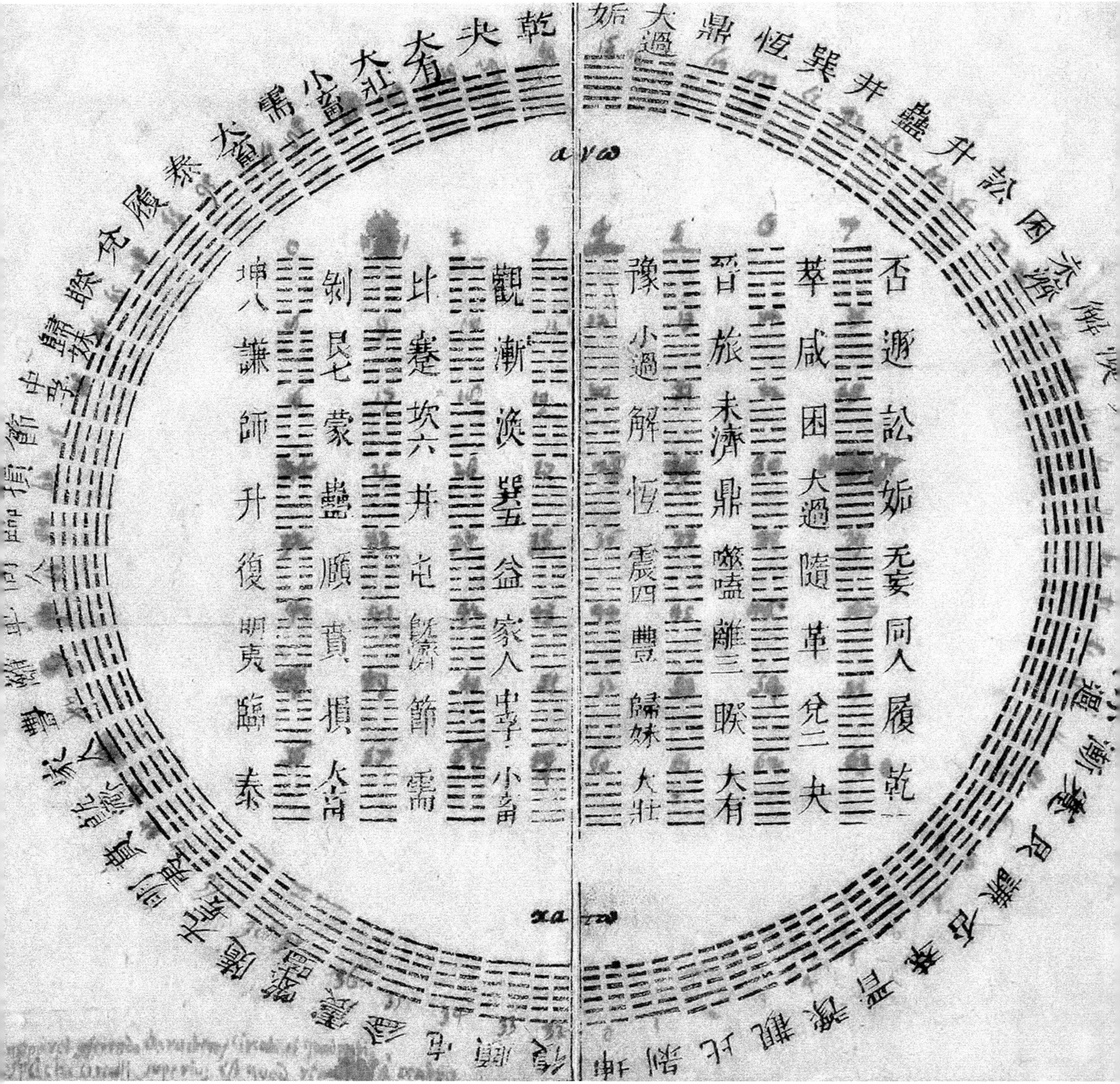

否 遯 訟 姤 无妄 同人 履 乾一
萃 咸 困 大過 隨 革 兌二 夬
晉 旅 未濟 鼎 噬嗑 離三 睽 大有
豫 小過 解 恆 震四 豐 歸妹 大壯
觀 漸 渙 巽五 益 家人 中孚 小畜
比 蹇 坎六 井 屯 既濟 節 需
剝 艮七 蒙 蠱 頤 賁 損 大畜
坤八 謙 師 升 復 明夷 臨 泰
乾 夬 大有 大壯 小畜 需 大畜 泰 履 兌 睽
姤 大過 鼎 恆 巽 井 蠱 升 訟 困 未濟 解

hexagram; some urge perseverance, others recommend marriage or warn of misfortune. Wen's poet son, the Duke of Zhou, is said to have gone a step further and composed separate interpretations for each of the six lines of the hexagram.

The first written *I Ching* text probably appeared around 800 BC, based on oral accounts from the past. By 300 BC, philosophical and ethical comments known as the Ten Wings were added to the *I Ching*, transforming it from a divination manual into a book of wisdom – a handbook on how to live a positive and meaningful life through self-knowledge and self-improvement. Most experts have discounted the theory that the Ten Wings were written by the great philosopher Confucius, but it is said that he consulted his copy of the *I Ching* so often that the binding had to be replaced three times. Confucius said that if he lived for 100 more years, he would spend half of them studying the *I Ching*. The handbook in use today dates to 136 BC, when Emperor Wu of the Han dynasty combined various versions into one standard text.

As time passed, oracle bones gave way to more accessible fortune-telling aids. Instead of going to a diviner, questioners could use items like coins, as people still do today when they consult the *I Ching*. Three coins are tossed six times. After each toss, solid or broken lines are drawn based on how the coins land. After six tosses, a hexagram corresponding to one of the 64 in the *I Ching* is created and the questioner can refer to the handbook to receive the advice that accompanies that particular hexagram; however, the problem remains of how to interpret this advice.

The *I Ching* draws on myth, proverbs, philosophy, history and poetry to explain the world. It has dominated life and thought in China and other parts of Asia for 3,000 years. Both branches of Chinese philosophy – Confucianism and Daoism – have been influenced by the *I Ching*, but it only reached Western consciousness in the late seventeenth century, when it was translated by Jesuit missionaries working in China.

Many modern trailblazers have turned to the *I Ching* for inspiration. Singer-songwriter Bob Dylan called it "the only thing that is amazingly true, period ... besides being a great book to believe in, it's also very fantastic poetry." The lyrics of the Beatles and Pink Floyd reflect the *I Ching*, as do the works of novelists such as Herman Hesse, Douglas Adams and Philip Pullman. But perhaps the final word on this encyclopaedia of oracles should go to the eleventh-century Chinese philosopher Cheng Yi: "*I Ching* is grand in its scope; it is all-encompassing. To those who contemplate its depth and practise its discipline, the text will provide everything."

OPPOSITE The I Ching *hexagram sent to the German mathematician Gottfried Wilhelm Leibniz by a Jesuit missionary in China. It became a model for Leibniz's new binary number system.*

ABOVE These ancient Chinese coins were tossed to get an I Ching *reading. They replaced the more cumbersome method of examining cracks in heated animal bones. Coins are still used today when consulting the* I Ching.

4

The *Mahabharata*

The *Mahabharata* has been described as an ancient encyclopaedia of Indian knowledge. One of the world's oldest and longest epic poems, it is to us the most important work of Indian literature ever written. It played a central role in the development of Hindu culture and has been ranked alongside the Bible, the Koran and the works of Homer and Shakespeare as one of world civilization's most influential manuscripts.

RIGHT A sixteenth-century Indian painting of a scene from the Mahabharata, *the ancient poem about a royal family's power struggle. It shows Prince Arjuna (centre), a leader of the Pandava family, racing towards the enemy Kaurava force in his chariot.*

When a dramatized version of the *Mahabharata* was shown on Indian television in 1998, streets around the country emptied. Entire communities crowded around TV sets to watch the mesmerizing and very familiar tale of two branches of a royal family locked in a bloody struggle to control ancient India. It took 139 episodes to capture the poem's nearly two million words.

The *Mahabharata* originated as an oral poem sometime around the eighth century BC. It was recited and enhanced by priests, professional story-tellers, singers and dance troupes. The first reference to the poem as a written

document was around the fourth century BC, but it was not until AD 350, more than 700 years later, that the *Mahabharata* became a unified text, written in Sanskrit, India's classical language. Some historians believe the work is based on a conflict that occurred during India's Vedic period (1500 to 500 BC). Its central tale is a bitter fight between two sets of cousins: the Pandavas and the Kauravas. Both are out to control the Bharata kingdom in northern India. Exactly who created the *Mahabharata* is not clear, but it is traditionally said to have been Vyasa, also known as Krishna, the great sage who Hindus believe is immortal. He plays a central role in the poem as grandfather to the warring cousins. A Hindu legend claims Vyasa narrated the epic to Ganesha, the elephant-headed deity, who wrote it down with one of his tusks.

The poem is made up of around 100,000 couplets and prose passages encompassing a great range of subjects. History, philosophy

LEFT A seventeenth-century painting of the Pandava prince Arjuna with his charioteer, the god Krishna, on horseback.

BELOW A copy of the Mahabharata *open at the Bhagavad Gita, one of the most revered texts of Hinduism. In its 700 verses, the god Krishna shares his philosophical beliefs with warrior Prince Arjuna.*

OPPOSITE A ninth-century depiction of the epic Battle of Kurukshetra, which lasted for 18 days. Soldiers ride into battle on horses and elephants.

and spiritual ideas are woven through the saga of the Pandava and Kaurava rivals. It bristles with romance, intrigue, chivalry, ethical conundrums and has numerous subplots. No wonder it has been dubbed an ancient version of *Game of Thrones*.

At the heart of the *Mahabharata* are 700 verses known as the *Bhagavad Gita*, or the *Gita*, one of the most revered texts of Hinduism. Most experts believe the *Gita* was composed later than the rest of the *Mahabharata*, probably after the third century BC – an unsettled period when the ethics of war were a preoccupation. It is a dialogue between Arjuna, a Pandava prince, and his charioteer Krishna, who gradually reveals himself to be a god. It takes place just before a momentous battle with the Kaurava family. Arjuna suddenly has doubts about killing his cousins and friends and he asks Krishna what to do. Krishna advises Arjuna to fulfil his dharma: to be true to his duty as a warrior. For one of the first times in Indian literature, there is a discussion about what constitutes a "just war". Krishna tells Arjuna that once a war breaks out, it should be fought if it is for a good cause. Krishna also offers insights about the purpose of life, reincarnation and many other philosophical and religious matters. Short and coherent, the *Gita* was easily understood by all social classes and it became a popular guide to Hindu duty, morality and salvation.

Prince Arjuna decides that it is his duty to fight, and one quarter of the *Mahabharata* is dedicated to recounting the cataclysmic 18-day Battle of Kurukshetra. Nearly four million soldiers from all over India take part in the conflict. The Kaurava army has eleven divisions; Arjuna's Pandava force has seven. They fight with arrows, swords, lances and maces. Nearly everyone on the battlefield dies. On one day alone, the poem describes how Prince Arjuna destroys a battle formation of huge numbers of chariots, elephants, cavalry and infantry. Both sides resort to tricks and deceit in the attempt to emerge victorious. In the end the Pandavas win the battle, but the appalling carnage makes it no cause for celebration. The poem's theme of the futility of war and violence has resonated with Indian leaders over centuries. It was a major influence on Mahatma Gandhi, who led India's non-violent independence movement against British rule in the early to mid-twentieth century.

The *Mahabharata* has been a source of entertainment as well as a spiritual guide ever since it was composed. It is still widely read, recited and performed in theatres, movies and on television. Children are still named after characters in the poem, and its messages remain as familiar today as they were thousands of years ago.

5

Homer's *Odyssey*

Homer's *Odyssey* is one of the greatest stories ever told. This fragment of papyrus dating from around 250 BC tells the story of the Greek hero Odysseus's adventurous voyage home to Ithaca. It was found in Egypt, which was part of the Greek-speaking Hellenistic world at that time. This tiny document demonstrates how Homer's poetry, which even then was 600 years old, has been preserved through the ages for future generations to read.

The story of the *Odyssey* has been told for nearly 3,000 years. Together with the *Iliad*, it has been a treasure of world literature since it was first compiled in around 700 BC. We say "compiled" because nobody knows who the author really was or how the narrative was passed down from generation to generation. We talk of someone called Homer who may have written these two great epics, but it is also possible that the captivating rhythm of the lines we read today is the gathering together of poems and songs conceived by different people in the early years of ancient Greece. Together, the *Iliad* and the *Odyssey* tell a story which may be truth or legend, or a mix of both, and comes from the earliest known period of Greek history.

Whatever its origins, the *Odyssey* recounts the heroic tale of the extraordinary adventures of the wily Greek warrior Odysseus (Ulysses in Latin) on his way back from the siege of Troy. The siege started when Paris, a Trojan prince, eloped to the city with the beautiful Helen, Queen of Sparta, and her furious husband Menelaus demanded that Troy be annihilated. The struggle between the attacking Greeks and the Trojan defenders, described in the *Iliad*, lasted 10 years. It ended in victory for the Greeks when Odysseus persuaded his compatriots to build a wooden horse and

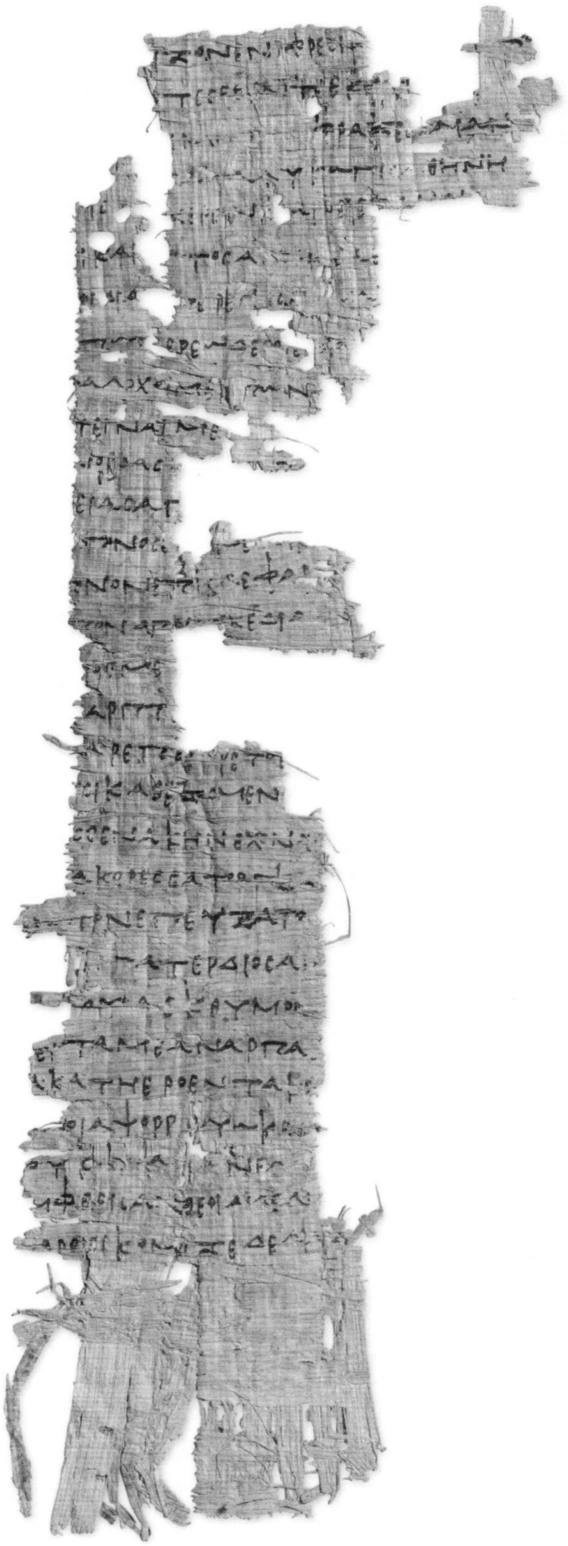

RIGHT The tiny fragment of a papyrus found in Egypt dating from around 250 BC. It is from Homer's Odyssey*, Book 20, lines 41–68. Odysseus confides in the goddess Athena.*

OPPOSITE The title page of George Chapman's 1616 translation. After reading it, the poet John Keats wrote: "Then felt I like some watcher of the skies. / When a new planet swims into his ken ..."

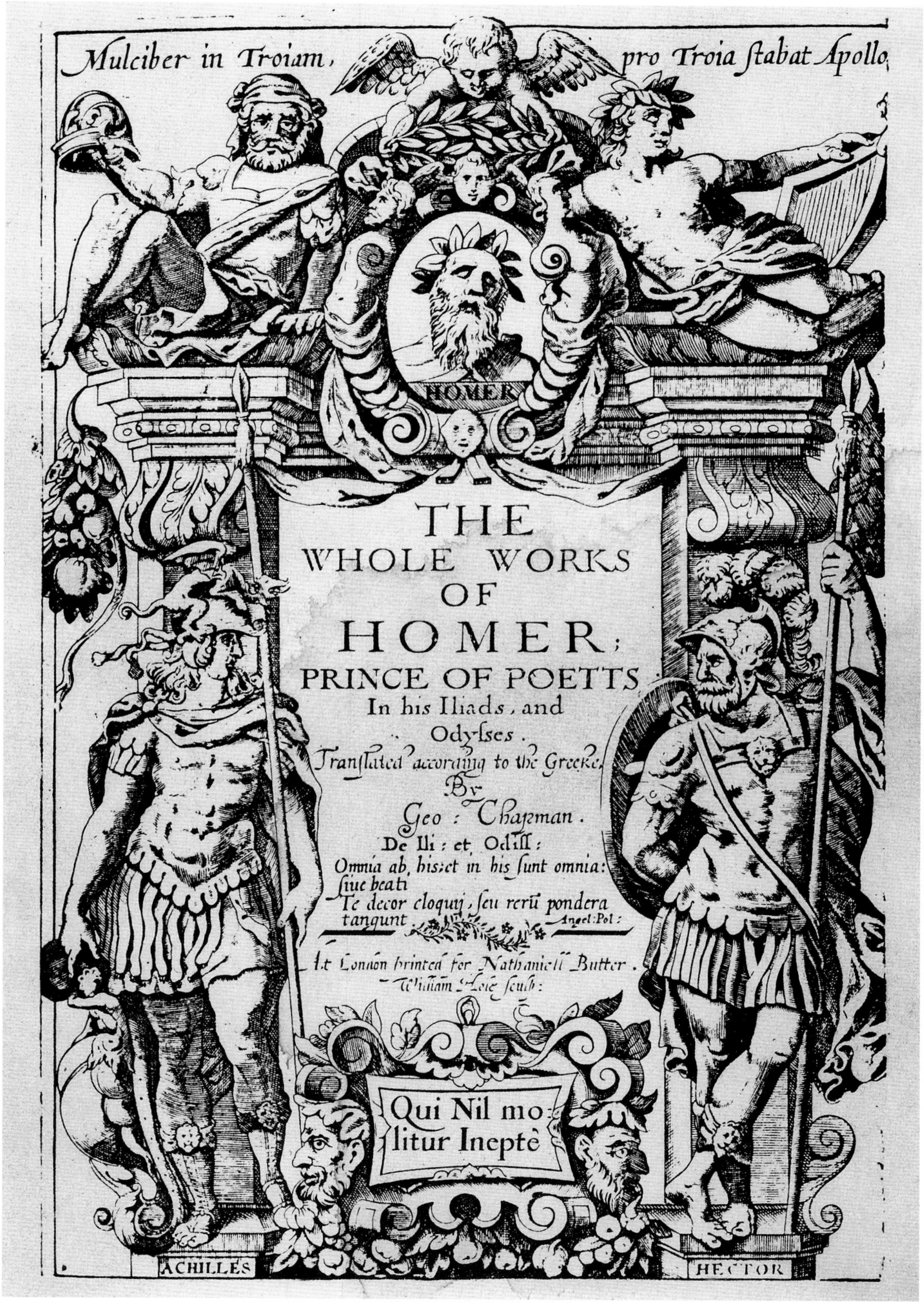
Mulciber in Troiam, pro Troia ſtabat Apollo
HOMER
THE
WHOLE WORKS
OF
HOMER;
PRINCE OF POETTS
In his Iliads, and
Odyſses.
Tranſlated according to the Greeke.
By
Geo: Chapman.
De Ili: et Odiſſ:
Omnia ab his: et in his ſunt omnia:
ſiue beati
Te decor eloquij, ſeu rerũ pondera
tangunt. Angel: Pol:
At London printed for Nathaniell Butter.
William Hole ſculp:
Qui Nil molitur Inepte
ACHILLES
HECTOR

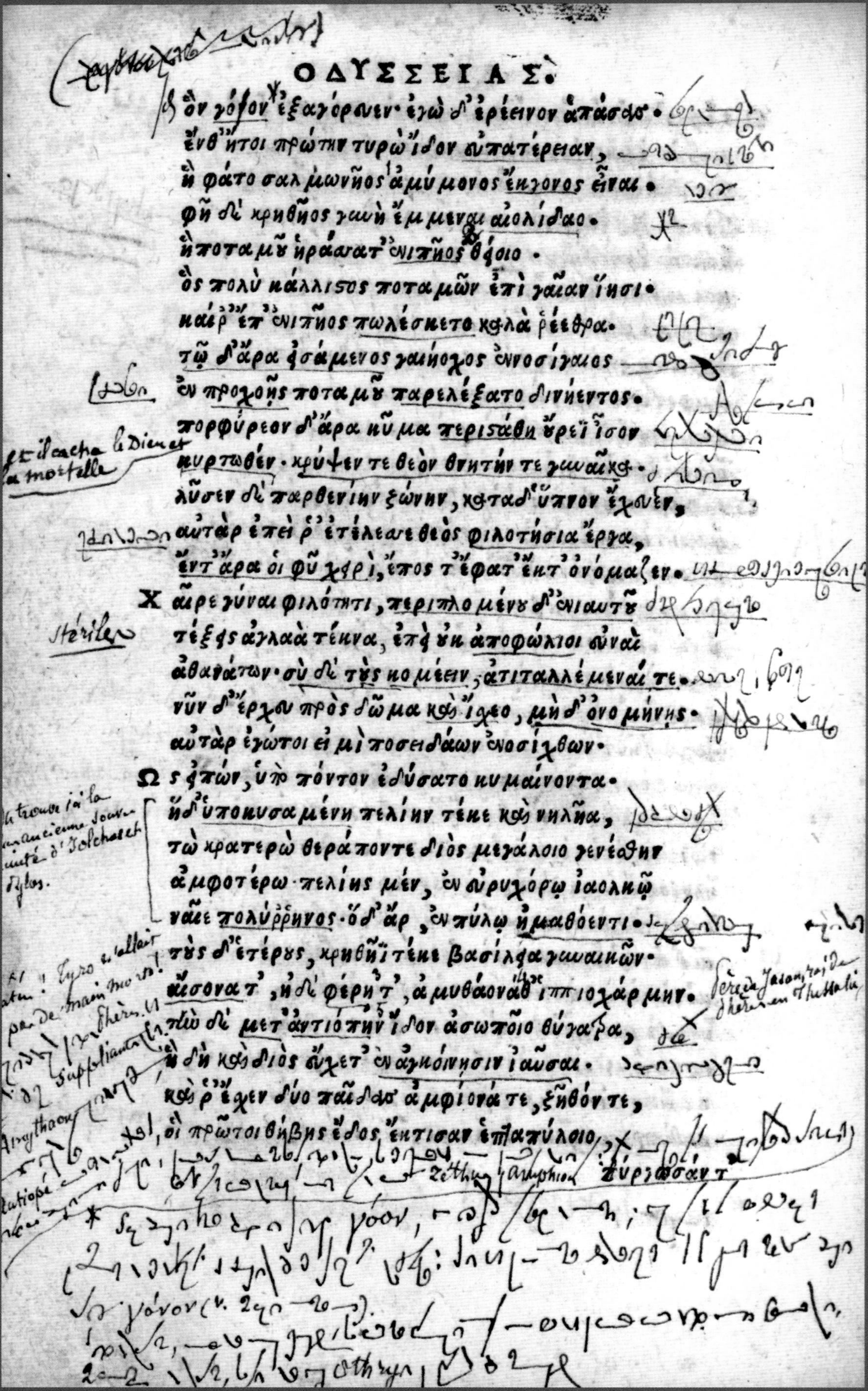

ΟΔΥΣΣΕΙΑΣ.

ὃν γόνον ἐξαγόρευεν· ἐγὼ δ' ἐρέεινον ἁπάσας.
ἔνθ' ἤτοι πρώτην Τυρὼ ἴδον εὐπατέρειαν,
ἣ φάτο Σαλμωνῆος ἀμύμονος ἔκγονος εἶναι·
φῆ δὲ Κρηθῆος γυνὴ ἔμμεναι Αἰολίδαο·
ἣ ποταμοῦ ἠράσσατ' Ἐνιπῆος θείοιο·
ὃς πολὺ κάλλιστος ποταμῶν ἐπὶ γαῖαν ἵησι·
καί ῥ' ἐπ' Ἐνιπῆος πωλέσκετο καλὰ ῥέεθρα.
τῷ δ' ἄρα ἐσάμενος γαιήοχος ἐννοσίγαιος
ἐν προχοῇς ποταμοῦ παρελέξατο δινήεντος·
πορφύρεον δ' ἄρα κῦμα περιστάθη οὔρεϊ ἶσον
κυρτωθέν· κρύψεν τε θεὸν θνητήν τε γυναῖκα·
λῦσεν δὲ παρθενίην ζώνην, κατὰ δ' ὕπνον ἔχευεν,
αὐτὰρ ἐπεί ῥ' ἐτέλεσσε θεὸς φιλοτήσια ἔργα,
ἔν τ' ἄρα οἱ φῦ χειρί, ἔπος τ' ἔφατ' ἔκ τ' ὀνόμαζεν·
Χαῖρε γύναι φιλότητι, περιπλομένου δ' ἐνιαυτοῦ
τέξεις ἀγλαὰ τέκνα, ἐπεὶ οὐκ ἀποφώλιοι εὐναὶ
ἀθανάτων· σὺ δὲ τοὺς κομέειν, ἀτιταλλέμεναί τε.
νῦν δ' ἔρχευ πρὸς δῶμα καὶ ἴσχεο, μηδ' ὀνομήνῃς·
αὐτὰρ ἐγώ τοί εἰμι Ποσειδάων ἐνοσίχθων.
Ὣς εἰπών, ὑπὸ πόντον ἐδύσατο κυμαίνοντα.
ἣ δ' ὑποκυσαμένη Πελίην τέκε καὶ Νηλῆα,
τὼ κρατερὼ θεράποντε Διὸς μεγάλοιο γενέσθην
ἀμφοτέρω· Πελίης μέν, ἐν εὐρυχόρῳ Ἰαολκῷ
ναῖε πολύρρηνος· ὁ δ' ἄρ', ἐν Πύλῳ ἠμαθόεντι.
τοὺς δ' ἑτέρους, Κρηθῆϊ τέκε βασίλεια γυναικῶν·
Αἴσονά τ', ἠδὲ Φέρητ', Ἀμυθάονά θ' ἱππιοχάρμην.
τὴν δὲ μετ' Ἀντιόπην ἴδον Ἀσωποῖο θύγατρα,
ἣ δὴ καὶ Διὸς εὔχετ' ἐν ἀγκοίνῃσιν ἰαῦσαι.
καί ῥ' ἔτεκεν δύο παῖδας Ἀμφίονά τε, Ζῆθόν τε,
οἳ πρῶτοι Θήβης ἕδος ἔκτισαν ἑπταπύλοιο,

OPPOSITE A much-annotated sixteenth-century Venetian text of the Odyssey, *Book 11, lines 234–63. Odysseus recounts meeting the ghosts of Tyro and Antiope, lovers of Neptune and Zeus.*

RIGHT Bust of Homer in the British Museum. All Homer's portraits are products of artists' imaginations, as no one knows whether the great poet ever existed.

pretend to sail away, leaving it behind. The Trojans dragged the horse into their city, not knowing that it contained a force of Greek warriors. Late at night they burst out of the horse and captured Troy. Homer's *Odyssey* – a word that has now come to describe any memorable voyage – takes up the story and tells of our hero's return to his palace on the island of Ithaca, to the west of continental Greece. The journey lasts another 10 years and Odysseus has a litany of terrifying experiences, the most striking of which is his and his sailors' confrontation with the giant one-eyed Cyclops called Polyphemus. They drive a red-hot stake into the monster's eye and escape, but Polyphemus's father, the sea-god Poseidon, promptly condemns Odysseus to yet more ordeals on his voyage home. When he finally reaches Ithaca, he has lost every man in his crew, yet he still has to tackle the crowd of suitors who are brazenly occupying his palace and demanding marriage to his wife Penelope.

It is at this moment that our treasured fragment of papyrus picks up the story. This short passage describes Odysseus worrying about the challenge he faces and complaining to his patron goddess Athena that he finds it difficult to sleep. Meanwhile, his faithful wife Penelope does not yet know that Odysseus is home. She laments that the future is so bleak that she would rather be far away or even dead. The great epic goes on to give the story a happy ending, but only after a violent scene in the palace. Odysseus makes himself

known to Penelope and to his son Telemachus and, together with one or two of their servants, they overcome the suitors in a bloody fight with swords and bows and arrows.

Our fragment of the *Odyssey* confirms that by around 250 BC there were written versions of this epic as far away as Egypt. To this day scholars and archaeologists argue about how much of the story is true. Was there really a siege of Troy? And did a host of warriors from Mycenae and other Greek towns really sail across the Aegean and capture the city after a long siege? There is no doubt there was a great Mycenaean civilization in Greece that lasted from around 1600 to 1100 BC. There is also proof that there was a city in north-western Turkey on the Dardanelles. Its remains are at Hissarlik and, as we saw on a recent visit, the ruins do stand on a slight rise separated from the sea by a plain some 7 kilometres (4 miles) wide, as the *Iliad* implies. What's more, one archaeological level of these ruins (known as Troy VIIA) dates to around 1200 BC and shows signs of destruction by fire.

All this is still the subject of intense debate among scholars, but it does raise the tantalizing possibility that this mound of Hissarlik comprises the remains of Troy. It's exciting to stand on the ruined walls today and imagine the great battles on the plain below, the fall of Troy and the subsequent lengthy wanderings of Odysseus which so caught the imagination of that ancient poet (or poets) and produced two of the great founding masterpieces of Western literature. Thanks to this ancient fragment of text and others like it, the story will never die.

OPPOSITE A fifteenth-century Italian painting of the triumphant Greek warrior Achilles in his chariot. He is dragging the dead body of the Trojan hero Hector around the walls of Troy.

ABOVE Odysseus, back home in Ithaca after his harrowing voyage, shoots dead the crowd of suitors who have abused the hospitality of his faithful wife Penelope.

6

The Ostracon

This small shard of pottery from ancient Athens is called an ostracon. It was the equivalent of today's voting slip. Megacles, the man whose name has been scratched on its surface, is the choice of this voter for ostracism: exile from Athens. This is fascinating evidence of the world's oldest democracy at work.

ABOVE Four examples of the ostracon used to identify an Athenian voter's choice of candidate for ostracism, or exile. The name of Megacles is scratched on three of them.

OPPOSITE Cleisthenes, one of the early founders of Greek democracy, invented ostracism at the end of the sixth century BC*. Ironically, Athenian voters used the ostracon to exile Cleisthenes' nephew, Megacles.*

FOLLOWING PAGES An artist's impression of the Agora or marketplace of ancient Athens lying below the Acropolis. Athenian democracy flourished when the city enjoyed full freedom from the sixth century BC*.*

It is the earliest example of direct democracy – people power – at its most absolute. Once a year any citizen of ancient Athens in the fifth century BC could walk to the Agora, the central marketplace, and drop an "ostracon", a fragment of pottery, into a pot. It was the ancient version of a modern ballot paper, but instead of a cross on a piece of paper, the Athenian voter scratched the name of a person on the pottery. The name they inscribed, far from being someone the voter wanted to represent them, was the person he wanted kicked out of power – and out of the city. As long as they received 6,000 of Athens' 30,000 or so citizens' votes, the unfortunate person named on the ostracon had to pack a bag and go into exile. This negative vote, the casting of the ostracon, was a citizen's exercise of direct power.

Ostracism was only one of the ways men in Athens and some other city states in ancient Greece could decide events. When voters gathered together in the Agora or in the Assembly on a great rocky platform within sight of the Acropolis, they were not voting as *representatives* of the people like today's parliamentarians. They *were* the people. Any big decision, any major appointment, had to be decided by direct popular vote. You can imagine the chaos this must have led to, with thousands clamouring to speak and heckle: the catcalls and the roars of approval, then the show of hands for the actual vote. It would be like modern governments having to put not just one rare question, but *all* decisions to an instant referendum of the whole population.

Athenian democracy was the outcome of a process of evolving reform that began in the 590s BC and ended nearly 300 years later, but it fell short of total democracy in an important respect. Women and slaves were not eligible to vote; only Athenians who were recognized as free men were enfranchised. Before we condemn the practice too harshly, however, we should remember that it was only at the end of the nineteenth century that women began to be given the vote in modern democracies, and no modern country's male citizens have ever enjoyed the voting power of ancient Athenians.

Democracy's heroes, the men who did more than anyone else to set the world on course for – in Abraham Lincoln's words – "government of the people by the people for the people", were the Athenian law-makers Solon and Cleisthenes. In the sixth century BC they established direct democracy by giving all free male citizens a direct say in making decisions and in choosing the officials to manage the everyday running of the country. Solon had begun the process by sweeping the old aristocracy aside. Cleisthenes perfected the arrangements in 508–7 BC. All male citizens of Athens were to have an equal chance of being selected to take their place in the ruling Council of 500. It was this council which, subject to the sovereign power

of the all-citizen Assembly, supervised the day-to-day running of the state. This was to be the shape of government that led to the golden age of Athenian democracy and prosperity that lasted on and off until Macedon brought all of Greece under its control nearly two centuries later.

Cleisthenes was also the inventor of the ostracon, the little piece of pottery that could bring banishment for even the highest and mightiest of Athenians. It was a powerful instrument of direct democracy, but it was sometimes used ruthlessly by the voters, who could turn on people who were out of favour. One victim of the ostracon was that innovative Athenian leader Themistocles, who planned the destruction of the immense Persian invasion of Greece in 480 BC. For a time a popular hero, he was thrown out of the city after being accused of corruption. And, by a telling stroke of irony which demonstrated the free-ranging nature of the democracy he had unleashed, Cleisthenes's own nephew Megacles was exiled only a decade after his uncle had been the toast of Athens.

Democracy in our modern world owes much to the way so many Athenians were given a decisive share in government, but one feature of the politics of Athens can never be repeated. Countries today may have widened the vote to include all citizens, but they are now far too populous to allow the scale of people power enjoyed in ancient Greece.

7

The Rosetta Stone

The Rosetta Stone provided the key to deciphering ancient Egyptian hieroglyphics. The priestly decree inscribed on the stone was written in 196 BC in three languages. Two of the texts, in Greek and ancient demotic script, are easily translated, which allowed experts to work out the meaning of the third, hieroglyphic, text.

Pierre François Bouchard was a 28-year-old engineer lieutenant in Napoleon's army in Egypt in 1799. The French emperor put Bouchard in charge of rebuilding an old fort in the Nile delta near the town of Rosetta (modern-day Rashid). In mid-July that year, he happened to find among the rubble a large dark stone over 1 metre (3 feet 4 inches) long and 0.75 metres (2 feet 6 inches) wide. It was made of granodiorite, a tough stone from eastern Egypt, and had an inscription in three languages cut into one of its sides. Bouchard was intrigued: the big stele was obviously important, and he immediately drew it to the attention of his colleagues – and to Napoleon himself.

What Bouchard had stumbled upon was in fact one of the most precious archaeological finds ever discovered. The stone had probably been used 300 years earlier by Egyptian Mameluke builders in the construction of the fort. They would have had no idea what it was or what was written on it. They had almost certainly salvaged it from a collapsed ancient Egyptian temple at the nearby ruins of Sais on the Nile.

The unfortunate Bouchard was later captured by the British, who threw Napoleon and his French army out of Egypt, but by this

ABOVE Sir Thomas Young, the British scientist whose breadth of knowledge and obsessive curiosity led him to tackle the challenge of deciphering Egyptian hieroglyphs in 1813.

RIGHT Jean-François Champollion, the French scholar who finally interpreted the Rosetta Stone. He worked with Young for a time but soon overshadowed him. Champollion published his detailed findings in 1824.

OPPOSITE The Rosetta Stone, with hieroglyphic text at the top, demotic in the centre and Greek at the bottom. The hieroglyphic cartouche (signature) of the Egyptian pharaoh Ptolemy V is highlighted.

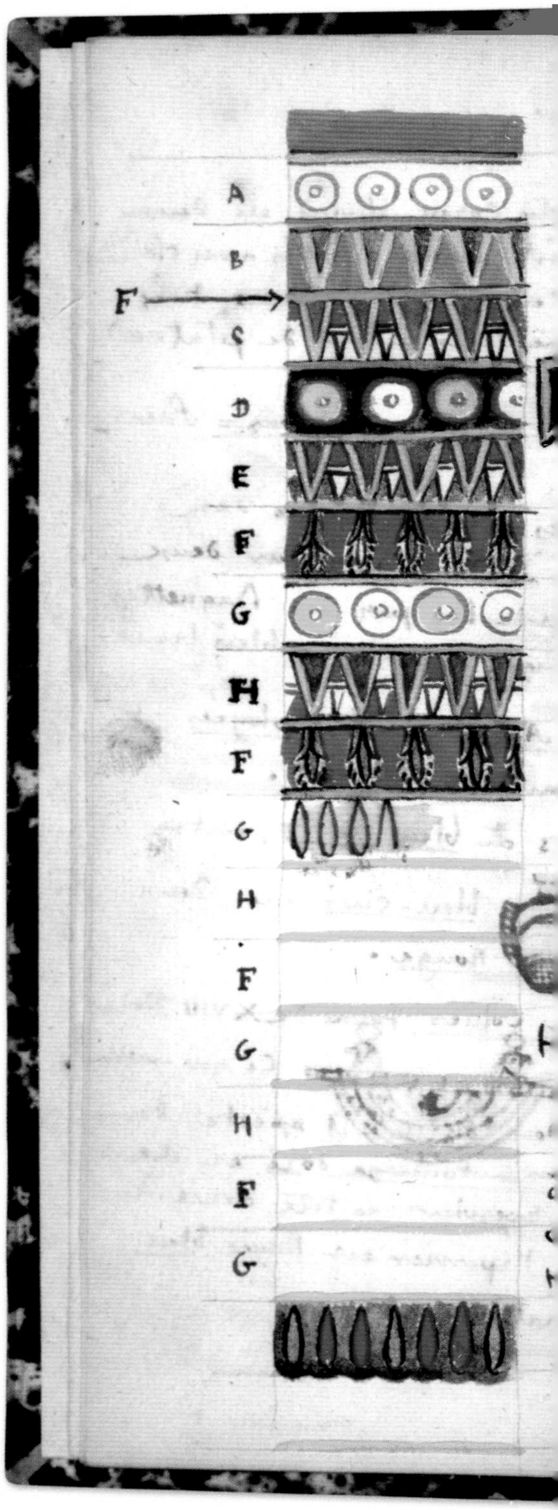

RIGHT Champollion's notebook reflects his painstaking work in deciphering the Egyptian hieroglyphs. His study of each symbol unlocked the forgotten language of ancient Egypt.

time experts, first French and then British, were enthusing about the new discovery they called the Rosetta Stone. They were quick to discern that it had some kind of a decree on it inscribed in three languages – Egyptian hieroglyphics at the top, Egyptian demotic script in the middle and ancient Greek at the bottom. If the words in the three scripts meant the same, then they knew that this could be the key to interpreting the previously indecipherable hieroglyphic script of ancient Egypt.

Bouchard had unearthed an inscription dating back to 196 BC, an uneasy year for Egypt. Ptolemy V had become pharaoh when he was only five years old, in 204 BC, after his parents were murdered. He was now 13 and his country was in a turbulent state. Parts of Egypt were in rebellion, and the decree inscribed on the stone reveals the extent to which the royal family depended on the priesthood for its own and the country's welfare. On the Rosetta Stone the priests promise that in return for the king's gift of grain and silver to Egypt's temples, they will ensure that the king's birthday and coronation days will be the occasion for annual festivities.

The value of the stone went much further than this trifling piece of dynastic history. It was to open the door to the written record of one of the world's most sensational cultures. All of those anonymous monuments and tombs in Giza, Saqqara, Luxor and the other great ancient Egyptian sites were soon to disclose their personalities. It took two decades of Anglo-French research and rivalry for the revelations to become a reality. However, the discord started in Egypt, where the victorious British had a frantic tussle with the French over the stone's ownership. According to one story, the defeated French army commander was found to have hidden the stone inside several carpets in his baggage as he left for France.

The stone was transported to England on a captured French frigate, HMS *Égyptienne*, and placed in the British Museum. Copies of its inscription were widely circulated at home and abroad, and an intellectual struggle between Britain and France followed. The two key protagonists were Thomas Young in London and Jean-François Champollion in Grenoble. Young in particular worked very hard on what were called the "cartouches", clearly framed phrases in the hieroglyphs that were thought to denote the names of the kings of Egypt. He managed to discover that a cartouche on the Rosetta Stone contained the symbols that spelled the name "Ptolemy". Both Young and Champollion made important contributions to the final deciphering of the hieroglyphs, but it was Champollion's publication of what amounted to a hieroglyphic dictionary in 1822 that was the springboard from which Egyptologists were able to understand the writings in Egyptian tombs and temples. These texts revealed the stories of the dynasties and their kings and high officials.

The rivalry between the two men took on international dimensions when visitors to the British Museum complained about the size of their portraits on display. In the early 1970s there were protests from French visitors to the Museum that the portrait of Young was larger than Champollion's and from British visitors that Champollion's was bigger, although apparently both pictures were exactly the same size.

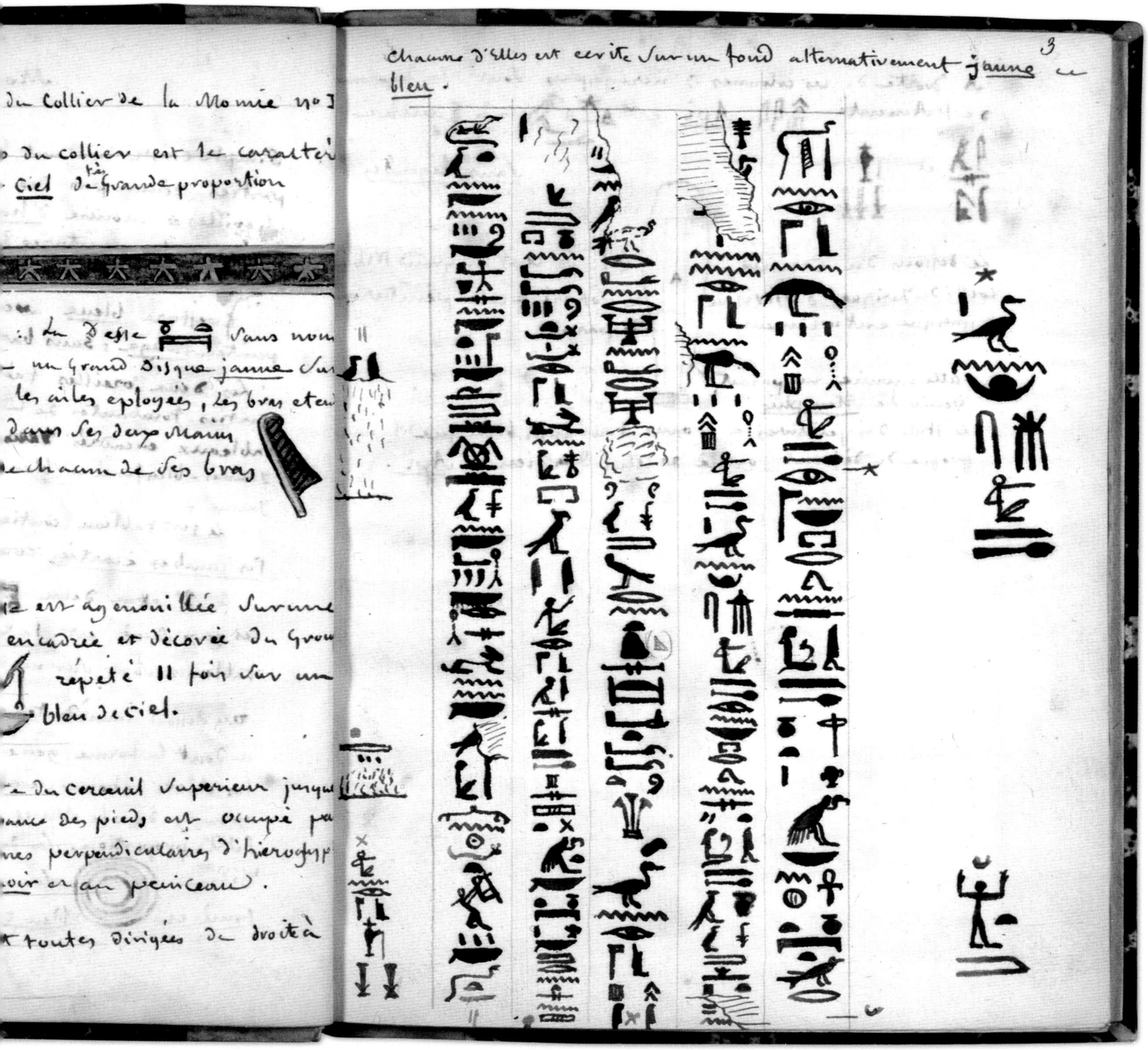
du Collier de la Momie no I
du collier est le caractère
Ciel de grande proportion
La Déesse sans nom
un grand disque jaune sur
les ailes éployées, les bras éten
dans ses deux mains
chacun de ses bras
est agenouillée sur une
encadrée et décorée du gran
répété 11 fois sur un
bleu de ciel.
du cercueil supérieur jusqu
ance des pieds est occupé pa
nes perpendiculaires d'hiéroglyp
noir et au pinceau.
toutes dirigées de droite à
Chacune d'elles est écrite sur un fond alternativement jaune
bleu.
3

8

The Dead Sea Scrolls

Accidentally discovered by a group of Palestinian shepherds in 1946–47 in caves at Qumran, just west of the Dead Sea, the Dead Sea Scrolls are an archaeological miracle. They record extensive passages from the Old Testament, the Hebrew Bible, copied some 2,000 years ago from even older texts by members of a strict Jewish sect called the Essenes.

RIGHT The tall narrow jars in which the Dead Sea Scrolls were discovered. The lids on the jars helped protect the scrolls from getting damp.

OPPOSITE A selection of the scrolls delicately unravelled by experts. There are around 1,000 texts altogether, mainly recording the Hebrew Bible.

A chance discovery just after the Second World War revealed a precious hoard of magnificently preserved biblical manuscripts. The Dead Sea Scrolls, created on papyrus – made from the stalk of a papyrus plant – contain the written words of the Old Testament or Hebrew Bible 1,000 years before any other surviving detailed texts. What the shepherds unearthed near the north-west corner of the Dead Sea reveals, in fascinating detail, what the Jewish world knew of its older biblical writings at around the time of the birth of Christianity.

The shepherds who found the first scrolls hawked them around local markets without prompting much interest and finally sold them for a handful of dollars. It was two or three years before scholars recognized them for what they were, and the caves were re-explored in 1949.

The people who wrote these texts (which must have been copied from earlier material) were members of a very strict Jewish religious sect living in isolation at a village called Khirbet Qumran, 40 kilometres (25 miles) east of Jerusalem. Scholars believe they were the Essenes, who endured an extreme form of monastic existence from around 300 BC until the Romans crushed the Jewish revolt in AD 73. The Roman author Pliny described the Essenes as "unique and admirable beyond all others in the world, without women and renouncing love entirely, without money and having for company only the palm trees". In their settlement these abstemious recluses had a scriptorium (a reading and writing room) where – day in, day out – they worked on their papyri before hiding them in jars in a dozen caves in the surrounding hillsides. The scrolls are now identified by the cave in which they were found. The Essenes wore white garments, ate simple food and pursued a strict routine, particularly on the Sabbath, when even excretion was forbidden. On weekdays they had to find a remote spot to go to the toilet and bury their faeces. Indecent exposure (it is unclear whether this included accidental or only deliberate exposure) meant at least 30 days' punishment.

What survives of the remarkable work these scribes carried out is some 950 manuscripts written mainly in Hebrew and Aramaic. They record varying lengths of passages from the Hebrew Bible (Old Testament), from Genesis through Exodus, Leviticus, Numbers and Deuteronomy to the prophets. The Great Isaiah scroll contains all 66 of its chapters.

One intriguing feature of this vast treasure house of biblical writing is how it varies from the medieval Masoretic text compiled 1,000 years later – which, until the discovery of the scrolls, was seen as the classical source of the scriptures. To take one fascinating example, the giant Goliath, whom David famously killed

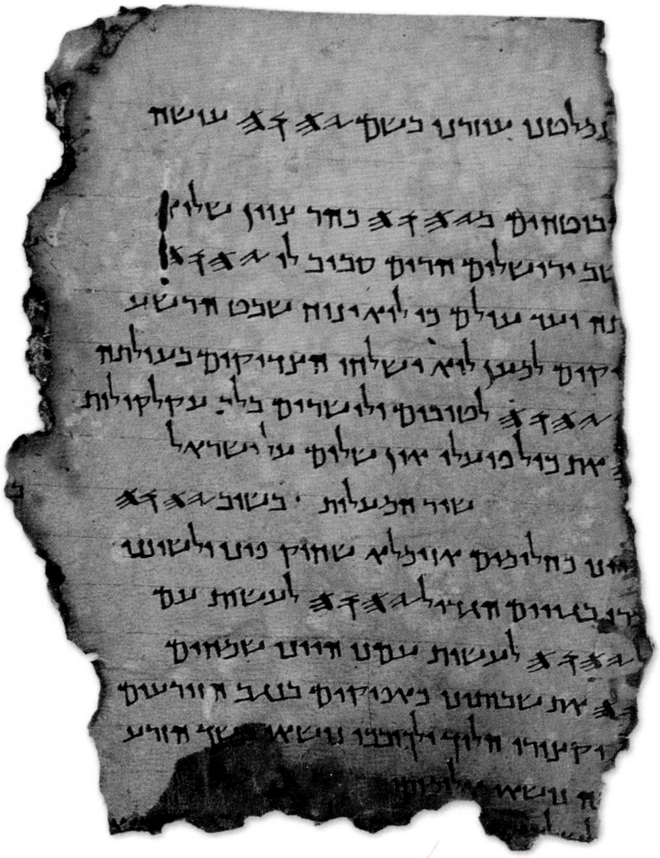

in single combat, is described in the authorized version of the Bible (derived from the Masoretic text) as having a height of 6 cubits and a span (I Samuel 17:4). That would make him 3 metres tall (9 feet 9 inches). The Samuel scroll from Cave No. 4 puts him at 4 cubits and a span – that's just over 2 metres (6 feet 6 inches).

It is not just the text itself that varies from the authorized Bible; the scrolls occasionally go further than that. For example, in Chapter 12 of the book of Genesis, Abraham is off to Egypt with his wife Sarah. He fears, however, that Pharaoh may be so attracted to her that he will kill Abraham to get him out of the way. The Bible says just that Sarah was "very fair". But the scrolls' writers go into much more detail: "How fine are the hairs of her head. How lovely are her eyes. How desirable her nose and all the radiance of her countenance ... no virgin or bride led into the marriage chamber is more beautiful than she ..." This extra description is oddly suggestive for the supposedly puritan Essenes!

Since the Essenes were still there in the three or four decades after Christ's life and crucifixion, scholars have scanned the scrolls in the hope of finding possible allusions to the new Christian religion. Some believe that a reference to a "slain messiah" may be a positive sign, but this and other hints of a link are not widely accepted.

The scrolls are now mostly housed in the Shrine of the Book in the Israel Museum in West Jerusalem. Tens of thousands of people visit every year. Each scroll spends only three to six months on display before it is packed off to "recover" from its exposure to even the gentlest of light. There is a timeless mystique to the story of the scrolls – whether you consider the nature of their discovery or the riddle of what they contain. They are a gift to the novelist, too: Dan Brown mentions them several times in his *Da Vinci Code*.

OPPOSITE The scrolls were discovered in caves in this parched landscape near the ancient settlement of Khirbet Qumran, north-west of the Dead Sea. Shepherds stumbled on the first jars in 1946.

LEFT Many of the scrolls are made up of small fragments of parchment or papyrus. Experts carefully piece them together using special instruments.

9

The Res Gestae of Augustus

This massive inscription known as the *Res Gestae Divi Augusti* ("The Deeds of the Divine Augustus") took up one whole wall of a Roman temple in Ankara, Turkey. Our document is a copy of it carved on a wall in Rome. It records all the achievements of Rome's first emperor, who ruled from 30 BC to AD 14.

RIGHT A man walks past the modern copy of the giant "Res Gestae" inscription in Rome that boasts the achievements of the Emperor Augustus. The text, in four sections, praises Augustus's political career; his gifts; his military deeds; and his claims of widespread popular support.

It is hardly surprising that the Emperor Augustus, who ruled Rome at almost exactly the same time as Jesus Christ lived in Judea, trumpets his own achievements so boastfully in this gigantic inscription. He is determined that no one anywhere in his huge empire will ever forget what he did. And he did indeed leave a legacy to be proud of. This was the man who inherited the combustible civil strife that plagued the collapsing Roman Republic and erected a new constitutional beacon of stability that was to survive for 1,500 years. The republic became an empire ruled by a succession of emperors who lasted – with varying fortunes – until the fall of Constantinople in 1453.

Augustus was the first emperor and one of the most competent and successful. He ended the republic's civil strife by ruthlessly crushing all his opponents, the last of them the unfortunate Antony, whose infatuation with Cleopatra of Egypt distracted him from grasping his opportunity to lead the Roman world. By 27 BC Augustus had no rivals. "I was", he says in one bare-faced claim in his Res Gestae, "in charge of all affairs." The result of Augustus's success was a largely peaceful rule of four decades that ended with his death in AD 14. It was the Augustan era, an age that saw an explosion of creativity in writing and other arts. It enriched the world with such paragons of artistic achievement as Virgil, Horace and Ovid and benefactors and architects who prompted Augustus to claim, in his biographer Suetonius's words: "I found Rome a city of bricks and left it a city of marble." Virgil, in his *Aeneid*, praises "Augustus Caesar, kindred unto Jove. He brings a golden age, he shall restore old Saturn's sceptre to our Latin land."

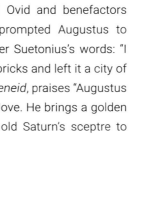

ERRARVM · IMPERIO · POPVLI · ROM

Map of the Roman Empire in the period roughly 20 BC to AD 10

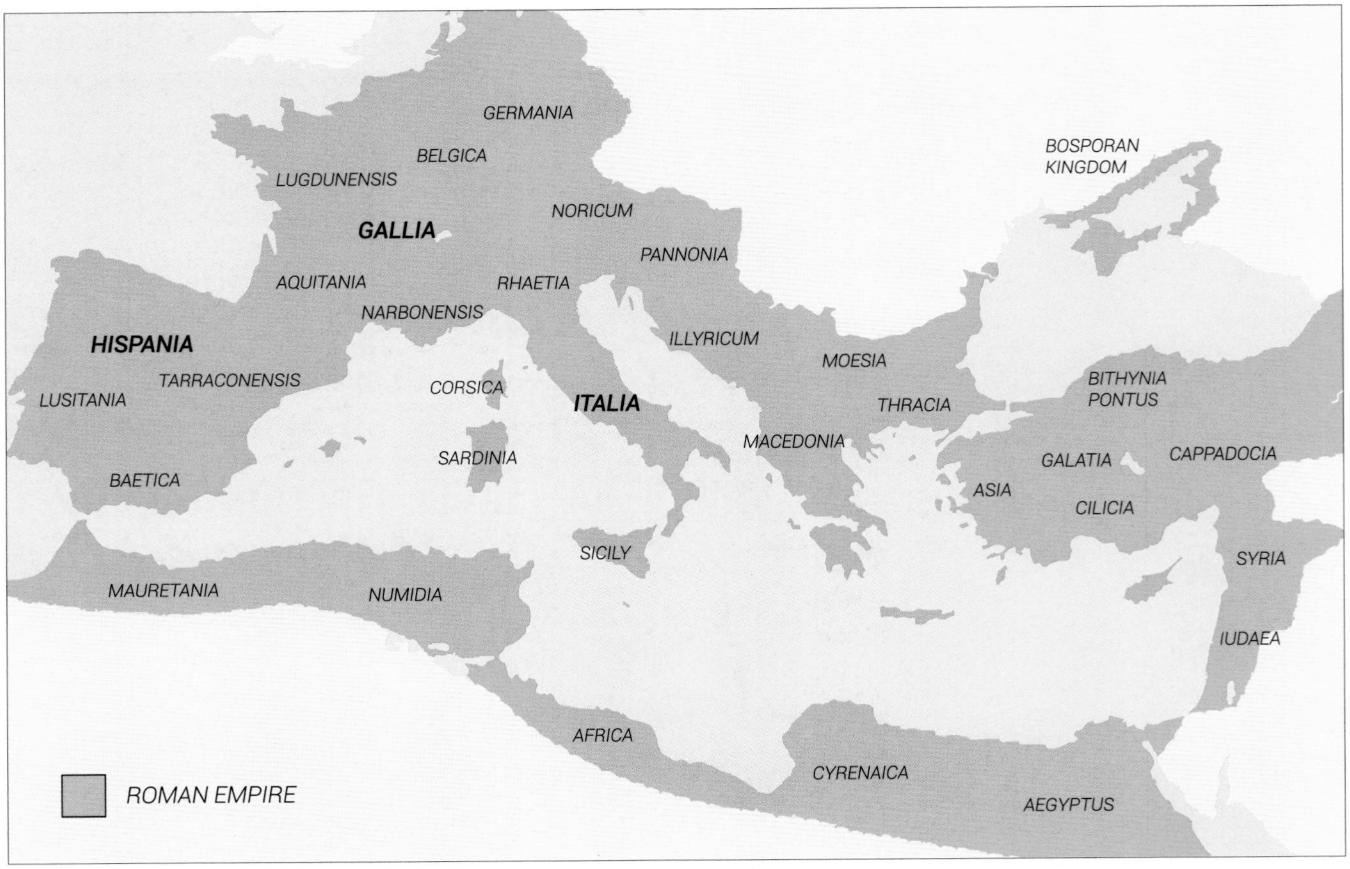

OPPOSITE One of the original, now incomplete, inscriptions of the Res Gestae on the Temple of Augustus at Ancyra (modern-day Ankara) in Turkey.

RIGHT This marble statue of Augustus was discovered in 1863 in the ruins of his wife Livia's villa and stands at 2 metres (6 feet 6 inches) high. Rome's first emperor, he ruled for 44 years from 30 BC to AD 14.

So how did Augustus manage to establish this "golden age" and launch that era of imperial governance that was to survive for so long? The answer is that he took his time to translate the institutions of the old republic into a machine that allowed him to build an entrenched and lasting dictatorship. It was a gradual process, throughout which he was always careful to underline his respect for venerable bodies such as the Roman Senate. Unlike his great-uncle Julius Caesar, who seized too much power too quickly, Augustus was cannily cautious.

In his first years in power the young undisputed leader gave the impression of respecting the right of senators and other office-holders to make the decisions that mattered, but he slowly took powers that emphasized his own authority. Augustus avoided anything that made him look like a king, but in 27 BC he became *princeps senatus* and *imperator* – leader of the senate and army commander. He soon acquired the power of a tribune for life, which allowed him to summon the Senate and preside over elections.

Suetonius, who wrote a century after Augustus, describes him as a "womanizer" who could act with great cruelty, but says he was also generous and able to show modesty and even disapproval when he was subject to undue flattery. Augustus was of below-average height with "clear and bright eyes. His eyebrows met above his Roman nose … and he had yellowish and rather curly hair". He disliked flowery oratory and spoke clearly and directly, and he "never drank more than three cups of wine and water at dinner".

Augustus did much to regularize the administration of Rome and Italy, and by the time of his death the Roman Empire completely encompassed the Mediterranean Sea and extended into the Balkans. As the Res Gestae inscription proclaimed, he added several provinces to the empire, including some that took Rome's northern frontier up to the Danube.

Under Augustus's successors, the ruling house of the Caesars sank into a mire of debauchery and incompetence, only to shine again nearly a century later under Trajan, Hadrian and the Antonine emperors in the second century. But the memory of what had happened under Rome's first emperor never faded. Britain in the early eighteenth century enjoyed a period of creative intellectual prosperity that became so famous for its novelists, philosophers and satirists that it was dubbed a second Augustan age.

WELTSYSTEM
oder
Darstellung des
nach der
des
Schütze
Skorpion
Steinbock
Wassermann
Fische
Widder
Stier
Zwillinge
Die Bahn des Saturn
SATURN
Die Bahn des Mars
MARS
Der Mond mit der unter ihm liegenden Welt.
Bahn der
VENUS
Bahn des Merkur
MERKUR
Bahn der Venus
Sonne, Venus und Merkur bewegt.
um Sonne, Venus und Merkur bewegt
dem Monde und den 4 Elementen um

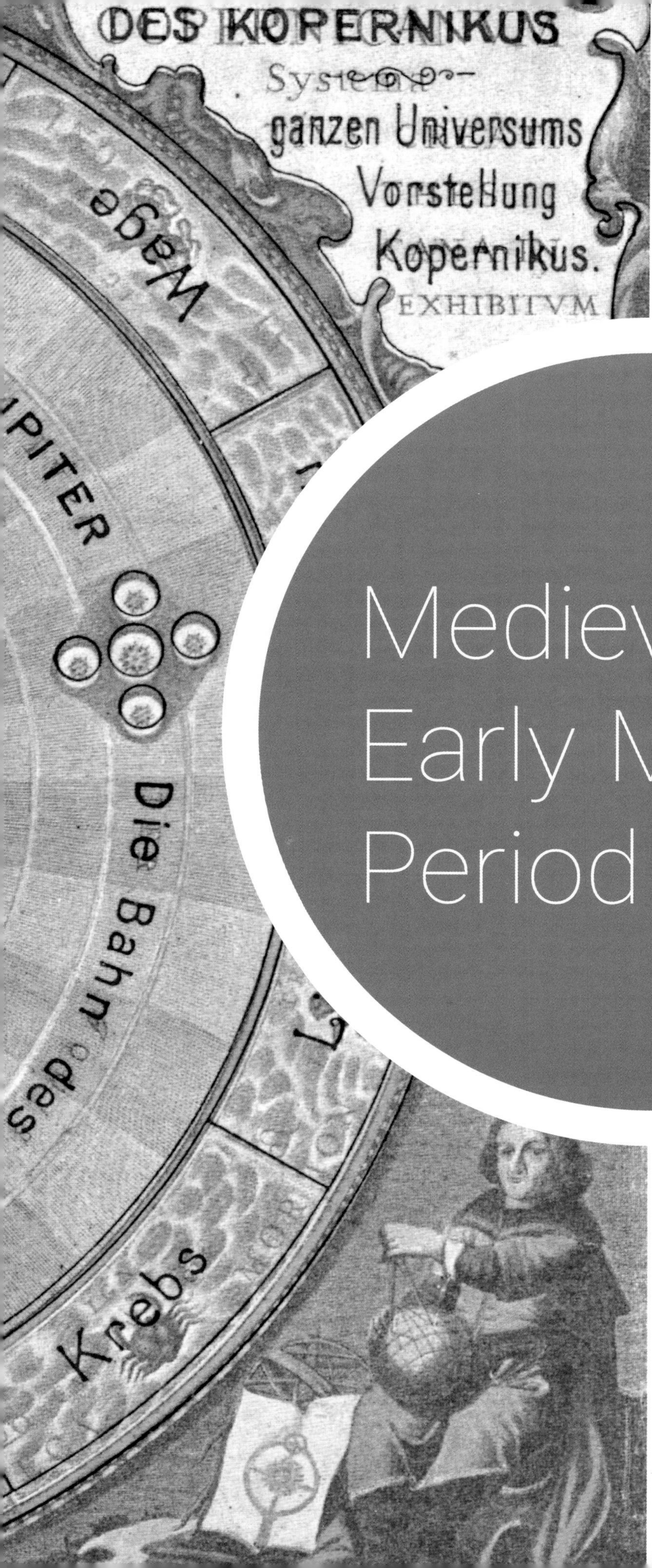

Medieval and Early Modern Period

c. 600–1648

10

The Koran

The Koran, the holy book of Islam, is the most widely read and recited manuscript in the world. Its philosophy, commandments and codes of behaviour have made Islam the religion of nearly one quarter of the world's population. Muslims consider it to be the word of God as revealed to the Prophet Muhammad by the archangel Gabriel between AD 610 and 632. They view Muhammad as the last and most important in a long line of prophets, which includes Adam, Noah, Abraham, Moses and Jesus, who received revelations from God.

Muslims believe that the archangel Gabriel came to 40-year-old Muhammad one night while he was on a spiritual retreat in the Cave of Hira near Mecca in AD 610. The angel announced that God had chosen Muhammad to be a prophet and recited three verses to him. When he awoke, the newly appointed messenger of God said the verses were inscribed on his heart. Over the next 22 years there were many more revelations in Mecca and Medina and, since Muhammad was illiterate, he memorized them. He shared these words of God by reciting them to his followers, some of whom knew how to write. They inscribed Muhammad's verses on tablets, palm leaves and animal bones. After the Prophet's death in 632, his father-in-law, Abu Bakr, was named his successor or caliph. Abu Bakr ordered scribes to collect as many written verses as possible and to compile a manuscript. As Islam expanded from the Arabian Peninsula into Persia, the eastern Mediterranean and North Africa, concern grew about recitations of the Koran being corrupted. According to one account, in around 650 the third caliph, Uthman (Muhammad's son-in-law), took Abu Bakr's manuscript and added verses which had been memorized by Muhammad's companions. He sent this updated Koran to all Islamic provinces and ordered all other texts to be destroyed. The Uthmanic code became the definitive written version, the holy text of Islam. It remains unchanged today.

The Koran consists of just over 77,000 words (the Christian Bible is 10 times as long). Muhammad's revelations appear in 114 chapters, called suras. Each sura is made up of several verses about subjects ranging from God's omnipotence to support for the poor. About one third of the suras are concerned with the afterlife and the Day of Judgement. The rest contain references to prayer, history, stories also found in the Bible, the study of nature and the moral and legal duties of believers. Some of the suras have proved controversial and open to different interpretations. For example, Sura 4, verse 34, says: "Men are the managers of the affairs of women because God has preferred one of them over the other … those [women] you fear may be rebellious admonish; banish them to their couches and beat them." This has led to great debate about the role and treatment of women in Islam. Punishment is also the subject of much discussion. Surah 5, verse 38, says of thieves: "cut off his or her hands: a punishment as a way of example." The rise of jihadism, militant Islam, has led to heated argument about whether the Koran sanctions the killing of non-Muslims. A few insist it does, though most authorities say the Koran prohibits aggression and that believers are only permitted to fight in self-defence.

There have been ruptures in Islam, notably the dispute over the succession to the Prophet Muhammad. A group which became known as Shias demanded that the caliph should be Muhammad's cousin, Ali, a direct blood relation. A larger group, the Sunnis, insisted that Muhammad's father-in-law, Abu Bakr, become the new leader. The Sunnis won the argument and today make up nearly 90 per cent of Muslims worldwide. The two sides have come into conflict in modern times in countries

OPPOSITE This seventh-century AD parchment, one of the world's oldest copies of the Koran, was found by workmen renovating Yemen's Great Mosque of Sana'a in 1972. It is a palimpsest, written over, erased, and then written over again.

اموالهم ابتغاء مرضات الله وتثبيتا
من انفسهم كمثل جنة بربوة اصابها وابل
فاتت اكلها ضعفين فان لم يصبها وابل
فطل والله بما تعملون بصير ايود احد
كم ان تكون له جنة من نخيل واعنب تجر
ي من تحتها الانهر له فيها من كل الثمرت و
اصابه الكبر وله ذرية ضعفا فاصابها
اعصار فيه نار فاحترقت كذلك يبين الله
لكم الايت لعلكم تتفكرون يايها الذ
ين امنوا انفقوا من طيبت ما كسبتم
ومما اخرجنا لكم من الارض ولا تيمموا
الخبيث منه تنفقون ولستم باخذيه
الا ان تغمضوا فيه واعلموا ان الله
غني حميد الشيطن يعدكم الفقر ويامر
كم بالفحشا والله يعدكم مغفرة منه و
فضلا والله وسع عليم يؤتي الحكمة من
يشا ومن يؤت الحكمة فقد اوتي خير
كثيرا وما يذكر الا اولوا الالبب
وما انفقتم من نفقة او نذرتم من نذر فان
الله يعلمه وما للظلمين من انصار ان تبد
وا الصدقت فنعما هي وان تخفوها
وتؤتوها الفقرا فهو خير لكم ويكفر عنكم
من سياتكم والله بما تعملون خبير

21

المص كتب انزل اليك

فلا يكن في صدرك حرج منه لتنذر به وذكرى للمؤمنين
اتبعوا ما انزل اليكم من ربكم ولا تتبعوا من دونه اولياء
قليلا ما تذكرون وكم من قرية اهلكنها فجاءها باسنا
بيتا او هم قائلون فما كان دعوىهم اذ جاءهم باسنا
الا ان قالوا انا كنا ظلمين فلنسئلن الذين ارسل اليهم ولنسئلن
المرسلين فلنقصن عليهم بعلم وما كنا غائبين والوزن
يومئذ الحق فمن ثقلت موزينه فاولئك هم المفلحون ومن

خفت موزينه فاولئك

الذين خسروا انفسهم بما كانوا بايتنا يظلمون ولقد
مكنكم في الارض وجعلنا لكم فيها معيش قليلا ما
تشكرون ولقد خلقنكم ثم صورنكم ثم قلنا للملئكة
اسجدوا لادم فسجدوا الا ابليس لم يكن من السجدين قال
ما منعك الا تسجد اذ امرتك قال انا خير منه خلقتني من نار
وخلقته من طين قال فاهبط منها فما يكون لك ان تتكبر
فيها فاخرج انك من الصغرين قال انظرني الى يوم يبعثون

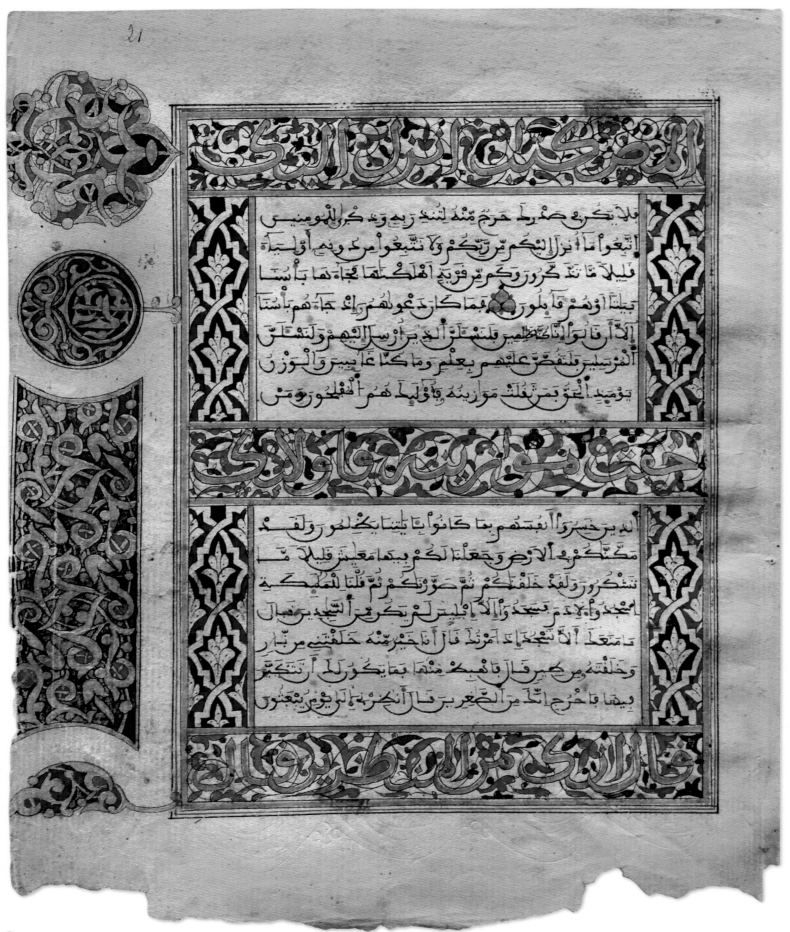

قال انك من المنظرين قال

Map of the Arab empire at its peak

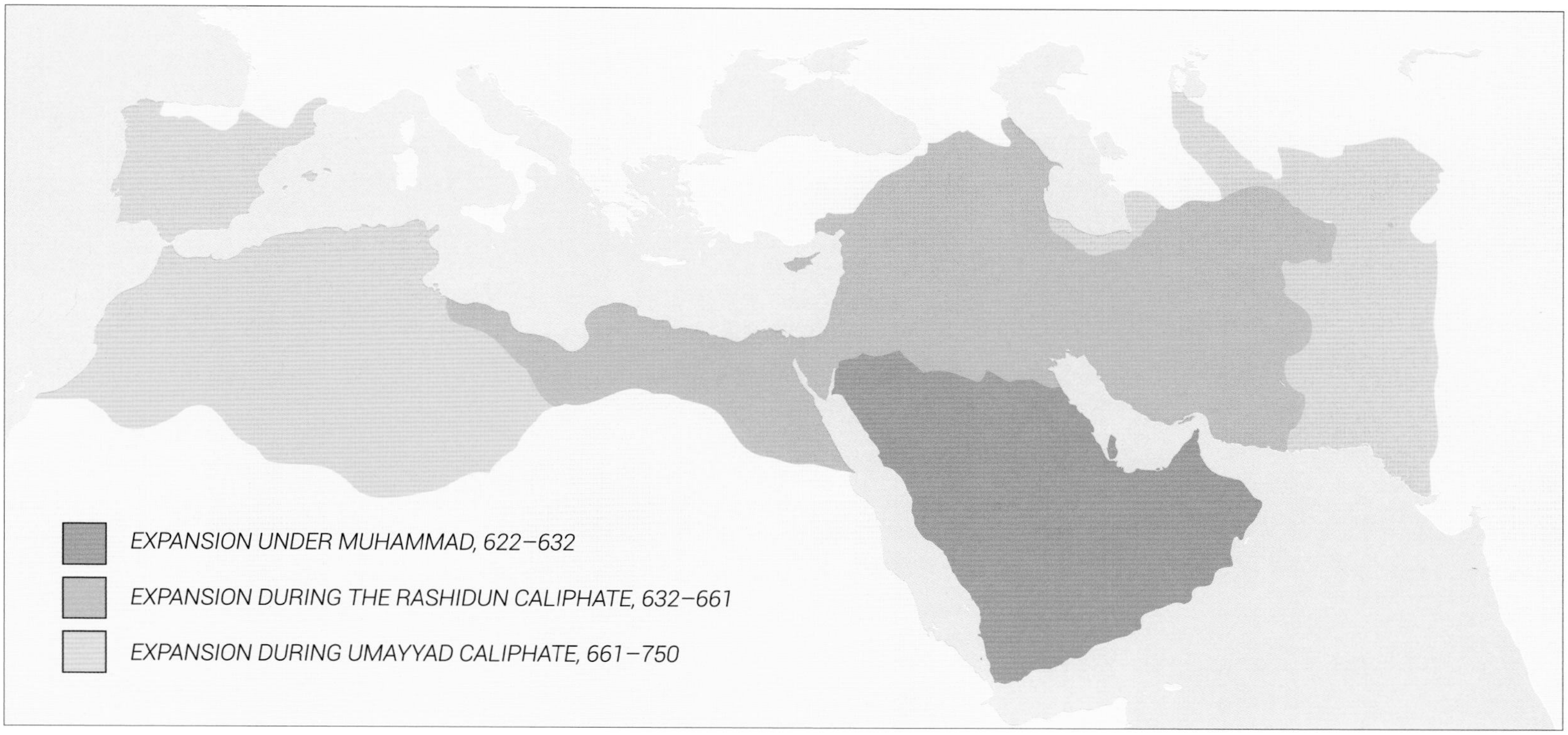

like Saudi Arabia – a Sunni regime – and Iran, a Shia stronghold. Whatever their differences, both branches of Islam accept the official Uthman version of the Koran.

Muhammad is seen as a reformer who replaced pagan tribal beliefs in the Arabian Peninsula with his Islamic teaching, which affects religion, family relationships, business practices and politics. Within 80 years of his death, the Muslim conquests began to create one of the great empires in world history. The inhabitants of conquered lands did not convert to Islam immediately, but as Muslim schools were set up and mosques were built, the Arabic language, customs and Islamic belief spread. The religion continued to move along trading routes into Africa and Asia. Muslim armies occupied the whole of North Africa, invaded Spain and expelled Christian crusader forces in the Middle East in 1291. The Ottomans, whose Muslim empire lasted from the thirteenth to the twentieth century, captured Constantinople in 1453 and advanced as far as the gates of Vienna. Today there are nearly two billion Muslims in the world. That number is expected to increase to three billion by 2060, when Islam will overtake Christianity as the world's largest religion.

OPPOSITE The decorative patterns in the Oppenheim Koran reflect the spread of Islam. Similar patterns can be found in Spain's Alhambra Palace and in Morocco.

11

The Book of Kells

The Book of Kells is an illuminated medieval manuscript recording the four gospels of the Christian Bible. It is the work of monks living around AD 800 who copied and ornamented texts they had acquired from even earlier times. Our choice shows a full-page picture of the Virgin Mary and child in all its colourful detail.

The Book of Kells, which tells the stories of the four New Testament gospels in the Christian Bible, is widely regarded as one of the most beautiful books in existence. There is some doubt about exactly where it was produced, but the likeliest story is that it is the achievement of an exceptional team of calligraphers and pictorial artists who lived on the Scottish island of Iona in around AD 800. The abbey where they worked was founded by the Irish missionary St Columba (or St Colmcille) in the sixth century. It was ravaged by the Vikings in AD 806 and scores of monks were killed. It seems probable that some of the surviving monks crossed back to Ireland with the book and took refuge in the monastery of Kells, 70 kilometres (43 miles) from Dublin. It was there that the book was kept and perhaps completed in far safer surroundings, although the Vikings roamed over parts of Ireland too. Somehow the monks managed to preserve this magnificent illuminated manuscript.

The monks who wrote and illustrated the Book of Kells were meticulous professionals.

Their version of the gospels, taken from the so-called Vulgate, the Latin text, is decorated with the most glorious ornamental extravagance, a great swirling profusion of patterns, dotted with pictures of people, plants and animals. The animals in particular are depicted with great imagination and humour, up to all sorts of tricks and sometimes so small you need a magnifying glass to spot them.

Many of the capital letters at the beginning of sentences in the text are composed of small animals in various twirling acrobatics. In the picture of the Virgin Mary and Child that appears very early in the book, the top of Mary's

ABOVE The abbey on the Scottish island of Iona. Founded by St Columba (St Colmcille) in AD 563, it was the home of Columban monks who fled from the Danes in AD 806. Completely reconstructed in the twentieth century, it is now the home of the Christian Iona Community.

RIGHT The ruins of the Abbey of Kells 70 kilometres (43 miles) north-west of Dublin. The monks of Iona sought refuge here in the early ninth century AD.

OPPOSITE The Virgin and Child surrounded by angels take pride of place in the Book of Kells. Devotion to the Virgin Mary began particularly early in Ireland.

LITERARIA INSTRUX

chair-back is in the form of a fearsome-looking beast obligingly protecting mother and child by biting off the heads of two snakes. It's thought that many of the human figures in the pictures may be cartoon-like representations of other monks in the abbey. Indeed, it does strike us, as it has many others, that the face of the child in Mary's arms is distinctly unbaby-like.

Experts have identified that four separate scribes composed the text, and each has a slightly different style. One in particular has a passion for a more florid version of the capital letters than the others, but all four have clearly been influenced by the elaborate designs of a wide range of schools of handwriting in other parts of Europe. The Irish prided themselves on what became known as the "insular style" of calligraphy, which was developed by Irish scribes on the fringes of Europe as early as the time of St Columba.

The book is written on vellum, specially prepared calfskin. It was a form of parchment highly prized in the damp atmosphere of Ireland where other materials might have been less hardy. The wonderful colours which have lasted so miraculously are the product of several different pigments. The blue pigment came from the indigo plant or from woad, a European member of the cabbage family which was common in northern Europe. The yellow came from a mineral substance called orpiment (yellow arsenic sulphide), the red from red lead.

The Book of Kells is in four parts, one for each gospel, and each one is now kept in a separate box. The original book was very large, with an elaborately worked cover which has been lost together with 30 folios of the text. A four-part introductory illustration depicts the four evangelists as four live creatures: Matthew as a man; Mark as a lion, the king of beasts; Luke as an ox, the king of domestic animals; and John as an eagle, the king of the birds.

No one knows exactly what the Book of Kells was used for during its monastic life in the Middle Ages. It was so large that it was probably not heaved out for daily services, but saved for special ceremonial occasions only. It is a wonder that it survived the Vikings and its seizure by robbers in the year 1007. The thieves appear to have ripped off the cover and then buried the treasured book under some grass, where it was recovered a few months later. After the monastery of Kells was abandoned in the mid-sixteenth century, the Book of Kells was removed to Trinity College Dublin for safe-keeping, and there it has remained ever since.

Some half a million people visit the Book of Kells in Trinity College Library every year. Two of the volumes are kept on display at any one time and their pages are turned about once a month. One will show a page of text, the other a full-page illustration.

OPPOSITE The magnificent old library at Trinity College Dublin is 65 metres (213 feet) long. The Book of Kells is the most celebrated of its 200,000 books.

ABOVE "The Four Evangelists" page from the Book of Kells. Three are represented as animals: Mark as a lion; Luke as a calf; and John as an eagle. Only Matthew is a man.

12

Magna Carta

Magna Carta, or the Great Charter, is the seminal English legal document that established for the first time that no one – not even the king – was above the law. Called the bible of the English constitution, Magna Carta is seen as a foundation document, a first step in establishing individual rights against the arbitrary use of power. Over the course of eight centuries it has shaped legal systems, parliamentary democracies and our concept of liberty around the world.

ABOVE The seal of King John was used to authenticate his royal documents. On the front of the seal the king holds a sword and sceptre. On the back, he is riding a horse. This seal appears on all original copies of the 1215 Magna Carta.

OPPOSITE This is the 1225 version of the Magna Carta, the third to be issued by Henry III and the first to bear his own seal. The previous two had been issued while he was still a boy. Clause 29 (which was Clause 39 in the original, 1215 version) is five lines up from the second hole in the manuscript. It guarantees that "no free man shall be taken or imprisoned ... except by the lawful judgment of his peers or by the law of the land".

The medieval Latin words of Magna Carta, scratched with a quill pen on a sheepskin parchment, have become synonymous with justice and liberty. They may have been written more than 800 years ago, but they continue to resonate today.

Magna Carta dates back to 1215. It was a contract designed to curb the power of a most unpopular monarch, King John, who ruled England from 1199 to 1216. "A tyrannous whelp" according to one of his contemporaries, he spent most of his reign fighting and losing battles in France, expecting his barons (major landowners) to pay for them. After a final, humiliating and very expensive military defeat in 1214, some of those barons rebelled and captured London. The king was forced to give in to many of their demands when he met the barons on 15 June 1215 at the traditional safe meeting place of Runnymede, on the banks of the river Thames. The result of that meeting was the Great Charter of Liberties, subsequently known as Magna Carta.

Most of its 63 clauses dealt with specific grievances about issues such as land ownership, taxes and freedom of the Church, but there were some radical new rules that made it clear that, for the first time, the monarch had to obey the law of the land. The most important clause, number 39, reads: "No free man shall be seized or imprisoned, or stripped of his rights or possessions, or outlawed or exiled, or deprived of his standing in any way, nor will we proceed with force against him, or send others to do so, except by lawful judgement of his equals or by the law of the land."

King John reluctantly agreed to the charter but then sent it to Pope Innocent III, England's feudal overlord, who declared it to be "illegal, unjust, harmful to royal rights and shameful to the English people", ruling it "null and void of all validity forever". Magna Carta had been valid for just 10 weeks. Chaos ensued, with a civil war between the king and his barons. King Louis of France invaded England and King John died of dysentery. His nine-year-old son Henry III succeeded to the throne in 1216. In order to win the barons' support in the fight against the French, Henry's advisers issued a revised version of Magna Carta which omitted some of the more controversial clauses but was true to the spirit of the original. Yet another version was produced in 1217 after the French had been thrown out of England.

In 1225, King Henry reissued Magna Carta in return for a tax that had been granted to him by the nation. It was put on the statute book in 1297 and finally became law. The original charter applied only to free men, a small proportion of England's population at the time, but, over the centuries, the very adaptable Magna Carta became a symbol of freedom and justice for all.

In 1776, American colonists who opposed, among other things, being taxed by the British

TOP A stained-glass window in the Massachusetts State House reflects Magna Carta's influence on the American Declaration of Revolutionary War. An American rebel holds a sword in one hand and Magna Carta in the other.

ABOVE King John signs Magna Carta. He is surrounded by the noblemen whose rebellion forced him to submit to their demands.

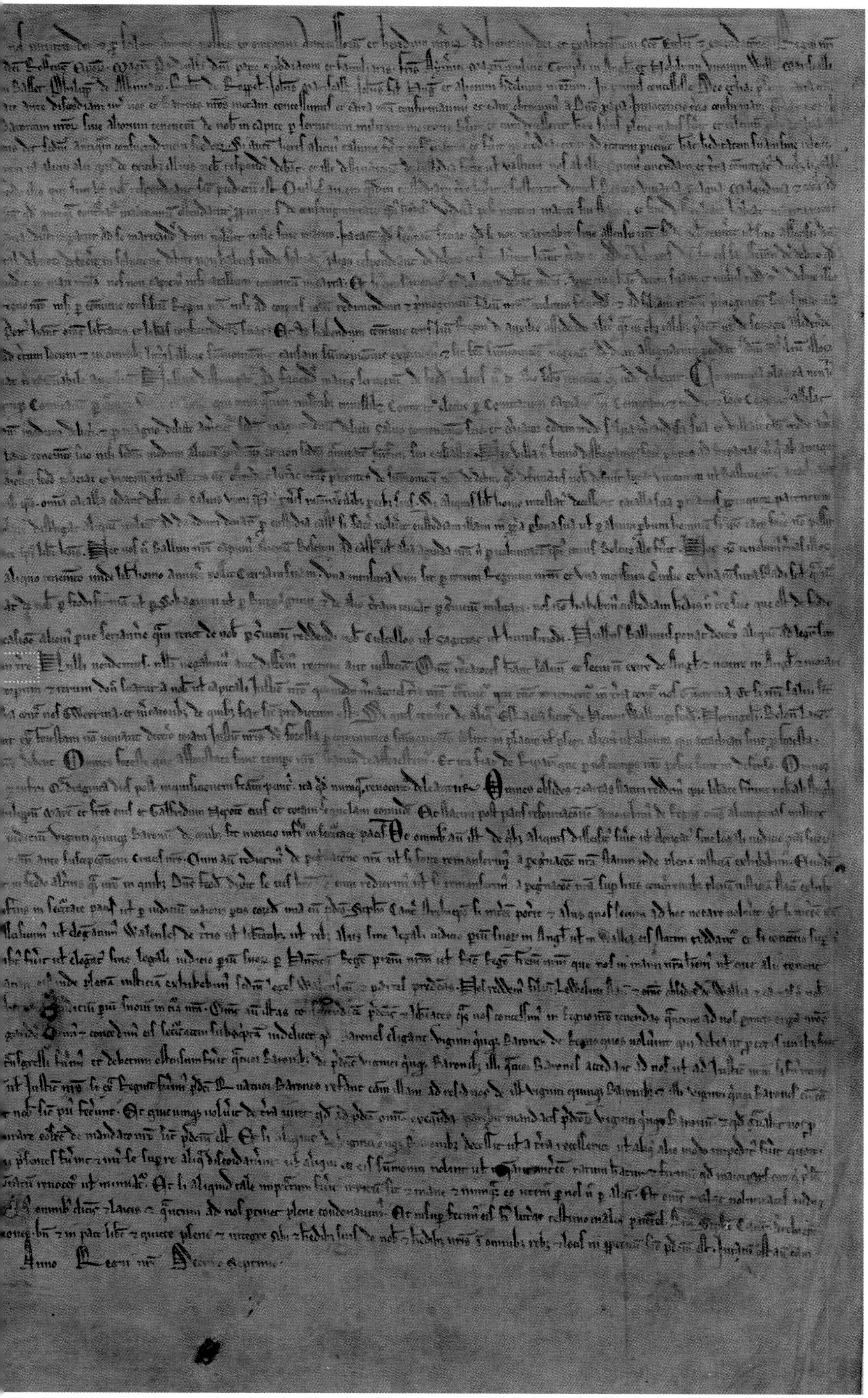

parliament used Magna Carta as their rallying cry. United States founding father Benjamin Franklin declared that his fellow countrymen could only be taxed "by their common consent … as declared by Magna Carta". The US Declaration of Independence, the Constitution and the US Bill of Rights all reflect its principles. The Constitution's fifth amendment guarantees that "no person shall be deprived of life, liberty, or property, without due process of law", a direct reference to the Charter's famous Clause 39. The constitutions of 17 American states incorporate terms from Magna Carta. The laws and constitutions of Canada, Australia, India and other countries which were part of the British Empire also echo the Great Charter.

Nelson Mandela (see page 202), who was imprisoned for opposing the apartheid regime in South Africa, said in his famous 1964 courtroom speech that Magna Carta was "held in veneration by democrats throughout the world". Human rights charters are modern legacies of Magna Carta. Eleanor Roosevelt, a driving force behind the 1948 Universal Declaration of Human Rights, hoped the declaration would become "the international Magna Carta of all men everywhere". The Great Charter is also reflected in the European Convention on Human Rights of 1950.

An unknown number of copies of Magna Carta were issued in 1215 and sent to officials around England. Just four survive today. Two copies are in the British Library in London, one is in Salisbury Cathedral and the other in Lincoln Cathedral. All were briefly reunited at the British Library in London in 2015. It was the first time they had been seen together in 800 years, and was a fitting tribute to a document that has transcended history.

LEFT The British Library's original 1215 Magna Carta. We have highlighted the significant Latin words "nullus liber homo capiatur, vel imprisonetur … nisi per legale judicium parium suorum vel per legem terrae", which translate: "no free man shall be seized or imprisoned, or stripped of his rights or possessions … except by the lawful judgement of his equals or by the law of the land."

13

Leonardo da Vinci's Notebooks

Leonardo da Vinci's inventions are as famous as his paintings. He always had a piece of paper handy to jot down his thoughts, and he filled thousands of pages with his observations on nature, astronomy, painting, architecture, mathematics, the human body and the flight of birds. His notebooks, known as codices, are a treasure trove of fact, fancy and the future.

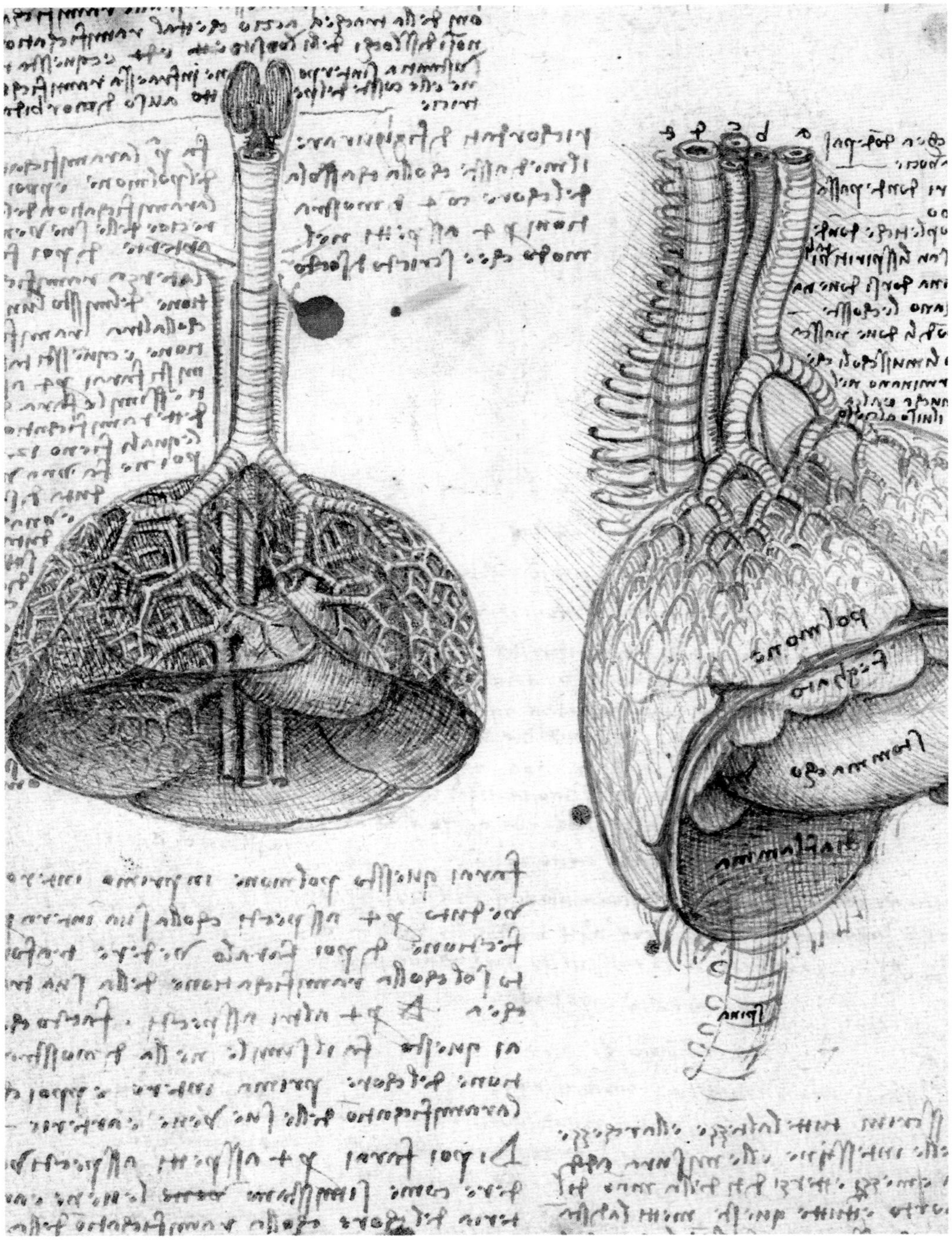

RIGHT Leonardo's drawing (left) of a lung. On the right, he labels separate organs: spine, lung, diaphragm, spleen, stomach and liver. It is thought that his subject was a pig.

OPPOSITE Many of Leonardo's drawings explore flight. On the left is a flying machine powered by a man. On the right is a propeller.

Fortunately for us, Leonardo da Vinci tried to understand things by describing them minutely in writing. His notebooks or codices reflect the brilliant combination of an artist's eye with a scientist's curiosity. One of his great passions was the miracle of flight. He produced 500 sketches and 35,000 words about how birds glide, balancing themselves with wings and tail. He envisioned flying machines, "ornithopters", without engines, where a human pilot controlled the flapping of the wings. He never put these ideas to the test, and it is highly unlikely they would have got off the ground, but Leonardo showed a basic understanding of air as a fluid, which made him a pioneer in the study of aerodynamics. It was nearly 400 years before the Wright brothers (see page 150) made the first successful flight, after which they paid tribute to Leonardo's vision, calling him "one of the greatest artists and engineers of all time".

Flight was just one among the wide range

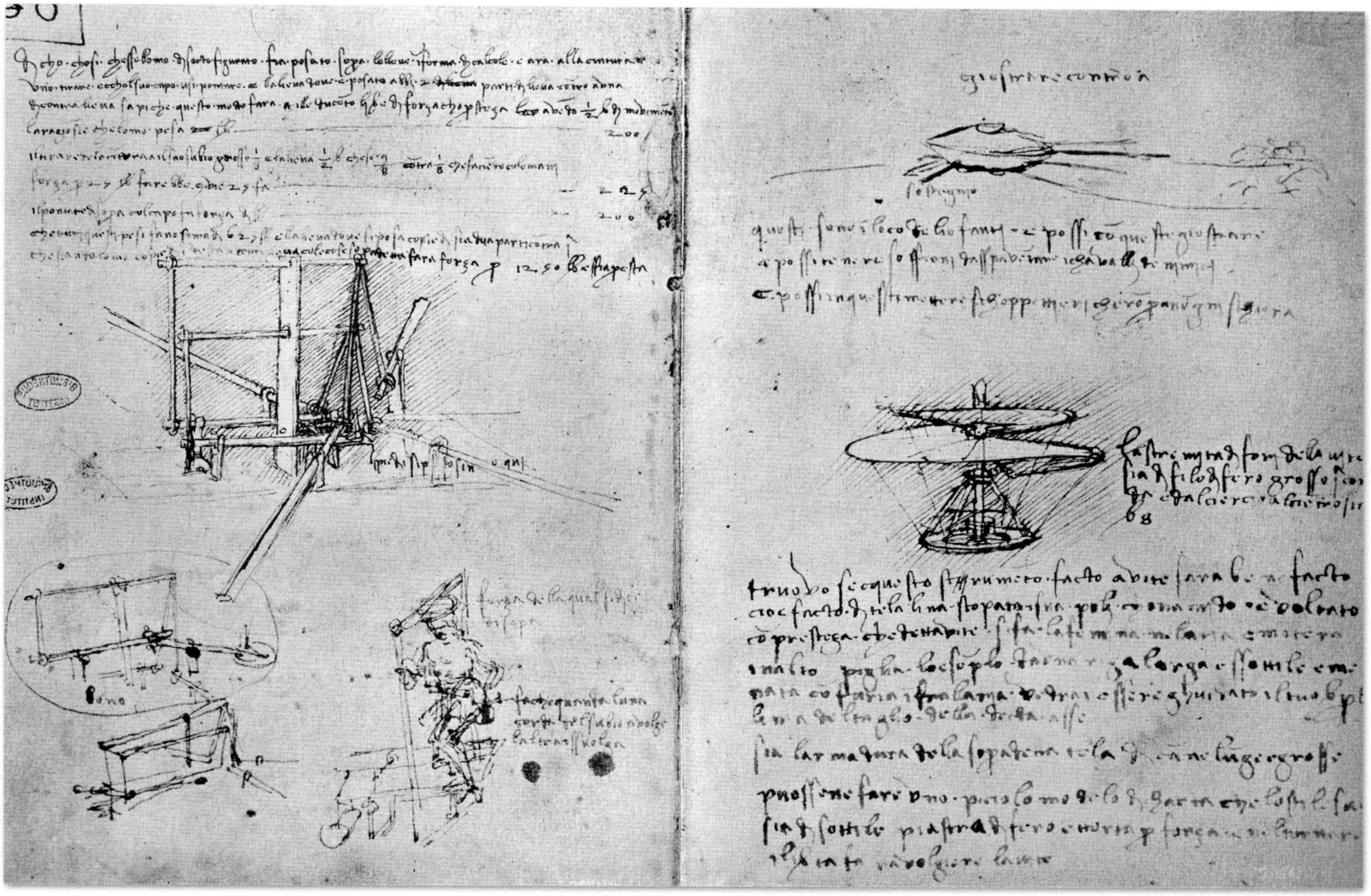

of Leonardo's interests. His notebooks are also full of subjects as diverse as solar power, bridge-building and the anatomy of the human lip. There are more mundane entries too: shopping lists, notes about a book he wants to borrow and people who owe him money.

Scholars believe that Leonardo's early life had a profound effect on his genius. He was born in 1452, the illegitimate son of a Florentine notary. He was mainly self-educated, but his father noticed his artistic talents and apprenticed him, aged 15, to the painter and sculptor Andrea del Verrocchio. Verrocchio insisted that his students understood the anatomy of the human body, so Leonardo became an expert at drawing limbs, muscles and other body parts. He was given permission to dissect human corpses in Florence and in Milan and Rome, where he later lived. Leonardo's notebooks contain more than 240 detailed drawings and 13,000 words on anatomy. He was the first to describe what we now call arteriosclerosis as a part of the ageing process, and he also identified cirrhosis of the liver.

This true Renaissance man appears to have started jotting down his observations in the mid-1480s. He had moved to Milan after offering his services to the local ruler as a military engineer. He wrote in "mirror writing" which reads from left to right, probably because he was left-handed. Experts believe that he worked on loose sheets of paper which were later folded

LEFT This is widely believed to be Leonardo's self-portrait, drawn in red chalk. Now in Turin's Royal Library, it is seldom displayed due to its fragile condition.

OPPOSITE Leonardo's studies of the foetus and an arm reveal his advanced understanding of the human body. He is credited with being the first to draw an embryo correctly.

into notebooks. He spent 17 years in Milan, constantly jotting down the thoughts, ideas and inventions that raced through his brilliantly unconventional mind. There are weapons of war – such as a chariot that could slice up men with whirling blades, an adding machine, shoes for walking on water, a mechanical organ, costume designs for elaborate pageants, notes about hydraulic engineering, town planning, architecture – the list goes on and on. Painting is often mentioned, too. A description of the way people sit in a group around a table may have been a study for *The Last Supper* fresco he started in around 1495. Although one of the outstanding artists of the Renaissance, Leonardo's preoccupation with the world about him meant that he often left paintings unfinished. He was also a perfectionist. He started his masterpiece *Mona Lisa* in 1503 and continued working on it year after year, adding a stroke here, a new glaze there.

As he grew older, Leonardo spent less time painting and concentrated more on his "studies". It seems likely that he planned to publish his notes, because many of his observations about specific subjects are contained on a single page. Sadly, the great man died in 1519, at the age of 67, before his notebooks were published. He left them to his devoted follower (and possible lover) Francesco Melzi, who managed to put all of Leonardo's thoughts about painting into one work, *Treatise on Painting*, but did little else. It was more than 200 years after Leonardo's death that the notebooks came to public attention. Seven thousand pages are known to have survived in 17 notebooks – about 20 per cent of the material the Renaissance visionary produced. The notebooks, with one exception, are now kept in museums in Italy, Spain, France and Britain. The only private copy is owned by Bill Gates, who digitized some of its pages as a screen-saver on his Microsoft operating system.

On 5 March 2012, *Curiosity*, a NASA rover, landed on Mars. On board were digital copies of a portrait of Leonardo da Vinci and his *Codex on the Flight of Birds*.

To us, Leonardo is more than a treasure; he is one of the great heroes in the history of human creativity.

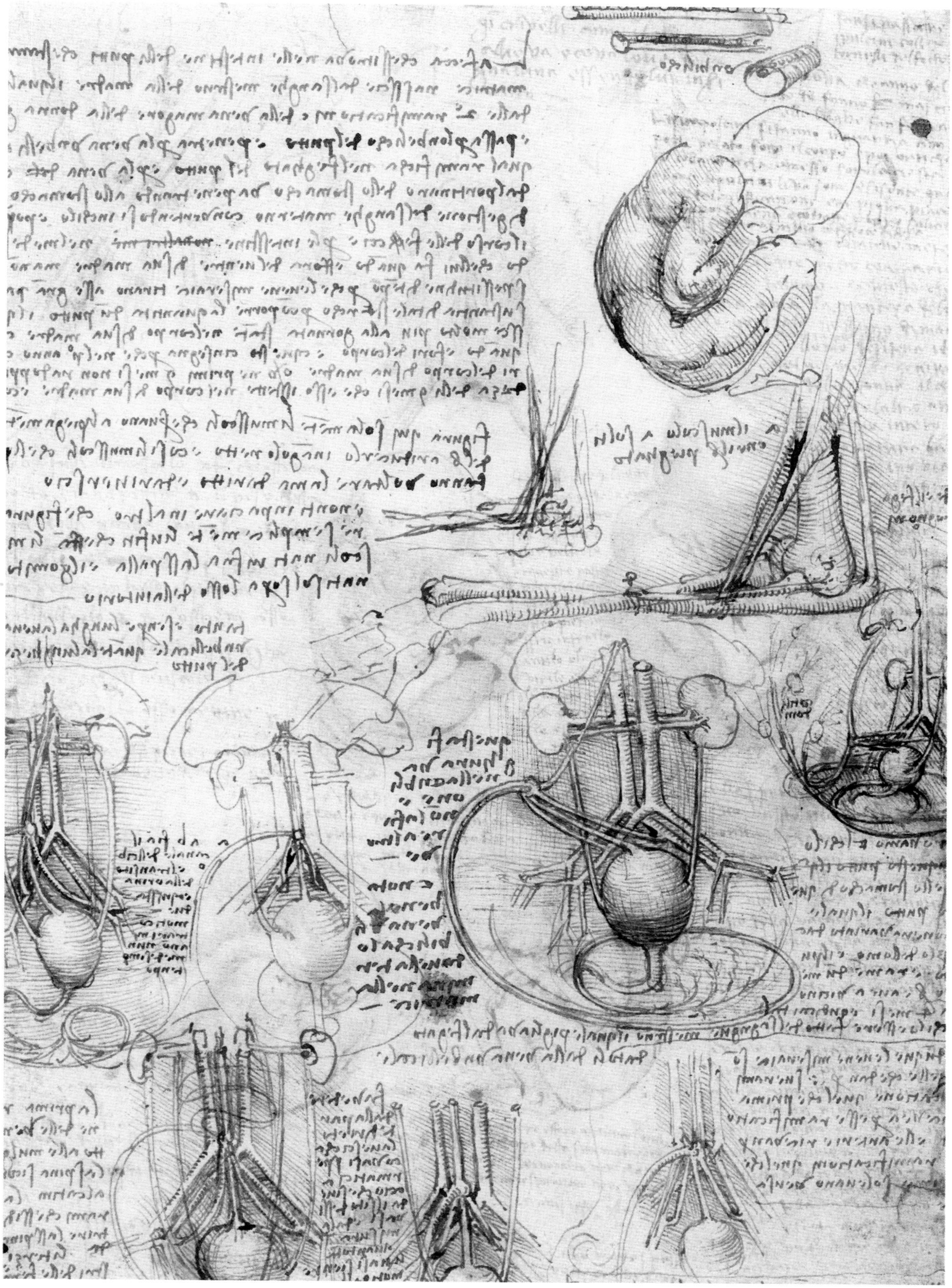

14

The Treaty of Tordesillas

The Treaty of Tordesillas created the first worldwide empires. It entrenched the right of the two earliest colonial powers, Spain and Portugal, to plant their flags in designated areas across the globe. It was proposed in 1494 by Pope Alexander VI, who was concerned about the growing tension between the two countries as their explorers ventured west to the Americas and south and east to Africa, India and beyond.

ABOVE The fierce debate between representatives of the Vatican, the Spanish states and Portugal about how to carve up the map of the known world. The treaty of 1494 divided it roughly in half.

To anyone without fluent Spanish, the town of Tordesillas may be as hard to pronounce as its nearby provincial capital of Valladolid, a bit further up the river Douro. But the name Tordesillas has a historical ring to it that outshines almost any other, for it was in this town, 120 kilometres (75 miles) from Spain's Portuguese border, that the world was divided between two empires for the first time. Long before Britain, Holland and France painted their imperial colours on the map, the two Iberian powers had sent their explorers way beyond Europe, and the inevitable friction between them led to the Treaty of Tordesillas.

The Portuguese were the first to dispatch their ships beyond the horizons. They reached Madeira in 1400, the Azores two years later, and for the rest of the century the Portuguese royal family enthusiastically backed adventurers who planted their flag further and further round the coast of Africa. The invention of the caravel, a sailing ship which could move much more safely and closer to the wind, allowed sailors to reach the Cape Verde Islands and go on to the Gulf of

RIGHT King John II of Portugal (left) and Pope Alexander VI (right) – key players in the shaping of the treaty.

OPPOSITE The text of the treaty between King John II of Portugal (whose name is at the top) and his Spanish rivals. The two empires dominated the world for more than a century, but by the eighteenth century their pact was ignored by later imperial powers.

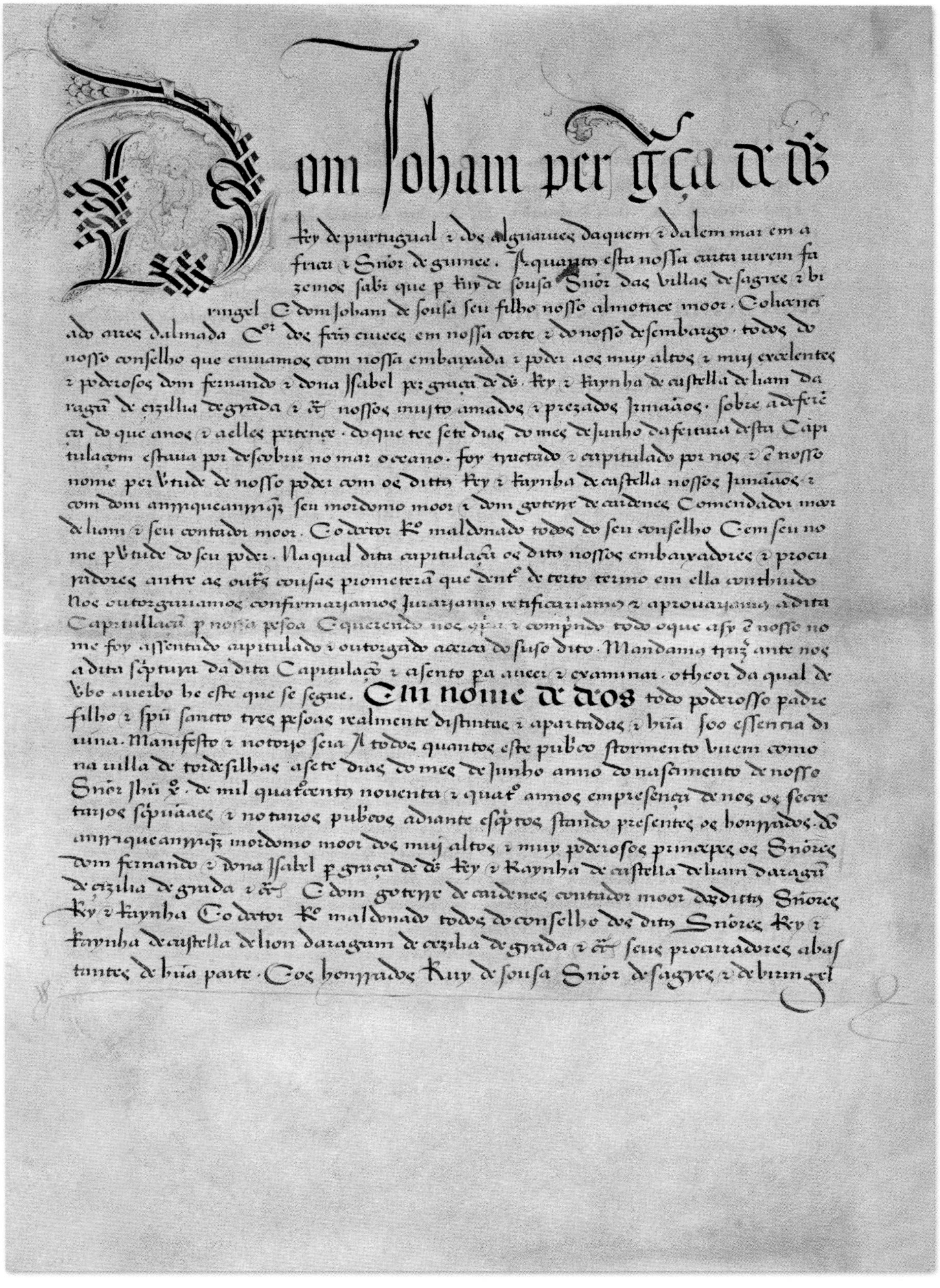

Dom Joham per graça de deus
Rey de purtugual e dos algarves daquem e dalem mar em a
frica e Senhor de guinee. A quantos esta nossa carta virem fa
zemos saber que per Ruy de sousa Senhor das villas de sagres e bi
ringel. E dom Joham de sousa seu filho nosso almotacee moor. E o lecenci
ado aires dalmada Corregedor dos feitos civees em nossa corte e do nosso desembargo. todos do
nosso conselho que enviamos com nossa embaixada e poder aos muy altos e muy excelentes
e poderosos dom fernando e dona Isabel per graça de deus Rey e Raynha de castella de liam da
raguam de cizilia de granada etc. nossos muyto amados e prezados Irmaãos. sobre a deferē
ca do que a nos e a elles pertence. do que tee sete dias do mes de Junho da feitura desta Capi
tulaçom estava por descobrir no mar oceano. foy tractado e capitulado por nos e ē nosso
nome per virtude de nosso poder com os ditos Rey e Raynha de castella nossos Irmaãos. e
com dom anrrique anrriquez seu mordomo moor e dom gutierre de cardenes Comendador mayor
de liam e seu contador moor. E o doctor Rodrigo maldonado todos do seu conselho E em seu no
me per virtude do seu poder. Na qual dita capitulaçã os ditos nossos embaixadores e procu
radores antre as outras cousas prometerã que dentro de certo termo em ella contheudo
Nos outorgariamos confirmariamos Jurariamos retificariamos e aprovariamos a dita
Capitullaçã per nossa pessoa. E querendo nos guardar e comprir todo o que asy ē nosso no
me foy assentado capitulado e outorgado acerca do suso dito. Mandamos trazer ante nos
a dita scriptura da dita Capitulaçã e asento pera a veer e examinar. o theor da qual de
verbo a verbo he este que se segue. **Em nome de deos** todo poderosso padre
filho e spiritu sancto tres pessoas realmente distintas e apartadas e hũa soo essencia di
vina. Manifesto e notorio seja A todos quantos este publico stormento virem como
na villa de tordesilhas a sete dias do mes de Junho anno do nascimento de nosso
Senhor Jhesu Christo de mil quatrocentos noventa e quatro annos em presença de nos os secre
tarios scrivaães e notarios publicos adiante scriptos stando presentes os honrrados dom
anrrique anrriquez mordomo moor dos muy altos e muy poderosos principes os Senhores
dom fernando e dona Isabel per graça de deus Rey e Raynha de castella de liam daraguam
de cizilia de granada etc. E dom gutierre de cardenes contador moor dos ditos Senhores
Rey e Raynha. E o doctor Rodrigo maldonado todos do conselho dos ditos Senhores Rey e
Raynha de castella de lion daragam de cezilia de granada etc. seus procuradores abas
tantes de hũa parte. E os honrrados Ruy de sousa Senhor de sagres e de beringel

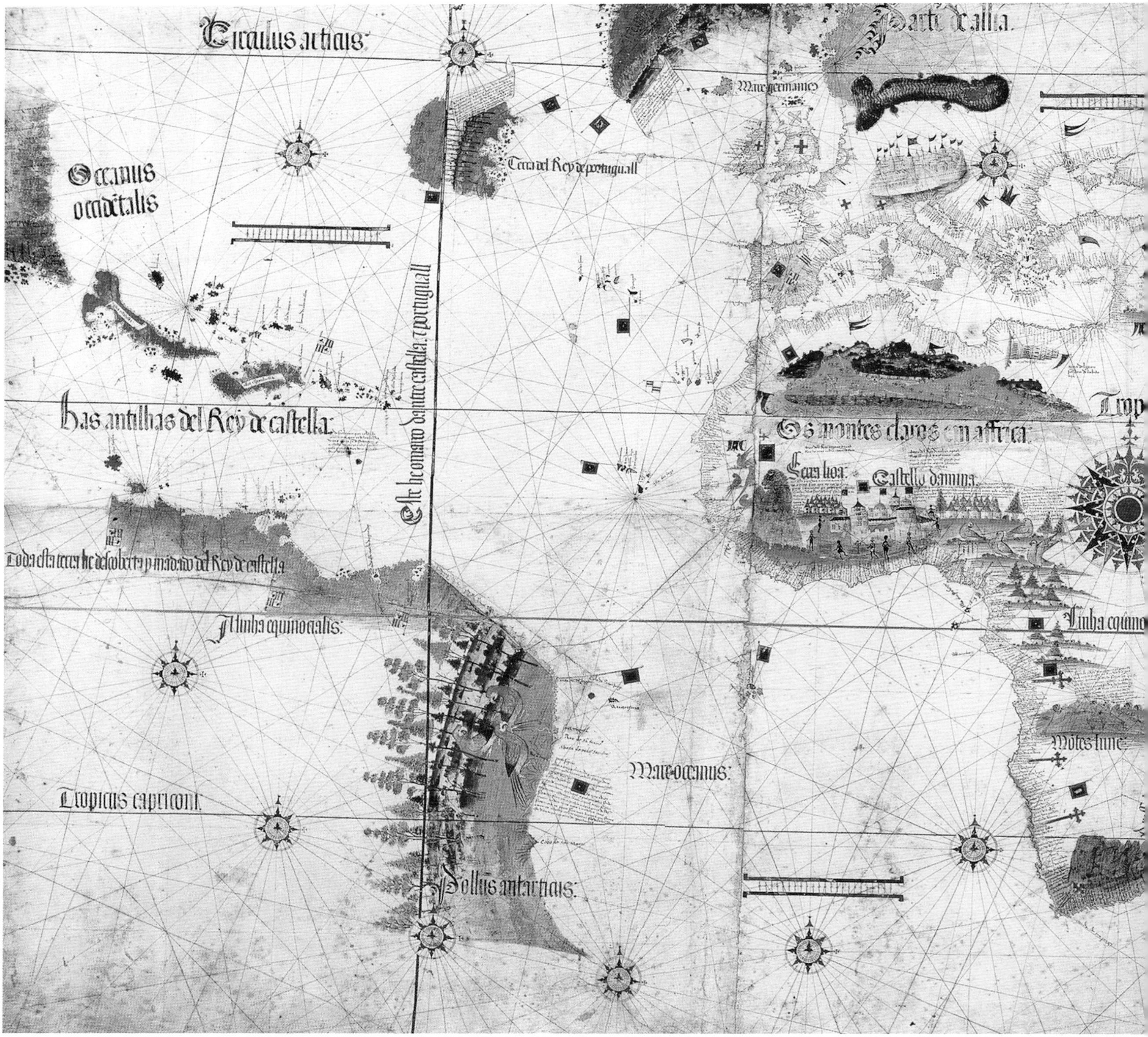

Guinea by the 1470s. By 1488, Bartolomeu Diaz had rounded the Cape of Good Hope, and Vasco da Gama was in India by 1498. There seemed to be no limit to Portuguese expansion. It was only when the king turned down Christopher Columbus's request for the cash to sail a fleet westwards across the Atlantic that the Spanish took up the challenge and financed the man who discovered America. With the return of Columbus from his first voyage in 1493 and the news that Portugal was reaching beyond Africa, the tension between Europe's two most adventurous powers demanded resolution.

The first to offer a compromise was the Pope in Rome, Alexander VI. The Vatican had a useful role in those early days of international affairs in declaring a form of religious fiat, a papal bull, to resolve disputes. Pope Alexander drew a pole-to-pole line from north to south in the Atlantic 100 leagues west of the Azores and Cape Verde Islands. He pronounced that Spain could settle

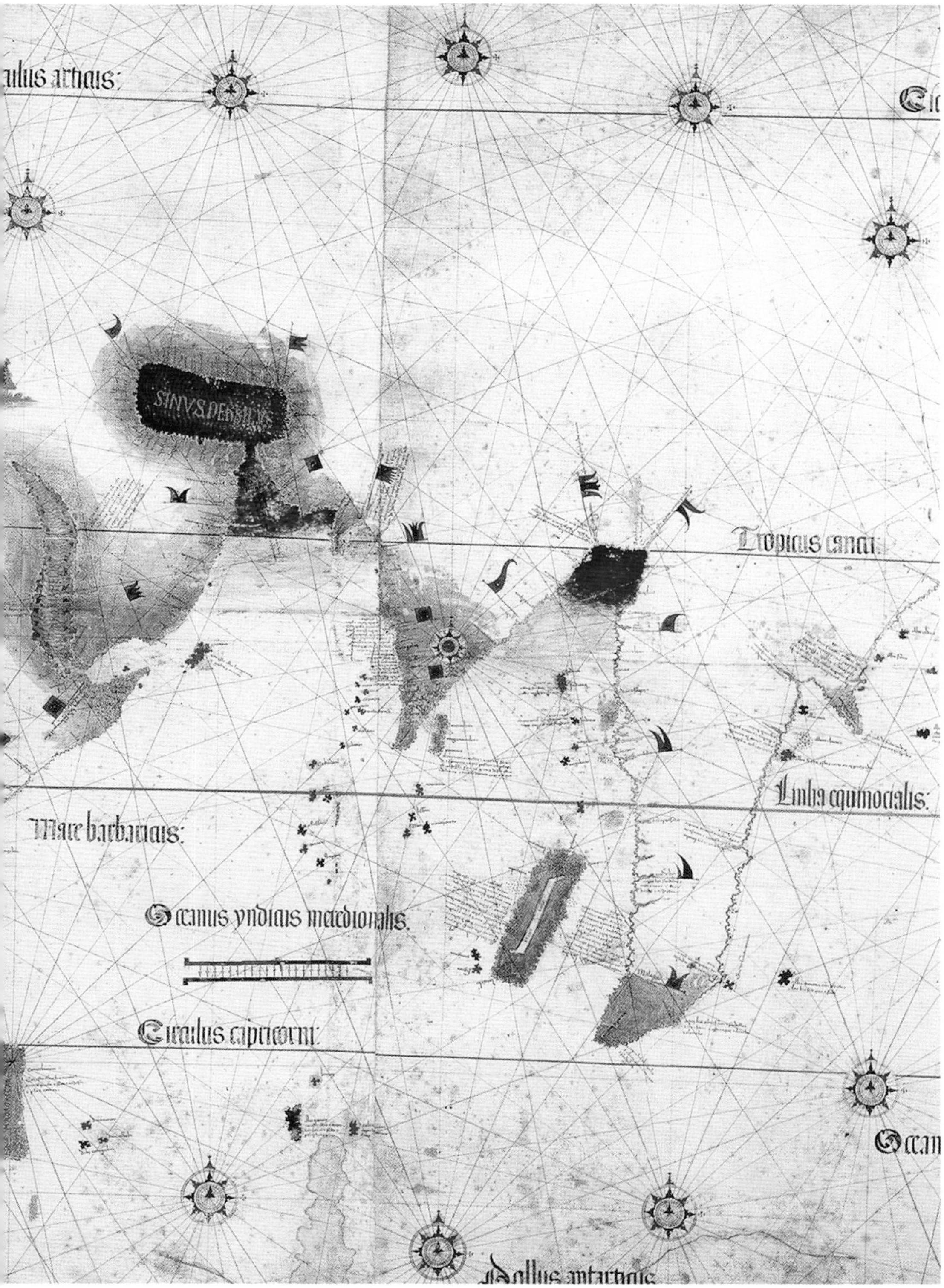

LEFT A contemporary map of the known world showing the agreed line of demarcation between the Spanish and Portuguese empires. Portugal expanded much further into Brazil than depicted on this map.

on any non-Christian territory to the west of the line. There was no mention of Portugal. King John II of Portugal, not a man to be pushed around, was none too happy with this. He had already personally stabbed his brother-in-law to death for allegedly conspiring against him and so the Spanish were quick to agree when he insisted on a new treaty that would define the boundary between the two empires more fairly.

The two sides met at Tordesillas in 1494 and the outcome did much to satisfy Portugal. The line in the Atlantic was shifted another 270 leagues further west. It was clearly agreed that Portugal would have the same opportunities east of this line as Spain would have to the west of it. Conveniently for Portugal, this new line embraced a large chunk of Brazil, which bulged out into the South Atlantic. It wasn't long before a Portuguese seaman, Pedro Cabral, landed in Brazil on his way to India and planted the Portuguese flag there with the clear intent to expand into the interior.

Tordesillas gave Portugal the right to stretch into the Indian Ocean and beyond. But how far beyond? The treaty did not provide for an eastern limit to Portugal's reach. The uncertainty was compounded when Portuguese seamen reached the Moluccas in what is now Indonesia. These "Spice Islands" would become famous for their excellent nutmeg trees and cloves, which ships were able to carry back to Europe at a considerable profit. Portugal got there first in 1511, but the Spanish arrived shortly after and the two nations soon came to blows. A new treaty would have to be drawn up to determine where the new dividing line should be. It was agreed in the Treaty of Saragossa to draw a line down the Pacific, as had been done earlier in the Atlantic, and tempers cooled. Portuguese outposts were soon established in the western Pacific in the Moluccas, in Macao and even as far north and east as Nagasaki in Japan.

The irony of this massive piece of empire-building is that it was soon ignored by the other powers in Europe which were hungry for colonies across the world. Spain and Portugal lost their footholds first to rivals and later to independence movements, but the Treaty of Tordesillas was the first major attempt to define power on a global scale. An echo of it rang through subsequent centuries, with Argentina citing it as one element in its claim to the British Falkland Islands and Chile's claim to part of the Antarctic.

15

The Codex Mendoza

The Codex Mendoza is a unique historical record. It is the nearest the world has come to a history of the Aztec civilization based on the evidence of the Aztecs themselves. Since these early inhabitants of central Mexico did not read or write, their Spanish conquerors persuaded them to record their memories in pictures, and this is the result. The Codex dates from the mid-sixteenth century and provides an illustrated story of the Aztecs who flourished from the 1320s to the Spanish conquest in 1521.

The Aztecs' civilization in Mexico has to be one of the most fascinating landmarks in world history. Yet sadly they left us no written legacy, no record of their own history or how they lived. That is why this "codex", a 71-page manuscript written only 20 years or so after the Aztec empire was annihilated by the Spanish conquest in 1521, is a precious and almost magically revealing account of that mysterious era of American history. The Codex Mendoza is so valuable because it is the product of people who were there before the Spanish arrived. It is a story told in pictures. Indigenous artists illustrate their history, their method of government and their culture; Spanish clerics add their written commentary on what the Aztecs are telling them. Each page explains something about the doomed Emperor Moctezuma's city of Tenochtitlán and the people (who called themselves "Mexica") who lived there and in the surrounding provinces. We visited Mexico City, which stands on the ruins of Tenochtitlán, and were captivated by the magnificent display of Aztec civilization in the archaeological museum. Whether or not you've visited the museum, the Codex Mendoza is a revealing guide to how the Aztecs lived.

This opening page of the manuscript is a glorious technicolour introduction to this remarkable story. An eagle stands on a cactus in the centre, symbolizing the legendary event which led the Aztecs to found their city early in the fourteenth century. They were told by their patron god Huitzilopochtli that they should place their city where they found an eagle standing on a cactus. That turned out to be on an island in Lake Texcoco. The island was dissected by waterways into four sections, as the frontispiece shows with the large blue "X". The Spanish invaders called it the "Venice of the West". The expanding Aztec empire is represented underneath by two Aztec warriors dwarfing their defeated opponents.

The Codex was inscribed on the orders of the Spanish viceroy of newly conquered Mexico, Antonio de Mendoza, who took over as Governor in 1535. Only 14 years earlier, Hernán Cortés and his small Spanish army had invaded the Aztec empire and overthrown Moctezuma II. Mendoza

RIGHT A delightful glimpse of everyday Aztec life, where getting drunk was a privilege. An upper-class woman is served "pulque", a liquor made from cactus.

OPPOSITE The title page of the Codex shows the Aztecs' subject peoples bringing tribute to the capital of Tenochtitlán. The skull on a pole (centre right) is a reminder of the penalty for not paying up.

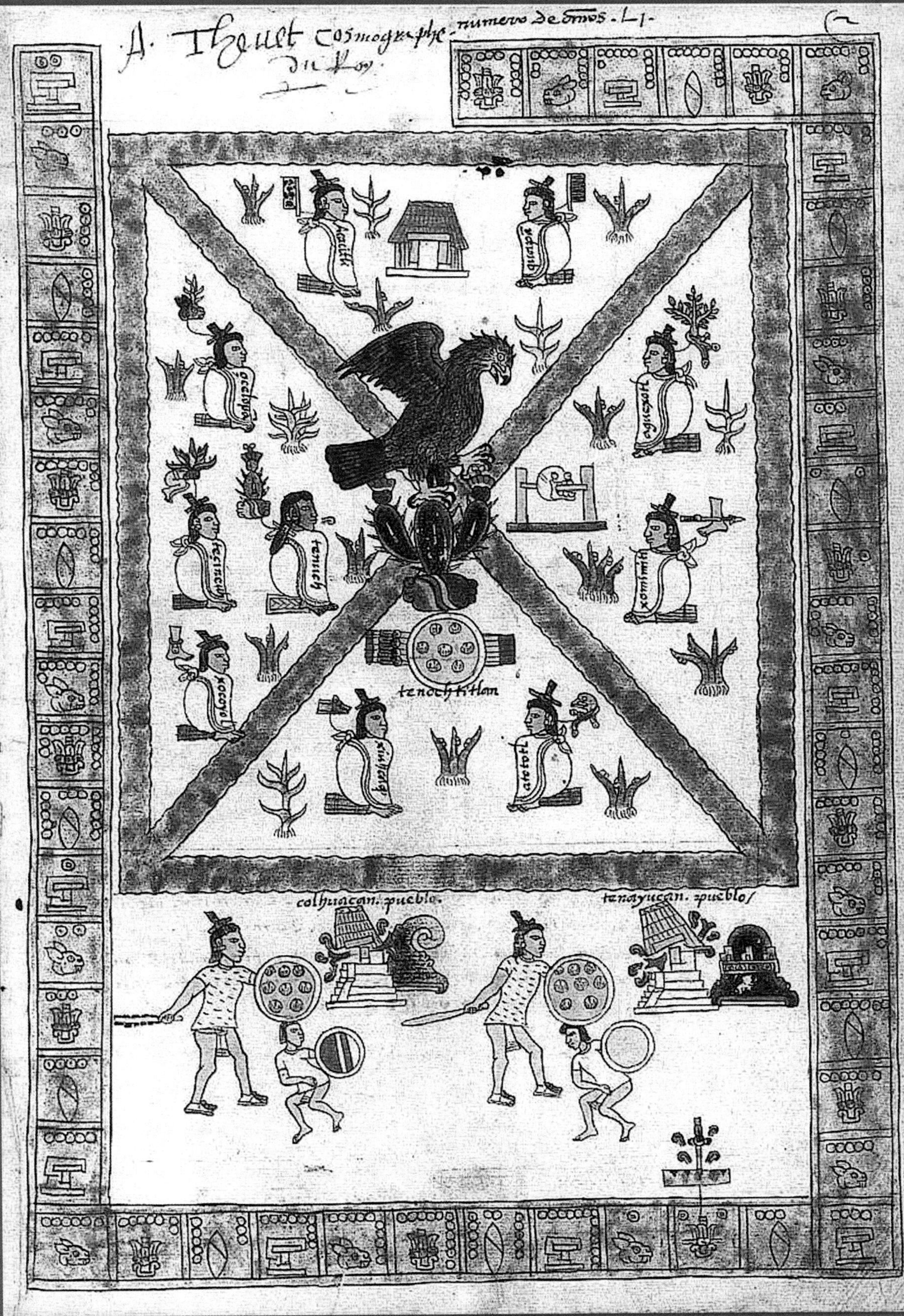

A. Thevet cosmographe du Roy
numero de años .LI.
tenochtitlan
colhuacan. pueblo.
tenayucan. pueblos

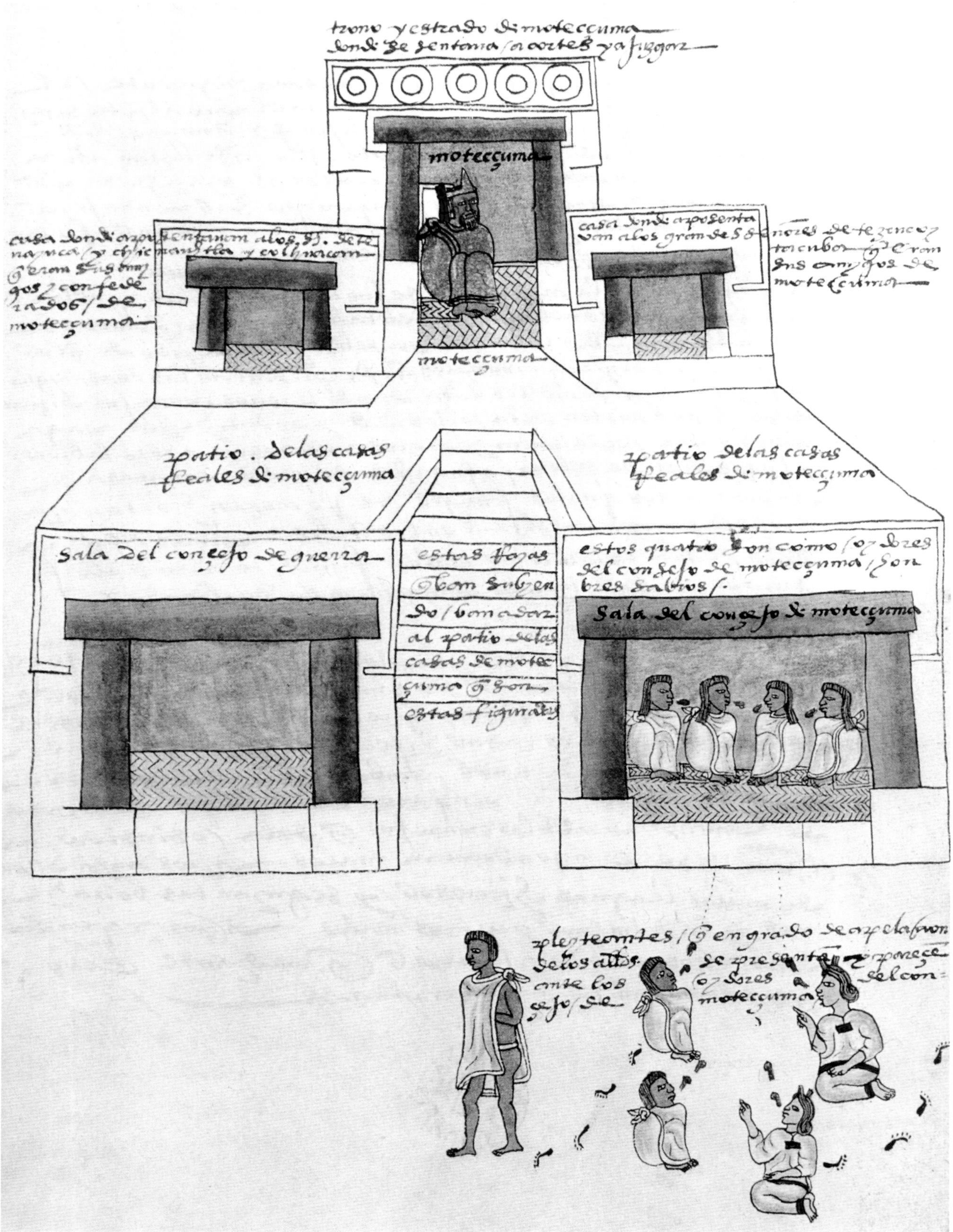

ABOVE A plan of the Aztec ruler's palace. Moctezuma himself sits in the throne room at the top.

OPPOSITE ABOVE A display of types of tribute paid by subject peoples to the Aztec regime. Feathers and jaguar skins were common forms of payment.

OPPOSITE BELOW Hernán Cortés, Spanish conqueror of Mexico, is offered a gift by the Aztec ruler. It didn't pay off. Within months Moctezuma was dead and Mexico Spanish.

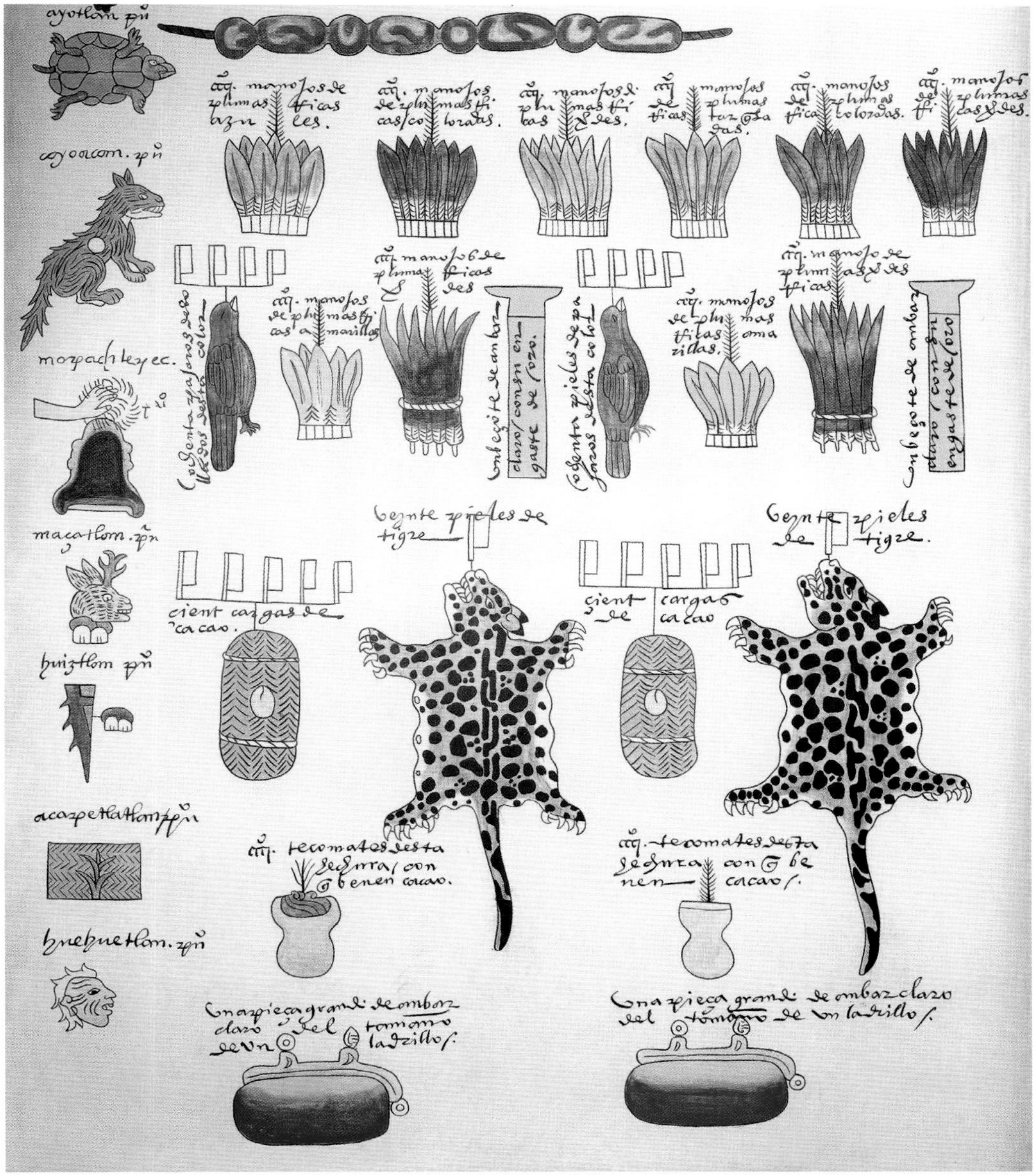

wanted to record the story of pre-Spanish Mexico and dispatch it to the Spanish king, Charles V. On its way back to Spain, however, the Codex was snatched by pirates, sold to France and then bought by an Englishman in Paris called Richard Hakluyt. He took it home to England and it ended up in the Bodleian Library in Oxford, where it remains today.

The Codex tells the story of how Aztec kings built their empire by ruthlessly suppressing neighbouring cities and forcing them to pay tribute to Tenochtitlán. They did this over just two centuries, from the 1320s to 1521. It tells us that one of the greatest Aztec kings was Moctezuma I, who reigned from 1440 to 1469. He brought the city to a level of prosperity that lasted until the Spanish conquest. By coincidence, that last century or so of Aztec power in Mexico was matched by the flowering of the Inca empire in Peru, Ecuador and Chile, which was also crushed by Spanish conquistadors in the early 1500s.

For us, the most interesting material in this beautifully illustrated manuscript is the picture it presents of Aztec culture and everyday life. For example, there are illustrations of the fabulous costumes that people wore to denote how senior they were in the strict hierarchy of Aztec society. We learn that difficult children had their heads shaved and women often married at the age of 15 and faced severe penalties for being unfaithful to their husbands. Human sacrifice was common, symbolized on the first page of the Codex by the rack of skulls just to the right of centre. The most revealing and detailed account of this grisly tradition is in another document which describes how several people were sacrificed at the dedication of a temple in the capital. It recounts how, with the population watching, the king himself "drove the knife into the victim's breast and ripped it open". Experts estimate that one king alone killed thousands of people in this way.

Terrible though some of the Aztec traditions were, it's also worth remembering the brutality with which the Spanish conquerors in both Mexico and Peru brought these ancient empires to an end.

16

Copernicus's *Revolutions of the Celestial Spheres*

The landmark scientific thesis *On the Revolutions of the Celestial Spheres* changed the way we humans view our world. Nicolaus Copernicus challenged the accepted belief that the earth was the centre of the universe around which the sun, planets and moon revolved. His revelation in 1543 that it was in fact the earth that circled the sun – his helio-centric breakthrough – established him as a pioneer of the Scientific Revolution.

ABOVE A German stamp commemorating the 500th anniversary of the birth of Nicolaus Copernicus. A Polish citizen, he is thought to have had German ancestry.

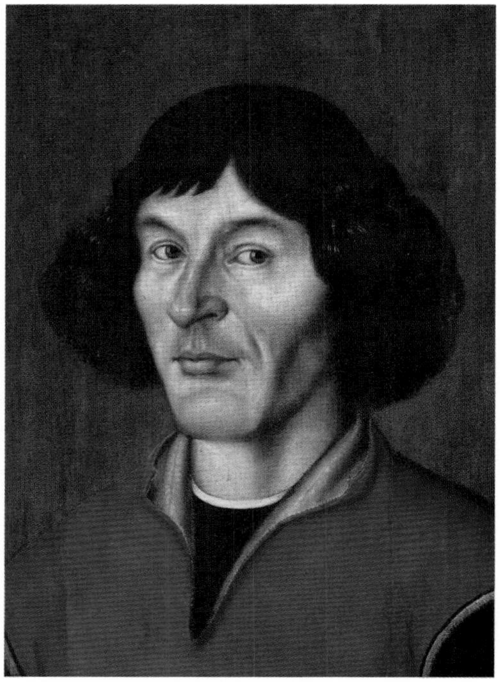

RIGHT Note the broken nose and slight scar above his left eye in this self portrait by Copernicus. They helped archaeologists identify his skull in 2005.

OPPOSITE An ancient copy of the thesis in which Copernicus shattered the accepted belief that the centre of the universe was the earth around which the sun and other planets revolved.

The first time Nicolaus Copernicus saw his masterwork in published form was on 24 May 1543, the day that he died. He had suffered a stroke. A friend rushed to his bedside clutching the newly published work. Copernicus opened his eyes, glanced at his book and serenely passed away. At least that is the poignant, probably romanticized, tale commonly told about the brilliant and modest man who dedicated his life to showing that planets revolved around the sun in elegant harmony.

Copernicus was born in Poland in 1473. He studied astronomy, astrology, mathematics, medicine and law at universities in Poland and Italy, returning to Poland to work as secretary to his uncle, a Roman Catholic bishop. By day, he collected rents from Church-owned properties, oversaw the chapter's financial matters and attended to his uncle's medical needs. At night, he gazed at the stars. The telescope had yet to be invented, so Copernicus made his observations with the naked eye.

At the time it was widely believed that the universe was geo-centric, with the earth stationary at its centre, circled in a uniform manner by the sun, moon and planets. This theory, put forward by the Greek philosopher Aristotle in the fourth century BC, was elaborated by Ptolemy, another Greek, 400 years later. One of the obvious problems with this model was that sometimes planets appeared to travel backwards across the sky in what astronomers called retrograde motion. By 1514, Copernicus had produced a handwritten work, *Commentariolus* (*Little Commentary*), in which he theorized that this retrograde motion was caused by the earth moving through space. He also suggested that changes in sunrise and sunset times and the seasons were caused by the earth's revolutions around the sun. A tiny handful of others had previously suggested the universe was helio-centric, but what made Copernicus stand out was that he produced an impressive array of facts and figures to back his claims.

His friends urged Copernicus to publish his findings, but he resisted, saying that he wanted to gather additional data for a more detailed book. It's thought he was also worried about upsetting the Church, which insisted that God created the universe with the earth as its centre.

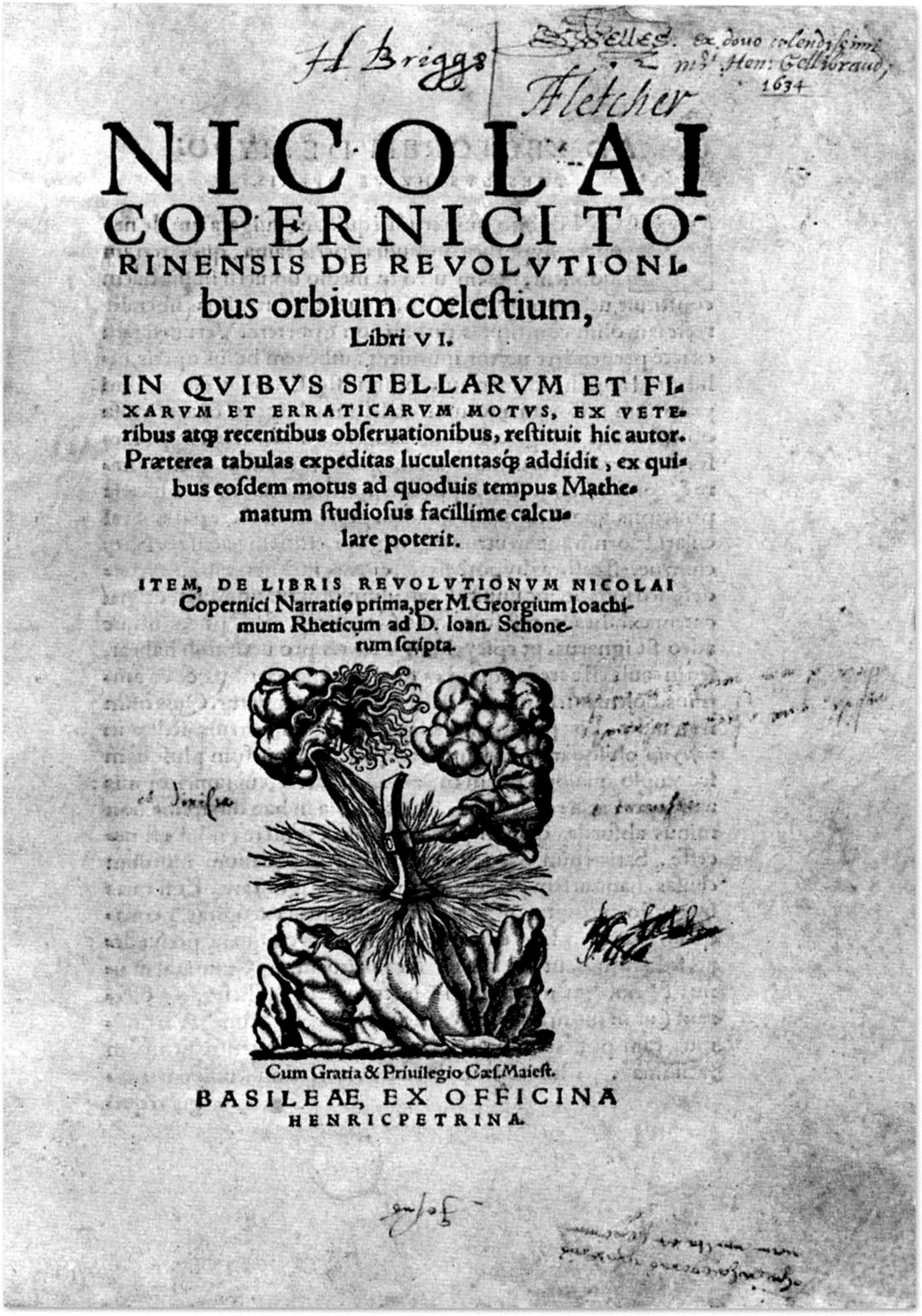

H Briggs

Fletcher

NICOLAI COPERNICI TORINENSIS DE REVOLVTIONIbus orbium coelestium, Libri VI.

IN QVIBVS STELLARVM ET FIXARVM ET ERRATICARVM MOTVS, EX VETEribus atque recentibus obseruationibus, restituit hic autor. Praeterea tabulas expeditas luculentasque addidit, ex quibus eosdem motus ad quoduis tempus Mathematum studiosus facillime calculare poterit.

ITEM, DE LIBRIS REVOLVTIONVM NICOLAI Copernici Narratio prima, per M. Georgium Ioachimum Rheticum ad D. Ioan. Schonerum scripta.

Cum Gratia & Priuilegio Caes. Maiest.

BASILEAE, EX OFFICINA HENRICPETRINA.

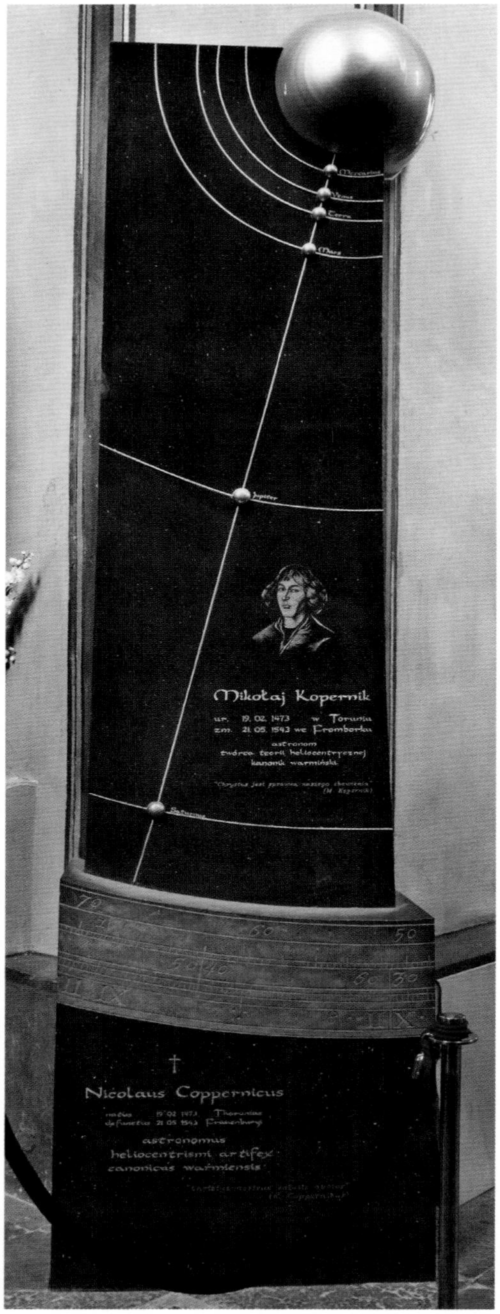

LEFT This black granite tombstone rises about the grave of Copernicus. It features a model of his solar system – a golden sun surrounded by six planets.

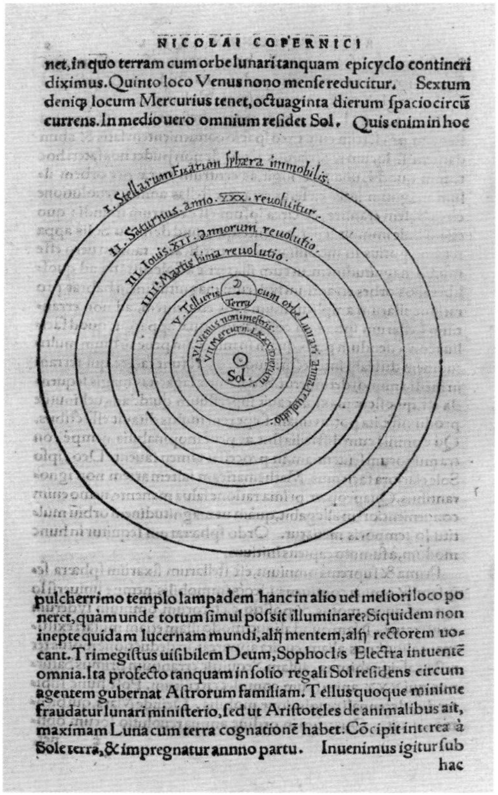
NICOLAI COPERNICI

net, in quo terram cum orbe lunari tanquam epicyclo contineri diximus. Quinto loco Venus nono mense reducitur. Sextum deniq; locum Mercurius tenet, octuaginta dierum spacio circũ currens. In medio uero omnium residet Sol. Quis enim in hoc

pulcherrimo templo lampadem hanc in alio uel meliori loco poneret, quàm unde totum simul possit illuminare? Siquidem non inepte quidam lucernam mundi, alij mentem, alij rectorem uocant. Trimegistus uisibilem Deum, Sophoclis Electra intuentẽ omnia. Ita profecto tanquam in solio regali Sol residens circum agentem gubernat Astrorum familiam. Tellus quoque minime fraudatur lunari ministerio, sed ut Aristoteles de animalibus ait, maximam Luna cum terra cognationẽ habet. Cõcipit interea à Sole terra, & impregnatur annno partu. Inuenimus igitur sub hac

BELOW Copernicus's famous drawing of planets Mercury, Venus, Earth and moon, Jupiter and Saturn revolving around a stationary sun.

OPPOSITE This magnificent star atlas of the Copernican system is the work of Andreas Cellarius, a Dutch-German cartographer.

Even though Copernicus remained unpublished for another 30 years, his reputation as an exceptional astronomer spread. He was invited to travel to Pisa to join a discussion about a new church calendar to replace the Julian one, which dated back to the time of Julius Caesar. After the passage of so many years, it had fallen out of alignment with the position of the sun. Copernicus also developed economic theories about the value and use of money which are still important concepts today. Astronomy, however, remained his first love, and he worked unflaggingly on his magnum opus, developing – among other things – a method for ordering planets and calculating relative distances between them and the sun.

His major work, *On the Revolutions of the Celestial Spheres*, appears to have been completed about 1532, but, again, Copernicus refused to publish it because he feared the "novelty and incomprehensibility" of his theories would lead to scorn. It was not until the last year of his life that his 400-page manuscript appeared in public, laying out his model of the solar system and the path of the planets.

The momentous document was diplomatically dedicated to Pope Paul II. The Church banned the book in 1616, a whole 73 years after Copernicus's death. In 1633, 90 years after *On the Revolutions of the Celestial Spheres* was published, the Church convicted the Italian astronomer Galileo Galilei (1564–1642) of heresy for "following the position of Copernicus, which is contrary to the true sense and authority of the Holy Scripture".

The work which Copernicus pioneered was built on by scientists like Johannes Kepler (1571–1630) and Isaac Newton (1643–1727) and led to a new understanding of the universe and the nature of science. Copernicus was buried in Frombork, in Poland, in the cathedral where he worked as a canon. The exact location of his grave was unknown, and various searches over the years failed to find it. In 2005, archaeologists discovered what they were convinced were Copernicus's remains. DNA from the skeleton was matched to hair samples from a book owned by Copernicus, and on 22 May 2010 the illustrious star-gazer was given a second funeral. On the black granite tombstone is a model of his solar system: a golden sun circled by six planets.

SCENO SYSTE COPER
GRAPHIA MATIS NICANI.
ZODIACVS ET SPHÆRA STELLARVM FIXARVM IMMOBILIS ET CONSTANS
ÆQVINOCTIVM VERNVM
ÆQVINOCTIVM AVTVMNALE
GEMI NI
SAGIT TARIVS

17

Shakespeare's First Folio

No book about treasured documents would be complete without a contribution from William Shakespeare, widely regarded as the greatest writer in the English language. The First Folio, put together by two of the Bard's fellow actors, includes 18 of his plays which had never been published before. Without this manuscript, some of Shakespeare's most famous masterpieces might have been lost for ever. No wonder it is one of the most valuable printed books in the world.

Imagine a world without *Julius Caesar*, *Macbeth*, *As You Like It* or *Twelfth Night*. Incredibly, had it not been for the dedication and far-sightedness of two of William Shakespeare's contemporaries, these and many others of his works might not have survived. The two men who saved at least half of Shakespeare's plays from disappearing without a trace, John Heminges and Henry Condell, had acted in his company at London's Globe Theatre and were determined that future generations would enjoy his magnificent work. After Shakespeare's death in 1616, they set about gathering all his plays to be printed in a book worthy of their creator. The result was *Mr William Shakespeare's Comedies, Histories and Tragedies*, better known as the First Folio. It is without a doubt one of the most important documents in the English-speaking world.

In Shakespeare's day, a playwright first produced a handwritten draft known as a "foul copy". He or an assistant then transcribed that into a more legible "fair copy", adding notes for the staging of the play in prompt books. Although none of Shakespeare's original manuscripts survive, 18 of his 36 plays were printed in quarto books. The quartos, around the size of a modern paperback, were made of sheets of paper folded in half and then in half again. Quartos that seem faithful to Shakespeare's original work are known as "good" quartos, although there are also "bad" quartos. These are copies probably taken from rough drafts of the plays or based on the memories of actors. Rivalry among Elizabethan theatre groups was intense, so good plays were regularly pirated.

Heminges and Condell used "good" quartos to assemble the First Folio. They also turned

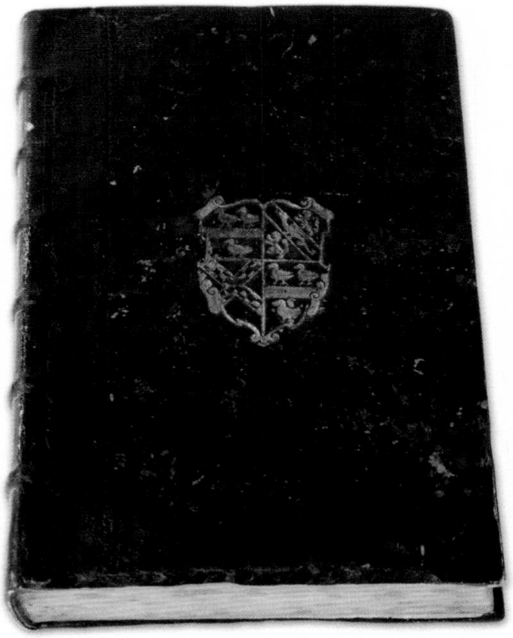

to any remaining "foul" and "fair" copies and prompt books, the production team's bibles. This was particularly important for transcribing the 18 plays that had not been published in quarto editions. Since both men had acted with Shakespeare, it is presumed that they asked members of his company, fellow actors and writers who collaborated with him to share their memories of individual plays.

Once the material was gathered, Heminges and Condell divided the plays into comedies, tragedies and histories, a decision that helped shape our understanding of Shakespeare's body of work. They also commissioned a Flemish engraver, Martin Droeshout, to produce a portrait of Shakespeare for the title page. As Droeshout had never met his subject, the illustration was probably copied from an earlier portrait, now lost. The writer Ben Jonson called it a good likeness and the Bard's trademark domed head is now familiar worldwide.

The plays were published in folio format, on large sheets of paper folded in half, reflecting the high esteem in which Shakespeare was held, as folios were usually reserved for important books like the Bible. The printing process was a massive undertaking, and it

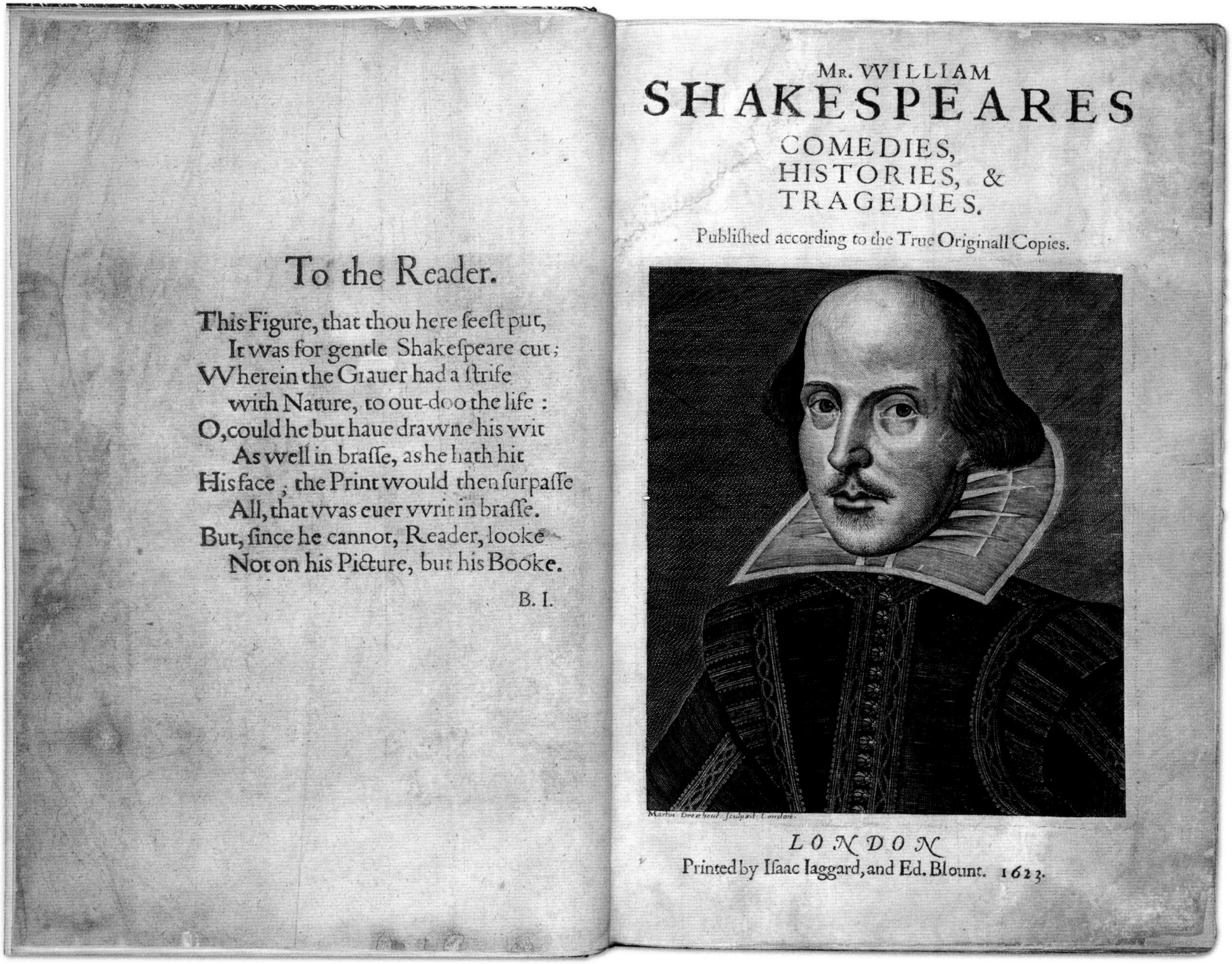

To the Reader.
This Figure, that thou here ſeeſt put,
It was for gentle Shakeſpeare cut;
Wherein the Grauer had a ſtrife
with Nature, to out-doo the life :
O, could he but haue drawne his wit
As well in braſſe, as he hath hit
His face ; the Print would then ſurpaſſe
All, that vvas euer vvrit in braſſe.
But, ſince he cannot, Reader, looke
Not on his Picture, but his Booke.
B. I.
Mr. WILLIAM
SHAKESPEARES
COMEDIES,
HISTORIES, &
TRAGEDIES.
Publiſhed according to the True Originall Copies.
LONDON
Printed by Iſaac Iaggard, and Ed. Blount. 1623.

OPPOSITE This book belongs to the world's largest collection of First Folios. US oil tycoon Henry Clay Folger and his wife Emily began collecting them in 1889.

ABOVE One of only four first folios to have Shakespeare's portrait in its original state. Later copies show minor changes were made to the Bard's features during the print run.

TO THE MOST NOBLE AND INCOMPARABLE PAIRE OF BRETHREN.

WILLIAM
Earle of Pembroke, &c. Lord Chamberlaine to the *Kings most Excellent Maiesty.*

AND

PHILIP
Earle of Montgomery, &c. Gentleman of his Maiesties Bed-Chamber. Both Knights of the most Noble Order of the Garter, and our singular good
LORDS.

Right Honourable,

WHilst we studie to be thankful in our particular, for the many fauors we haue receiued from your L.L. we are falne vpon the ill fortune, to mingle two the most diuerse things that can bee, feare, and rashnesse; rashnesse in the enterprize, and feare of the successe. For, when we valew the places your H.H. sustaine, we cannot but know their dignity greater, then to descend to the reading of these trifles: and, while we name them trifles, we haue depriu'd our selues of the defence of our Dedication. But since your L.L. haue beene pleas'd to thinke these trifles some-thing, heeretofore; and haue prosequuted both them, and their Authour liuing, with so much fauour: we hope, that (they out-liuing him, and he not hauing the fate, common with some, to be exequutor to his owne writings) you will vse the like indulgence toward them, you haue done

A 2   vnto

To the great Variety of Readers.

FRom the most able, to him that can but spell: There you are number'd. We had rather you were weighd. Especially, when the fate of all Bookes depends vpon your capacities: and not of your heads alone, but of your purses. Well! It is now publique, & you wil stand for your priuiledges wee know: to read, and censure. Do so, but buy it first. That doth best commend a Booke, the Stationer saies. Then, how odde soeuer your braines be, or your wisedomes, make your licence the same, and spare not. Iudge your sixe-pen'orth, your shillings worth, your fiue shillings worth at a time, or higher, so you rise to the iust rates, and welcome. But, what euer you do, Buy. Censure will not driue a Trade, or make the Iacke go. And though you be a Magistrate of wit, and sit on the Stage at *Black-Friers*, or the *Cock-pit*, to arraigne Playes dailie, know, these Playes haue had their triall alreadie, and stood out all Appeales; and do now come forth quitted rather by a Decree of Court, then any purchas'd Letters of commendation.

It had bene a thing, we confesse, worthie to haue bene wished, that the Author himselfe had liu'd to haue set forth, and ouerseen his owne writings; But since it hath bin ordain'd otherwise, and he by death departed from that right, we pray you do not envie his Friends, the office of their care, and paine, to haue collected & publish'd them; and so to haue publish'd them, as where (before) you were abus'd with diuerse stolne, and surreptitious copies, maimed, and deformed by the frauds and stealthes of iniurious impostors, that expos'd them: euen those, are now offer'd to your view cur'd, and perfect of their limbes; and all the rest, absolute in their numbers, as he conceiued thē. Who, as he was a happie imitator of Nature, was a most gentle expresser of it. His mind and hand went together: And what he thought, he vttered with that easinesse, that wee haue scarse receiued from him a blot in his papers. But it is not our prouince, who onely gather his works, and giue them you, to praise him. It is yours that reade him. And there we hope, to your diuers capacities, you will finde enough, both to draw, and hold you: for his wit can no more lie hid, then it could be lost. Reade him, therefore; and againe, and againe: And if then you doe not like him, surely you are in some manifest danger, not to vnderstand him. And so we leaue you to other of his Friends, whom if you need, can bee your guides: if you neede them not, you can leade your selues, and others. And such Readers we wish him.

A 3

Iohn Heminge.
Henrie Condell.

LEFT A 1997 reconstruction of Shakespeare's Globe Theatre built near the original structure which burned down in 1613.

BELOW The first line of Hamlet's soliloquy seen here in a First Folio is one of the most quoted sentences in the English language.

OPPOSITE The Preface to the First Folio starts with effusive thanks to two noble brothers who were Shakespeare's patrons. It continues with a light-hearted address to "the great Variety of Readers".

took the father-and-son team of William and Isaac Jaggard nearly two years to complete the task. Each folio was more than 900 pages long, and although most of the work had been edited before printing, around 15 per cent of the material shows signs of having been changed during typesetting, which accounts for the variations seen between individual copies of the First Folio. There are also printing errors, and one play, *Troilus and Cressida*, is in the book but not included on the contents page. Mistakes aside, John Heminges and Henry Condell could not have been more delighted with their masterpiece. In its Preface, they condemned "the stol'n and surreptitious copies, maimed and deformed by frauds and … imposters" and promised that the Shakespearean plays in their book were "cured … absolute in their numbers as he conceived them".

There is no record of how many copies were printed, but estimates range from 750 to 1,000. Just 235 survive today. The Folger Shakespeare Library in Washington, DC, holds 82, making it

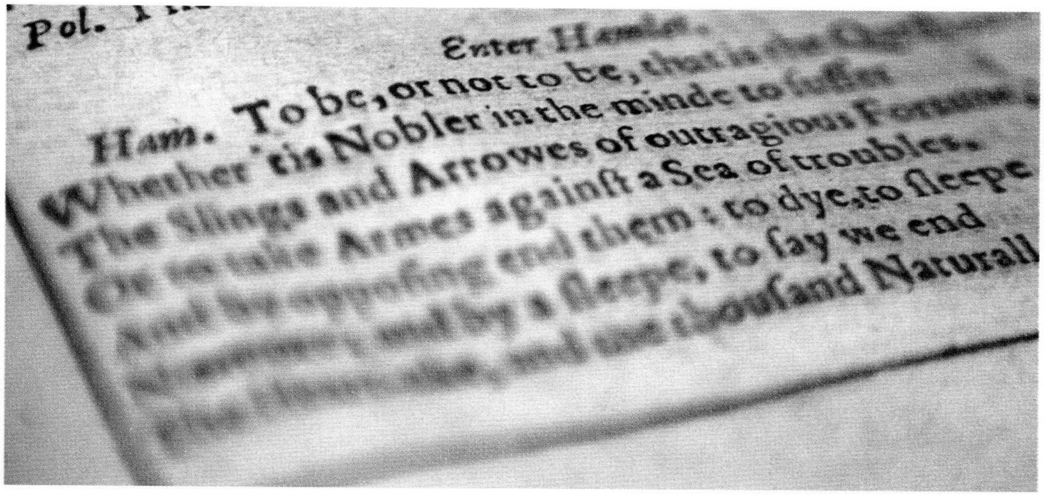

the possessor of the largest collection. Then there are also 12 copies at Meisei University in Tokyo. Copies of the First Folio are held in museums and libraries all over the world and they are still being found. In 2014, a librarian in St Omer, France, discovered one hidden away in a pile of English books. Another copy turned up in Mount Stuart House, a stately home in Scotland, in 2016.

When the First Folio was published in 1623, it sold for £1, around £180 in today's money. A copy sold at public auction in 2006 fetched nearly $5,000,000 (£3,800,000).

In the document's Preface, Shakespeare's contemporary Ben Jonson wrote: "He was not of an age, but for all time." We have the First Folio to thank for that.

18

The Peace of Westphalia

The Peace of Westphalia was a critical landmark in the history of Europe. This series of treaties was signed in 1648 by over 100 states in the centre of the continent exhausted by decades of savage conflict. Europe was soon consumed by other wars, but Westphalia set the pattern for peaceful coexistence and respect for national sovereignty that has been at the heart of international diplomacy ever since.

The Thirty Years War was one of the most devastating conflicts in history. It was fought between 1618 and 1648 within that curious conglomeration of hundreds of large, small and tiny states that made up the Holy Roman Empire, with outside powers such as France and Sweden involved as well. That great expanse of land stretched from the Baltic to northern Italy and across to what is today Romania. Around a third of the population died in the 30 years of bitter fighting and destruction. The multiplicity of small German states like Brunswick and Mecklenburg were ravaged by battle, disease and famine. To single out just one tragedy, Magdeburg in northern Germany lost 80 per cent of its population when an invading army inflicted a firestorm on the city. There were three decades of savage interstate battling aggravated by religious differences between Catholics and Protestants and by the ferocious intervention of foreign powers before all sides called for peace. It was not so much exhaustion as recognition of the strategic futility of continuing the struggle that led to the treaties that made up the Peace of Westphalia.

The Holy Roman Empire was ruled nominally by the Habsburg Emperor Ferdinand II, a Catholic zealot who was determined to

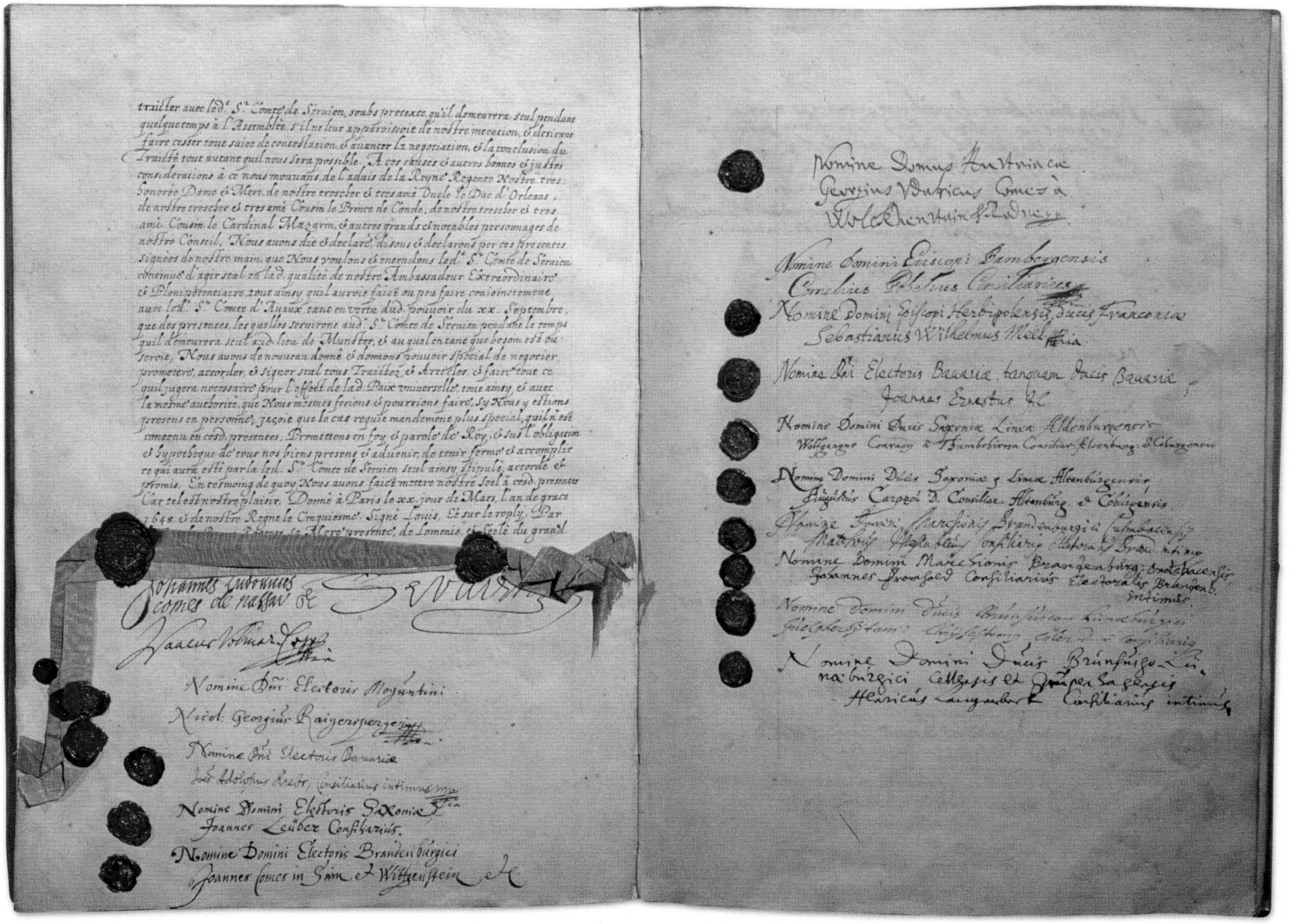

impose imperial authority on the fragmentary assortment of states, many of which were Protestant in the aftermath of the Reformation that had taken place 100 years earlier. The war started in 1618 in Bohemia, where the Protestants were foolish enough to throw two of Ferdinand's Catholic regents out of the window of the Prague governorate. Even though the two men survived the so-called Defenestration of Prague – reputedly having their falls broken by a dung heap – Ferdinand could not overlook the affront. When the Bohemians went further and rejected him as their emperor, he marched in and defeated the largely Protestant army at the Battle of the White Mountain in 1620.

Over the next few years, as an emboldened Ferdinand moved to exert his growing military power over states in his shambling empire, more and more outsiders muscled in looking for pickings. First came the Danes, then the Swedes, the French and the Spanish. Finally the Dutch in the Netherlands saw the war as their chance to entrench their independence. The most effective fighters were the Swedes under the dashing King Gustavus Adolphus. He was seen as the saviour of Protestant Europe. He crushed the imperial army at the Battle of Breitenfeld in 1631 but his intervention was short-lived and he was killed in the Battle of Lützen a year later. It wasn't long before Cardinal Richelieu's France was in the fray, his swashbuckling army commander, the Duke of Enghien, seizing territory that bordered France. Soon the French were attacking the Spanish, who had come in on the emperor's side. The fierce fighting continued and the horrific suffering of civilians dragged on into the 1640s.

OPPOSITE ABOVE The town hall door handle in Osnabrück, Germany, commemorates the "friede" (peace) of the 1648 Peace of Westphalia.

OPPOSITE King Gustavus Adolphus ruled Sweden from 1611 to 1632. A bold military commander, he made Sweden a major European power.

ABOVE The text of the Treaty of Westphalia. It was signed by a host of large and small central European states on 24 October 1648 and marks a pivotal moment in diplomatic history.

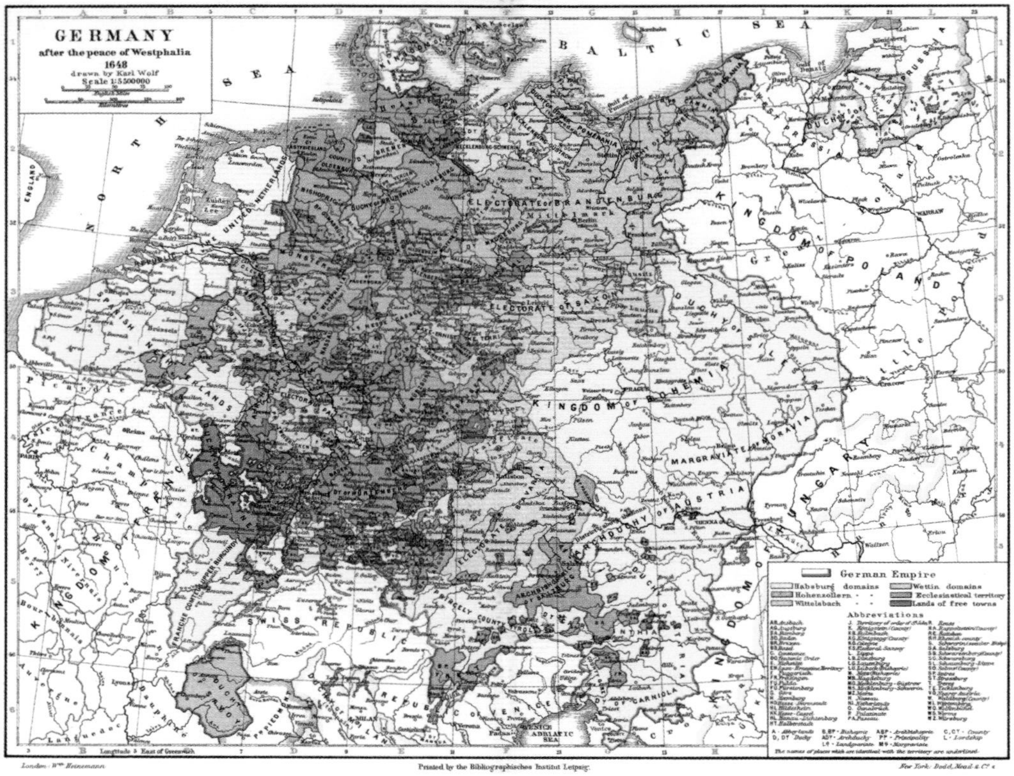

By 1648, all sides, particularly the emperor's regime in Vienna, felt that nothing further could be achieved by fighting.

Peace negotiations took place in the town of Münster in Westphalia and nearby Osnabrück. Delegates from over 100 states in the fractured but undefeated Holy Roman Empire took part, together with the other countries involved in the conflict. The outcome was a peace that did much to settle the frontiers of most Central European states. The Peace of Westphalia rewarded Sweden with territory in northern Germany on the shores of the Baltic; France received parts of Alsace and towns such as Metz and Verdun on its eastern border; and Switzerland and Holland became independent. But what was so innovative and lasting about this peace, making it a blueprint for future settlements, was how it enshrined exclusive national sovereignty within recognized borders. Westphalia established a new regime of international recognition of the right of all states to conduct their own domestic affairs without interference. Its effect was to reduce massively the authority of the ailing empire and its claim to represent Christendom. Unsurprisingly, Pope Innocent X in Rome was the only world leader to condemn the new peace outright and call it "null, void, invalid, iniquitous, damnable ... and devoid of all meaning for all time".

Somehow the Holy Roman Empire staggered on. Even the depredations of Frederick the Great, king of Prussia in the mid-eighteenth century, did not destroy the continuing hold of the Austrian emperors in Vienna on their great mass of principalities. All of those small German states had to await the genius of Bismarck a century later before they were made to unite as one Germany.

ABOVE The states of the Holy Roman Empire at the time of the Peace of Westphalia. The treaty established their right to live in peace with their neighbours. Most became part of Germany in the nineteenth century.

RIGHT An important precursor to the Treaty of Westphalia was the peace signed in Munster four months earlier by the Dutch (left) and Spanish (right).

The Age of Revolution

1776–1893

19

The Declaration of Independence

The Declaration of Independence by 13 British colonies in North America launched the people of the United States on their fight for freedom from British rule. It was proclaimed on 4 July 1776 and the new country was finally recognized by the Treaty of Paris in 1783. The American Revolution did much to inspire struggles for liberty in other parts of the world.

ABOVE LEFT Benjamin Franklin, one of five men who drafted the Declaration. When John Hankey told him and other revolutionaries: "We must not hang apart", Franklin replied: "We must indeed hang together, or, most assuredly, we shall all hang separately".

ABOVE RIGHT John Adams, another of the drafters of the Declaration, later second president of the United States of America.

OPPOSITE The US Declaration of Independence was signed by 56 men led by John Hancock, the US Congress president. His signature is larger than the others.

This bold document marks the birth of a superpower, although the flowering of that land of hope and promise was yet to come, around 100 years later. It was to suffer the agony of two internal wars – the Revolutionary War of 1775–83 and the Civil War of 1861–65 – before it could begin to shape the outside world in the twentieth century. However, the proud lines that begin this declaration have illuminated the history of the United States: "We hold these truths to be self-evident, that all men are created equal, that they are endowed by their Creator with certain unalienable Rights, that among these are Life, Liberty and the Pursuit of Happiness." The document was a beacon of idealism and hope that Americans took some time to live up to. It was, for example, nearly a century before they would abolish slavery, but by the 1900s the United States emerged for all its lesser faults as a world leader in providing its own people with freedom and prosperity. And while the nation's military muscle has landed it in some controversial wars, its economic power has won universal admiration.

It has been an astonishing journey from the days of Britain's 13 mismanaged American colonies in the 1770s and the growing resentment of their citizens. The government in London was unwise enough to impose a set of taxes on Americans who had no votes in the British parliament at Westminster. And men like Thomas Jefferson in Virginia, Benjamin Franklin in Pennsylvania and John Adams in Massachusetts were first demanding more self-government and then open rebellion.

Resentment spilled over into anger when Britain imposed a tax on tea in 1773. One large cargo of tea arrived in Boston Harbor and dozens of protesters, including the legendary Paul Revere, tipped 340 odd chests of it into the water. The British promptly closed the harbour, one of America's prime trading ports, and appointed the unpopular commander-in-chief in America, General Thomas Gage, as governor of Massachusetts. Gage's actions from then on did much to inflame American civic leaders and transform them from protesters into revolutionaries. In April 1775, he ordered the British army to the town of Concord to confiscate weapons that he understood American militiamen were stockpiling there. This was the match that lit the flame. Shots were fired and fighters were killed on both sides. The Revolutionary War had begun.

Even then, remarkably, most of the men who would lead the Revolution were counting on conciliation rather than war. They hoped that London would heed the voices of moderates like Edmund Burke who called for more generosity for the people he called "our English brethren in the American colonies". However, the declaration by King George III in August 1775 that Americans

IN CONGRESS, JULY 4, 1776.

The unanimous Declaration of the thirteen united States of America,

When in the Course of human events, it becomes necessary for one people to dissolve the political bands which have connected them with another, and to assume among the powers of the earth, the separate and equal station to which the Laws of Nature and of Nature's God entitle them, a decent respect to the opinions of mankind requires that they should declare the causes which impel them to the separation. —— We hold these truths to be self-evident, that all men are created equal, that they are endowed by their Creator with certain unalienable Rights, that among these are Life, Liberty and the pursuit of Happiness. — That to secure these rights, Governments are instituted among Men, deriving their just powers from the consent of the governed, — That whenever any Form of Government becomes destructive of these ends, it is the Right of the People to alter or to abolish it, and to institute new Government, laying its foundation on such principles and organizing its powers in such form, as to them shall seem most likely to effect their Safety and Happiness. Prudence, indeed, will dictate that Governments long established should not be changed for light and transient causes; and accordingly all experience hath shewn, that mankind are more disposed to suffer, while evils are sufferable, than to right themselves by abolishing the forms to which they are accustomed. But when a long train of abuses and usurpations, pursuing invariably the same Object evinces a design to reduce them under absolute Despotism, it is their right, it is their duty, to throw off such Government, and to provide new Guards for their future security. — Such has been the patient sufferance of these Colonies; and such is now the necessity which constrains them to alter their former Systems of Government. The history of the present King of Great Britain is a history of repeated injuries and usurpations, all having in direct object the establishment of an absolute Tyranny over these States. To prove this, let Facts be submitted to a candid world. —— He has refused his Assent to Laws, the most wholesome and necessary for the public good. —— He has forbidden his Governors to pass Laws of immediate and pressing importance, unless suspended in their operation till his Assent should be obtained; and when so suspended, he has utterly neglected to attend to them. —— He has refused to pass other Laws for the accommodation of large districts of people, unless those people would relinquish the right of Representation in the Legislature, a right inestimable to them and formidable to tyrants only. —— He has called together legislative bodies at places unusual, uncomfortable, and distant from the depository of their public Records, for the sole purpose of fatiguing them into compliance with his measures. —— He has dissolved Represtative Houses repeatedly, for opposing with manly firmness his invasions on the rights of the people. —— He has refused for a long time, after such dissolutions, to cause others to be elected; whereby the Legislative powers, incapable of Annihilation, have returned to the People at large for their exercise; the State remaining in the mean time exposed to all the dangers of invasion from without, and convulsions within. —— He has endeavoured to prevent the population of these States; for that purpose obstructing the Laws for Naturalization of Foreigners; refusing to pass others to encourage their migrations hither, and raising the conditions of new Appropriations of Lands. —— He has obstructed the Administration of Justice, by refusing his Assent to Laws for establishing Judiciary powers. —— He has made Judges dependent on his Will alone, for the tenure of their offices, and the amount and payment of their salaries. —— He has erected a multitude of New Offices, and sent hither swarms of Officers to harrass our people, and eat out their substance. —— He has kept among us, in times of peace, Standing Armies without the Consent of our legislatures. —— He has affected to render the Military independent of and superior to the Civil power. —— He has combined with others to subject us to a jurisdiction foreign to our constitution, and unacknowledged by our laws; giving his Assent to their Acts of pretended Legislation: — For Quartering large bodies of armed troops among us: — For protecting them, by a mock Trial, from punishment for any Murders which they should commit on the Inhabitants of these States: — For cutting off our Trade with all parts of the world: — For imposing Taxes on us without our Consent: — For depriving us in many cases, of the benefits of Trial by Jury: — For transporting us beyond Seas to be tried for pretended offences: — For abolishing the free System of English Laws in a neighbouring Province, establishing therein an Arbitrary government, and enlarging its Boundaries so as to render it at once an example and fit instrument for introducing the same absolute rule into these Colonies: — For taking away our Charters, abolishing our most valuable Laws, and altering fundamentally the Forms of our Governments: — For suspending our own Legislatures, and declaring themselves invested with power to legislate for us in all cases whatsoever. — He has abdicated Government here, by declaring us out of his Protection and waging War against us. —— He has plundered our seas, ravaged our Coasts, burnt our towns, and destroyed the lives of our people. —— He is at this time transporting large Armies of foreign Mercenaries to compleat the works of death, desolation and tyranny, already begun with circumstances of Cruelty & perfidy scarcely paralleled in the most barbarous ages, and totally unworthy the Head of a civilized nation. —— He has constrained our fellow Citizens taken Captive on the high Seas to bear Arms against their Country, to become the executioners of their friends and Brethren, or to fall themselves by their Hands. —— He has excited domestic insurrections amongst us, and has endeavoured to bring on the inhabitants of our frontiers, the merciless Indian Savages, whose known rule of warfare, is an undistinguished destruction of all ages, sexes and conditions. In every stage of these Oppressions We have Petitioned for Redress in the most humble terms: Our repeated Petitions have been answered only by repeated injury. A Prince, whose character is thus marked by every act which may define a Tyrant, is unfit to be the ruler of a free people. Nor have We been wanting in attentions to our Brittish brethren. We have warned them from time to time of attempts by their legislature to extend an unwarrantable jurisdiction over us. We have reminded them of the circumstances of our emigration and settlement here. We have appealed to their native justice and magnanimity, and we have conjured them by the ties of our common kindred to disavow these usurpations, which, would inevitably interrupt our connections and correspondence. They too have been deaf to the voice of justice and of consanguinity. We must, therefore, acquiesce in the necessity, which denounces our Separation, and hold them, as we hold the rest of mankind, Enemies in War, in Peace Friends. ——

We, therefore, the Representatives of the united States of America, in General Congress, Assembled, appealing to the Supreme Judge of the world for the rectitude of our intentions, do, in the Name, and by Authority of the good People of these Colonies, solemnly publish and declare, That these United Colonies are, and of Right ought to be **Free and Independent States**; that they are Absolved from all Allegiance to the British Crown, and that all political connection between them and the State of Great Britain, is and ought to be totally dissolved; and that as Free and Independent States, they have full Power to levy War, conclude Peace, contract Alliances, establish Commerce, and to do all other Acts and Things which Independent States may of right do. —— And for the support of this Declaration, with a firm reliance on the protection of divine Providence, we mutually pledge to each other our Lives, our Fortunes and our sacred Honor.

John Hancock

Button Gwinnett
Lyman Hall
Geo Walton.

Wm Hooper
Joseph Hewes,
John Penn

Edward Rutledge

Thos Heyward Junr.
Thomas Lynch Junr.
Arthur Middleton

Samuel Chase
Wm Paca
Thos Stone
Charles Carroll of Carrollton

George Wythe
Richard Henry Lee
Th Jefferson
Benja Harrison
Thos Nelson jr.
Francis Lightfoot Lee
Carter Braxton

Robt Morris
Benjamin Rush
Benja. Franklin
John Morton
Geo Clymer
Jas. Smith
Geo. Taylor
James Wilson
Geo. Ross

Caesar Rodney
Geo Read
Tho M:Kean

Wm Floyd
Phil. Livingston
Frans. Lewis
Lewis Morris

Richd. Stockton
Jno Witherspoon
Fras. Hopkinson
John Hart
Abra Clark

Josiah Bartlett
Wm Whipple
Saml Adams
John Adams
Robt Treat Paine
Elbridge Gerry
Step. Hopkins
William Ellery
Roger Sherman
Saml Huntington
Wm Williams
Oliver Wolcott
Matthew Thornton

were now in "open and avowed rebellion", and Thomas Paine's inspirational pamphlet *Common Sense*, which advocated an independent American republic, prompted American leaders to take the decisive step. In June 1776, nine of the 13 states appointed a committee of five men, including Jefferson, Adams and Franklin, to draft a Declaration of Independence. Two states, Pennsylvania and South Carolina, declined to participate; two others, New York and Delaware, hesitated. All but New York joined in by 2 July, when the declaration was voted into effect by America's Second Continental Congress meeting in Philadelphia, Pennsylvania. The declaration, its wording largely composed by Thomas Jefferson, was signed immediately by John Hancock, president of the Congress, whose name appears written large at the top of the signatures, and was issued on 4 July. It was some time before all the states' delegations, including New York, signed up in full.

The declaration has three main sections. There are the unforgettable words of the preamble and introduction, which assert the right of a people to throw off the bonds of a government that has pursued "a long train of abuses and usurpations". This is followed by the charge sheet of American complaints against George III's British government. It lists 28 ways in which Britain had opposed American democratic rights, imposed unjust taxation and waged war against the 13 colonies. The declaration concludes with the defiant words: "... that these united Colonies are, and of Right ought to be Free and Independent States; that they are Absolved from all Allegiance to the British Crown, and that all political connection between them and the State of Great Britain, is and ought to be totally dissolved." The die was cast, and it was to take seven years of fighting and finally negotiation with the British government before the United States became fully independent.

The publication of the Declaration of Independence was greeted with joy in most of America, though a few "loyalists" retained doubts for some time. Some "United Empire Loyalists" moved to Canada. But George Washington, who had been appointed America's army commander a year earlier, had the document read out to his troops in New York. One of the signatories, New Hampshire's William Whipple, felt bound by its words to free his slave. America's Declaration of Independence went on to inspire the French Revolution and independence movements in many other parts of the world.

ABOVE The five-man drafting committee of the Declaration of Independence present their plan to Congress President John Hancock on 28 June 1776. From left to right: John Adams (later the second president of the US), Roger Sherman, Robert Livingstone, Thomas Jefferson (third US president) and Benjamin Franklin.

LEFT Thomas Jefferson, the main author of the Declaration.

LEFT The British surrender at the Battle of Yorktown in 1781 is immortalized by John Turnbull's painting in the US Capitol. It is titled The Surrender of Lord Cornwallis, *although the British C in C did not actually turn up. He sent his deputy Gen O'Hara (red-coated centre left) to walk between the mounted commanders of the victorious Americans and their French allies. The US leader Gen George Washington (on the brown horse centre right) reacted by deputing his second in command Gen Benjamin Lincoln (centre) to take O'Hara's sword.*

20

The Tennis Court Oath

The Tennis Court Oath was the single most critical event that sparked the French Revolution. Exasperated representatives of the French lower classes who found themselves excluded from a meeting with the king in 1789 gathered on a tennis court in Versailles. There they made a historic declaration that would change the nature of French politics and the history of modern Europe.

The emergence of democratic politics in modern Europe went through several violent phases, beginning with the English Civil War in the mid-seventeenth century and ending with the defeat of Communism in Eastern Europe in the twentieth. In the broad sweep of history the French Revolution (1789–99) stands out for the sheer savagery of its violence and the extreme radicalism of its politics. The period of the so-called Terror between the summers of 1793 and 1794 saw the streets of Paris literally flowing with blood as some 20,000 people were guillotined. Maximilien Robespierre's Committee of Public Safety directed the violence, spurred on by the voracious public protests of the *sans-culottes,* "breeches-less" left-wing firebrands who demanded the extinction of the upper classes in the name of liberty and equality. *Culottes* were the smart knee breeches worn by the reviled upper classes. The *sans-culottes* were egged on by the committee's prominent hotheads like Bertrand Barère, who proclaimed: "The tree of liberty grows only when watered by the blood of tyrants." By the end of 1794, the Revolution had done its work in scything through the ranks of the French upper classes and the Catholic Church.

This ferocious crusade was set in motion by a gathering of the first revolutionaries on a tennis court in Versailles five years earlier, in 1789. Until then the French monarchy had reigned supreme, sustained by an aristocracy jealous of its own power and privilege. The king, Louis XVI, was an irresolute and poorly advised 35-year-old. He had the misfortune to be on the throne when absolute monarchy was being challenged by political thinkers like Jean-Jacques Rousseau and when there was deep public disquiet at France's severely weakened economy. Louis was also gravely compromised by the notorious extravagance

RIGHT Jean Sylvain Bailly, president of the National Assembly (wearing black centre), leads the crowd in the swearing of the Tennis Court Oath on 20 June 1789. It committed them to demand an "equitable constitution".

OPPOSITE The signatories to the Oath. There were nearly 600 altogether who demanded that power should pass from the monarchy to the people.

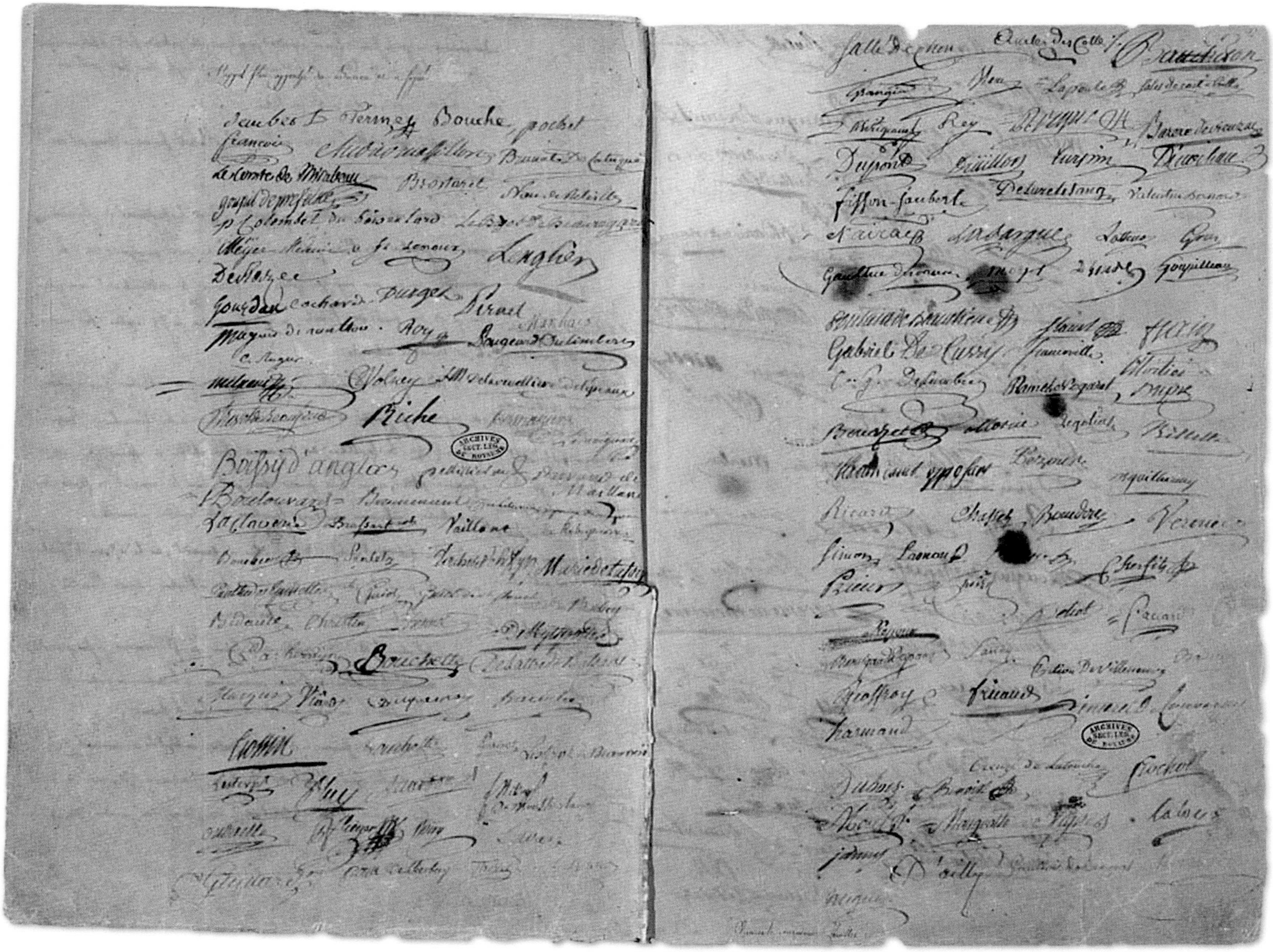

of his wife, Marie Antoinette, who is alleged to have said of people who faced starvation after a poor harvest left them without bread: "Let them eat cake."

Things got so bad that the king felt compelled to allow a measure of democratic reform in the summer of 1789. He tried to regenerate an age-old French gathering – the Estates General – which would draw together the three so-called "estates" in French society: the Church, the nobles and the commoners. The third estate, commoners who represented the majority of French people, refused his overture and proclaimed themselves the only body with the right to rule France. They called themselves the National Assembly. The king, torn between asserting his authority and being receptive to liberal reform, decided to invite all three estates to a grand meeting. This meant preparing the great salon in the palace of Versailles for the gathering, yet the reshuffling of furniture meant the doors were closed on the very day the commoners of the third estate were planning their own meeting there. They were furious. It was pouring with rain and one of the deputies remembered that there was a large indoor tennis court nearby which had been built a century earlier to allow Louis XIV to take some exercise. The 600 or so representatives, relieved to find shelter from the inclement weather, made a virtue of their absence from the king's formal meeting room by issuing a historic declaration in the form of an oath. Their president, Jean-Sylvain Bailly, stood on a crude table in the middle of the court and, with one hand over his heart and the other raised above his head, led the proclamation: "We swear to God and the Fatherland never to separate until we have formed a solid and equitable constitution ..."

Within two months the National Assembly enacted a number of reforms abolishing all vestiges of feudalism and privilege, curbing the power and wealth of the Church and publishing a Declaration on the Rights of Man

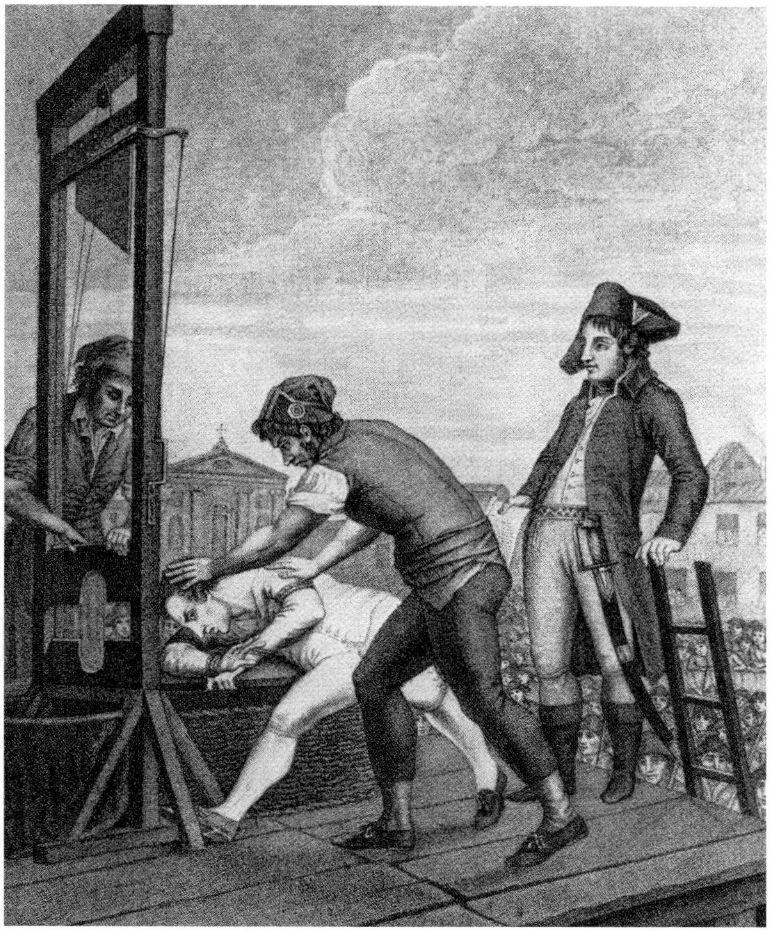

LEFT The storming of the Bastille. The great medieval fortress and prison in Paris was attacked by the revolutionaries on 14 July 1789. Its fall is celebrated in France every year on that day.

ABOVE TOP The 1794 execution of Maximilien Robespierre, the most prominent of the French revolutionaries behind the Reign of Terror. Reaction against his extreme policies finally sent him to the guillotine himself.

ABOVE Queen Marie Antoinette, wife of Louis XVI. She was sent to the guillotine along with her husband in 1793.

and the Citizen. At the same time, the growing mistrust between the king and his subjects led to rioting in the streets and the storming of the Bastille, the great symbol of royal power, on 14 July 1789. Successive groups of radical revolutionaries outbid each other in their violent struggle for power, and by the time the most extreme of all the Jacobins under Robespierre began the Terror in the summer of 1793, the leaders of the early days of the Revolution were viewed as dangerous conservatives. Bailly, the leader of the third estate who had launched the National Assembly and led his followers in the Tennis Court Oath, was guillotined at the height of the Terror in November 1793. King Louis XVI and his queen Marie Antoinette died on the guillotine that same year. Remarkably, one of the most bloodthirsty of all Robespierre's supporters, that firebrand Bertrand Barère, survived the Revolution and the rule of Napoleon that followed. He died quietly in his bed at the age of 85.

21

Mary Wollstonecraft's *A Vindication of the Rights of Woman*

This inspirational document challenged the traditional role of women in eighteenth-century Britain and served as a guiding light for the modern feminist movement. It is the first book written by a woman which argued that females were rational beings who were entitled to the same rights as men. The book, with its emphasis on the need for the proper education of women, established its unconventional author Mary Wollstonecraft as a leading British philosopher of the eighteenth century.

RIGHT A portrait of Mary Wollstonecraft five years after she published her book. It was painted in 1797, the year she died in childbirth.

OPPOSITE The 1792 first edition of Mary Wollstonecraft's ground-breaking A Vindication of the Rights of Woman *swiftly sold out.*

Mary Wollstonecraft was a rare female star in a firmament of male philosophers during the European Age of Enlightenment. She built on the ideas of radical thinkers like John Locke, Jean-Jacques Rousseau and Thomas Paine. For them, reason was the key to understanding and changing society for the better. What makes Wollstonecraft's manuscript extraordinary is that, unlike her male counterparts, she asserts that women

are just as capable of rational thought as men. In a society where women were regarded as second-class citizens, her call for females to take control of their lives through education and to end their "blind obedience" to men was revolutionary.

Many of Wollstonecraft's convictions came from her own experience. Born in London in 1759, she grew up in a wealthy family which had fallen on hard times. Her extravagant father was tyrannical and brutal. To protect her mother, Mary slept in front of her bedroom door. She watched her older brother Ned being sent to Cambridge to study law, while she and her sisters were taught how to be good housekeepers. Mary Wollstonecraft learned from bitter experience that if she was to be self-reliant, she needed to educate herself. She set up an unsuccessful school, worked as a lady's companion and as a governess – typical careers for impoverished middle-class women of the day. What changed her life was coming into contact with a group of dissenting Christians, later known as Unitarians. They believed that individuals could use reason to answer the great questions of life and act upon their findings to create a more just society. A member of the congregation, Joseph Johnson, asked Wollstonecraft to write for his political journal, *Analytical Review*. He published her masterpiece, *A Vindication of the Rights of Woman*, in 1792.

In this pioneering work, Wollstonecraft takes the view that, since men and women are equal in the eyes of God, they should be subject to the same moral law. She examines the cultural influences which made women value appearance and accomplishments like singing and sewing over rational thought.

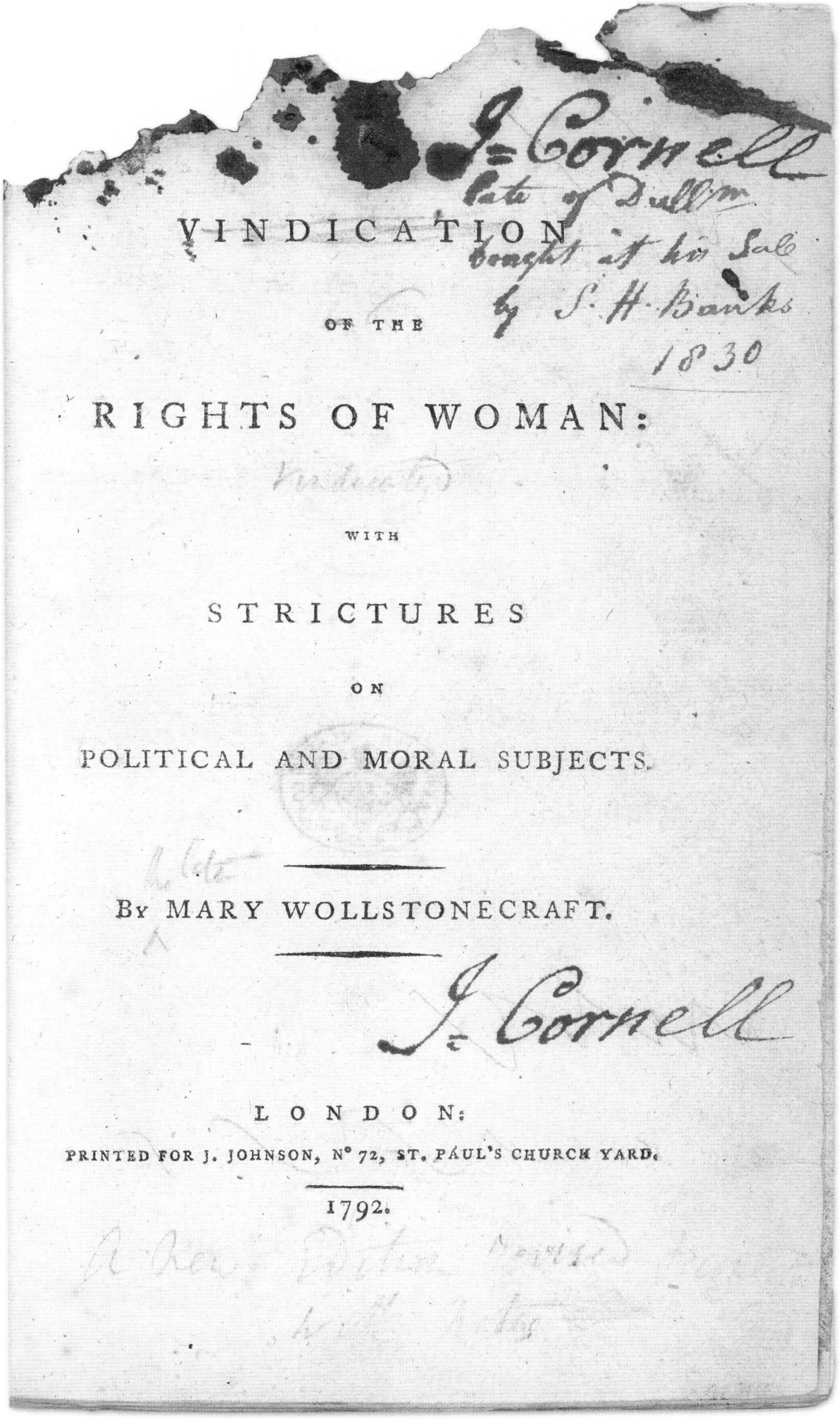
VINDICATION

OF THE

RIGHTS OF WOMAN:

WITH

STRICTURES

ON

POLITICAL AND MORAL SUBJECTS.

BY MARY WOLLSTONECRAFT.

J. Cornell

LONDON:

PRINTED FOR J. JOHNSON, N° 72, ST. PAUL'S CHURCH YARD.

1792.

LEFT Mary Shelley was only 11 days old when her mother Mary Wollstonecraft died. She ran away with the British poet Percy Bysshe Shelley when she was 17 and wrote her famous horror novel Frankenstein *four years later, in 1818.*

OPPOSITE Four pages from Wollstonecraft's book. Her theme that men and women are equal is repeated throughout.

She accuses men of encouraging women to be vain and superficial. In Chapter 3 she writes: "Taught from their infancy that beauty is a woman's sceptre, the mind shapes itself to the body and roaming around its gilt cage only seems to adorn its prison." In the book, women are urged to reject their traditional roles of "toys" and "spaniels" by becoming educated. The author says that she does "not wish women to have power over men; but over themselves" and insists that educating women in the same way as men will make them better wives and mothers and allow them to have careers.

When the book was first published, there were very few critics – perhaps surprising in a society where women were largely uneducated and had very few rights. One detractor called Wollstonecraft "a hyena in petticoats", but generally the book was well received. The first edition sold out and had to be reprinted, but the events of the next few years were to destroy the reputation of the author and her ground-breaking ideas.

Immediately after *A Vindication of the Rights of Woman* was published, 33-year-old Wollstonecraft left for Paris to support the French Revolution, which she believed would bring about much-needed political and social change. She arrived a few weeks before King Louis XVI was guillotined. She fell in love with an American businessman, Gilbert Imlay, and gave birth to his daughter, Fanny. When Imlay refused to marry her, she was distraught and attempted suicide twice. After returning to London in 1794, she made friends with the radical philosopher William Godwin and became his lover. Neither believed in marriage, but after Wollstonecraft became pregnant they became man and wife. In 1797 she gave birth to another daughter, Mary (who went on to become Mary Shelley, author of *Frankenstein*). Days later, Wollstonecraft died of an infection, aged 38.

Godwin wrote a biography of Wollstonecraft after her death. A firm believer in telling the truth, he chronicled her affairs, revealed her illegitimate child and reported that she had tried to commit suicide. He also published an unfinished novel his late wife had written, which, among other things, attacked the institution of marriage. People were horrified. Her tarnished reputation devalued her visionary ideas and they were largely ignored for the next century. It wasn't until women began demanding the vote in the late nineteenth century that Wollstonecraft's book resurfaced. As the feminist movement grew in the twentieth century, Mary Wollstonecraft was restored to her rightful place as the mother of feminism.

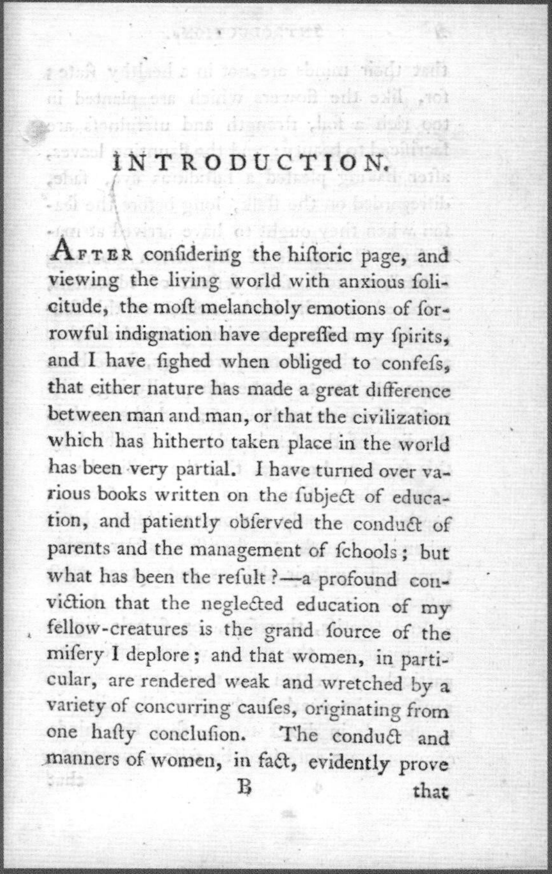

INTRODUCTION.

AFTER conſidering the hiſtoric page, and viewing the living world with anxious ſolicitude, the moſt melancholy emotions of ſorrowful indignation have depreſſed my ſpirits, and I have ſighed when obliged to confeſs, that either nature has made a great difference between man and man, or that the civilization which has hitherto taken place in the world has been very partial. I have turned over various books written on the ſubject of education, and patiently obſerved the conduct of parents and the management of ſchools; but what has been the reſult?—a profound conviction that the neglected education of my fellow-creatures is the grand ſource of the miſery I deplore; and that women, in particular, are rendered weak and wretched by a variety of concurring cauſes, originating from one haſty concluſion. The conduct and manners of women, in fact, evidently prove

B that

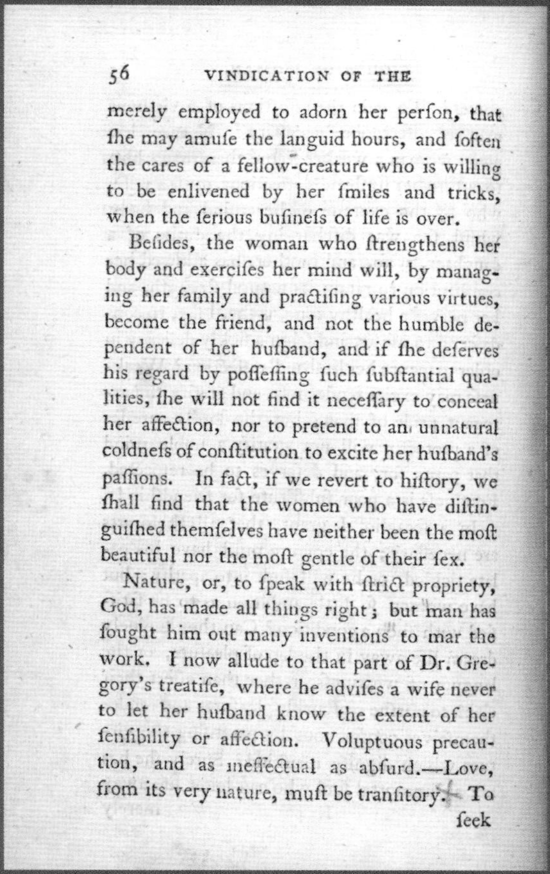

merely employed to adorn her perſon, that ſhe may amuſe the languid hours, and ſoften the cares of a fellow-creature who is willing to be enlivened by her ſmiles and tricks, when the ſerious buſineſs of life is over.

Beſides, the woman who ſtrengthens her body and exerciſes her mind will, by managing her family and practiſing various virtues, become the friend, and not the humble dependent of her huſband, and if ſhe deſerves his regard by poſſeſſing ſuch ſubſtantial qualities, ſhe will not find it neceſſary to conceal her affection, nor to pretend to an unnatural coldneſs of conſtitution to excite her huſband's paſſions. In fact, if we revert to hiſtory, we ſhall find that the women who have diſtinguiſhed themſelves have neither been the moſt beautiful nor the moſt gentle of their ſex.

Nature, or, to ſpeak with ſtrict propriety, God, has made all things right; but man has ſought him out many inventions to mar the work. I now allude to that part of Dr. Gregory's treatiſe, where he adviſes a wife never to let her huſband know the extent of her ſenſibility or affection. Voluptuous precaution, and as ineffectual as abſurd.—Love, from its very nature, muſt be tranſitory. To

ſeek

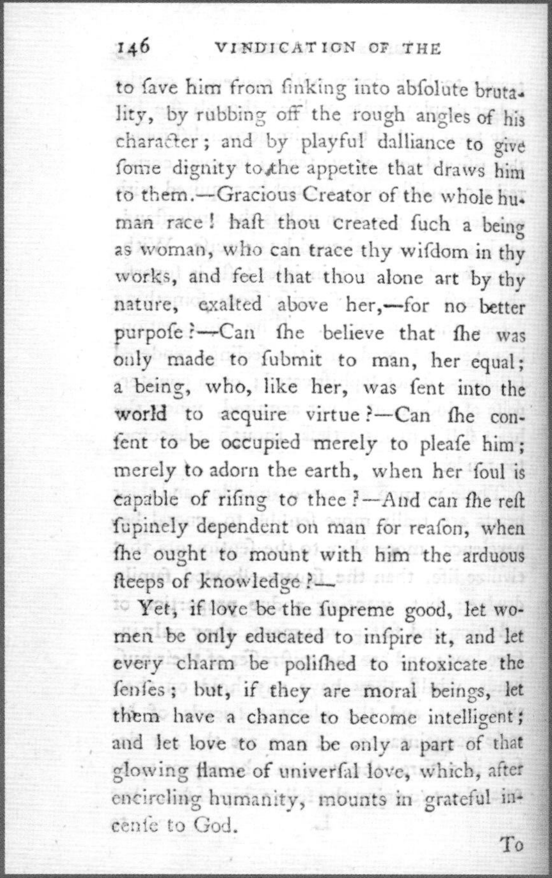

to ſave him from ſinking into abſolute brutality, by rubbing off the rough angles of his character; and by playful dalliance to give ſome dignity to the appetite that draws him to them.—Gracious Creator of the whole human race! haſt thou created ſuch a being as woman, who can trace thy wiſdom in thy works, and feel that thou alone art by thy nature, exalted above her,—for no better purpoſe?—Can ſhe believe that ſhe was only made to ſubmit to man, her equal; a being, who, like her, was ſent into the world to acquire virtue?—Can ſhe conſent to be occupied merely to pleaſe him; merely to adorn the earth, when her ſoul is capable of riſing to thee?—And can ſhe reſt ſupinely dependent on man for reaſon, when ſhe ought to mount with him the arduous ſteeps of knowledge?—

Yet, if love be the ſupreme good, let women be only educated to inſpire it, and let every charm be poliſhed to intoxicate the ſenſes; but, if they are moral beings, let them have a chance to become intelligent; and let love to man be only a part of that glowing flame of univerſal love, which, after encircling humanity, mounts in grateful incenſe to God.

To

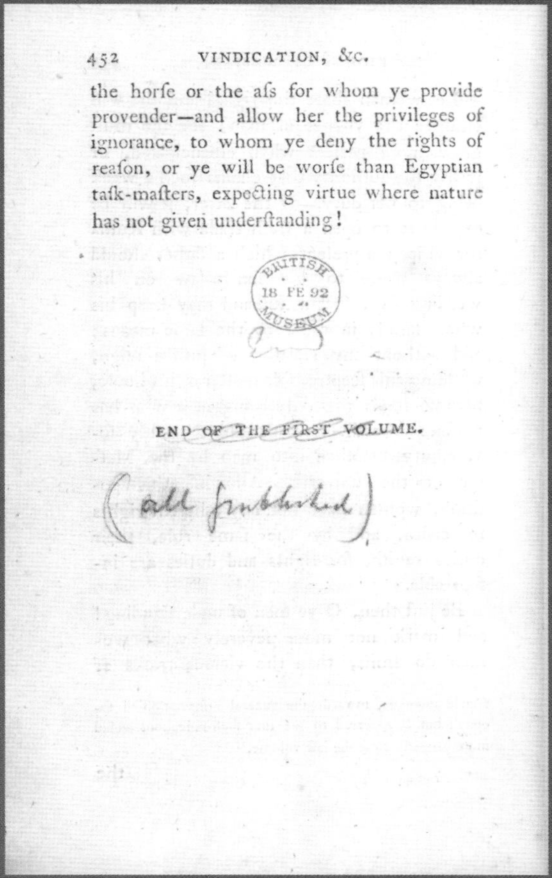

the horſe or the aſs for whom ye provide provender—and allow her the privileges of ignorance, to whom ye deny the rights of reaſon, or ye will be worſe than Egyptian taſk-maſters, expecting virtue where nature has not given underſtanding!

END OF THE FIRST VOLUME.

(all published)

22

Beethoven's Fifth Symphony

When we decided to include a musical manuscript in this book, the choice was obvious – Beethoven's Fifth Symphony. Its distinctive four-note (da, da, da, DUM!) opening is one of the most memorable musical sounds of all time. What makes Ludwig van Beethoven's masterpiece even more remarkable is the way its thrilling, innovative moments have inspired future generations of composers, from Johannes Brahms to Chuck Berry.

"It will be generally admitted that Beethoven's Fifth Symphony is the most sublime noise that has ever penetrated into the ears of man." The opening line of Chapter 5 of *Howard's End* by E. M. Forster sums up our view of this symphony perfectly. It is one of the most popular and frequently played works in the world, but its towering score did not come easily to the man who composed it. Beethoven spent four years working on his Fifth Symphony during a time of great personal anxiety. His notes bear witness to the fact that he wrote and rewrote

RIGHT Beethoven composing his "Missa Solemnis" in 1820. He restricted German artist Joseph Karl Stieler to four sittings. When the maestro refused to give him more time, Stieler had to paint the hands from memory.

OPPOSITE Beethoven's handwritten score of his Fifth Symphony starts with the famous four-note opening. At the top of the list of instruments on the left, "flute" is crossed out because he judged it too delicate for the powerful opening.

certain passages up to 20 times. Emil Ludwig, his biographer, called the Fifth Symphony "the greatest portrait that Beethoven has given us of himself".

In 1804, when he began his Fifth Symphony at the age of 34, Beethoven was surrounded by turbulence. Napoleon's armies were marching on Vienna, where the composer lived, and he was going deaf. His increasing deafness was so devastating that he had contemplated suicide. He also suffered from tinnitus, a continuous ringing in his ears. As a pianist as well as a composer, it must have been agonizing gradually to lose the ability to hear certain notes on his keyboard. Beethoven's secretary Anton Schindler said the composer told him that the opening four-note motif was "the sound of fate knocking at the door". The symphony is often referred to as the Fate Symphony, but there is debate about whether the "fate" in question was Beethoven's loss of hearing or the Napoleonic

Wars. The composer had been an enthusiastic supporter first of the French Revolution and then of Napoleon. He had planned to dedicate his Third Symphony to his hero but became disillusioned after the French leader named himself emperor of France. Beethoven crossed out Napoleon's name on the title page and rededicated the work "to the memory of a great man". When Napoleon's army bombarded Vienna in 1805, Beethoven covered his ears with pillows in case the noise of explosions further damaged his hearing.

The Fifth Symphony was first performed at the Theater an der Wien on 22 December 1808, with Beethoven himself conducting. It received a lukewarm response. The orchestra played badly after just one rehearsal, the overall programme was more than four hours long and the concert hall unheated. The audience was puzzled by the new work, which offered several novelties: two movements were joined together; the melody from one movement was reprised in another; and a trombone was used for the first time in symphonic music. Most importantly, Beethoven had changed the accepted symphonic form. Usually symphonies ended in the same key as they started, but the Fifth starts in C minor and ends in C major, putting the emphasis on the last movement instead of the first. This novel transposition took listeners on an emotional journey from grim adversity to glorious triumph. The composer wrote of his progression from minor to major key: "Many assert that every minor piece must end in the minor. On the contrary, I find that … the major has a glorious effect. Joy follows sorrow, sunshine – rain."

It was not until the score was published 18 months later that rave reviews began to appear. In 1810, music critic E. T. A. Hoffmann (who later wrote the children's book *The Nutcracker and the Mouse King*) waxed positively poetic: "How this wonderful composition, in a climax that climbs on and on, leads the listener

imperiously forward into the spirit world of the infinite! ... where grief and joy embrace him in the form of sound."

Beethoven was recognized as a revolutionary force who changed the way music was performed and listened to. He set a new standard for big musical forms and became a key influence on composers like Brahms, Tchaikovsky and Mahler. All followed his minor-to-major, darkness-to-light lead. During the Second World War, his Fifth Symphony served as a very different inspiration. It became known as the Victory Symphony after its association with the famous "V for victory" sign. "V" is the Roman numeral for five, and the Morse Code for the letter "V" is three dots and a dash, just like the first four notes of the first movement. The BBC used the first four notes of Beethoven's Fifth as its call sign for broadcasts to occupied Europe throughout the war.

More recently, Chuck Berry purloined the melody for his hit song "Roll Over Beethoven". Echoes of the first movement can be heard in films, like Walt Disney's *Fantasia 2000*, in video games, TV theme tunes and in the UK science-fiction series *Doctor Who*. Beethoven's Fifth Symphony even went into outer space in a recording on board the 1977 *Voyager* spacecraft, a fitting tribute to a composer who is supremely universal.

OPPOSITE Beethoven's Fifth Symphony was premiered at Vienna's historic Theater an der Wein. A memorial on an outside wall commemorates the composer who lived in the theatre rent free in 1803–4 while composing his opera Fidelio.

ABOVE The lavish interior of the Theater an der Wein was one of the wonders of nineteenth-century Europe. But when Beethoven's Fifth Symphony was first played here on 22 December 1808, there was a decided chill because the heating was not working.

23

Francis Scott Key's "Star-Spangled Banner"

The handwritten poem that became the national anthem of the United States of America was composed by a young poet named Francis Scott Key as he stood watching the British attacking Baltimore in September 1814. He was so inspired by the sight of the US stars-and-stripes flag still flying on the harbour fortress after a night bombardment that he wrote these lines in a surge of national pride.

ABOVE Fort McHenry under British bombardment on the night of 13/14 September 1814. The guns and rockets of the Royal Navy failed to suppress it.

OPPOSITE Francis Scott Key jotted down a poem on this piece of paper as he watched the dawn come up on 14 September 1814. More than a century later it became the US national anthem.

The story of how the lyrics of the US anthem were written is almost as uplifting as the words themselves. They are the work of a young American lawyer and poet who put pencil to paper at the end of a dark episode in American history. The United States had been free of British rule for over 30 years, but on 13 September 1814 it was again fighting for its life with the country whose army it had thrown out at Yorktown in 1781. Britain, which had been humbled in that war, was now back wreaking a remorseless act of vengeance. The British were incensed that the Americans had declared war on them in 1812 and even invaded the British territory of Canada at the height of Britain's conflict with the French emperor Napoleon. It was not until the summer of 1814, with Napoleon apparently crushed and exiled to Elba, that the British felt strong enough to take on America. A fleet of over 30 warships and troop carriers was dispatched across the Atlantic to give the Americans what the British government called "a good drubbing". The objective of the task force was not to re-establish British rule in America, but to punish the former colonists for – as British ministers saw it – stabbing them in the back.

The British army that landed in Maryland in August 1814 advanced inland with ruthless efficiency. The United States administration reacted with startled incompetence. President James Madison, a man of sharp intellect and one of the fathers of the US Constitution, was no great war leader. He was poorly served by his military commanders, whose attacks on Canada were failing miserably and who were now at a loss as to how to respond to this new British threat. What followed was one of the most shameful chapters in US military history. The British redcoats, grizzled veterans of the war with Napoleon, easily defeated America's enthusiastic but poorly trained forces guarding Washington, and within hours the public buildings in the capital were ablaze. President Madison and his plucky wife Dolley, who insisted on delaying her departure from the White House to rescue a fine picture hanging there of the first US president, George Washington, escaped across the Potomac River. British commanders Major General Robert Ross and Admiral George Cockburn found the White House abandoned, with the presidential meal still warm on the table. They and their officers promptly gobbled up the food, put the chairs on the dining table and set the building alight. Both Houses of Congress, the State Department and the Treasury were torched as well. It was the only time other than the 9/11 terrorist attack in

O say can you see ~~through~~ by the dawn's early light
What so proudly we hail'd at the twilight's last gleaming,
Whose broad stripes & bright stars through the perilous fight
O'er the ramparts we watch'd, were so gallantly streaming?
And the rocket's red glare, the bomb bursting in air,
Gave proof through the night that our flag was still there,
O say does that star-spangled banner yet wave
O'er the land of the free & the home of the brave?

On the shore dimly seen through the mists of the deep,
Where the foe's haughty host in dread silence reposes,
What is that which the breeze, o'er the towering steep,
As it fitfully blows, half conceals, half discloses?
Now it catches the gleam of the morning's first beam,
In full glory reflected now shines in the stream,
'Tis the star-spangled banner — O long may it wave
O'er the land of the free & the home of the brave!

And where is that band who so vauntingly swore,
That the havoc of war & the battle's confusion
A home & a Country should leave us no more?
— ~~[illegible]~~
Their blood has wash'd out their foul footstep's pollution.
No refuge could save the hireling & slave
From the terror of flight or the gloom of the grave,
And the star-spangled banner in triumph doth wave
O'er the land of the free & the home of the brave.

O thus be it ever when freemen shall stand
Between their lov'd home & the war's desolation!
Blest with vict'ry & peace may the heav'n rescued land
Praise the power that hath made & preserv'd us a nation!
Then conquer we must, when our cause it is just,
And this be our motto — "In God is our trust,"
And the star-spangled banner in triumph shall wave
O'er the land of the free & the home of the brave. —

2001 that outsiders have successfully struck America's capital.

It seemed that nothing could stop the British delivering further destruction and humiliation. On 12 September, the army landed a few miles short of Baltimore, and the navy's warships and gunboats moved up to bombard Fort McHenry, which guarded the entrance to the harbour. But Baltimore's redoubtable military commander, General Sam Smith, was determined not to allow his city to suffer the fate of Washington. Fort McHenry was the key. Its guns and ammunition were replenished. George Armistead, commander of the fort's garrison, had a huge new national flag made – a 30 x 40-foot stars-and-stripes banner – and flew it high above the battlements. Everything was done to fortify this symbol of Baltimore's resistance against the fearsome bombardment of artillery and rockets that was expected from British ships that night.

It happened that a young American lawyer, Francis Scott Key, was negotiating a prisoner release and was billeted on a nearby British ship as the massive attack on Fort McHenry began that evening. He was stunned at the ferocity of the cannon fire that pounded its walls and the great fiery arc of naval rocketry and mortar bombs that fell from the sky on the beleaguered garrison. As that dreadful night came to an end, Key was sure that the garrison must have succumbed, the American flag replaced by a British one. But as he peered through the misty dawn, he rubbed his eyes in surprise and delight. He was thrilled to see the stars and stripes still flying proudly over McHenry's battered walls. The attack had failed and the British were leaving. On a piece of paper, he quickly pencilled a poem: "Oh say, can you see, by the dawn's early light/What so proudly we hailed at the twilight's last gleaming? ... Oh say, does that star-spangled banner yet wave/O'er the land of the free, and the home of the brave?"

That evening Key showed his poem to a friend, who was so impressed that he insisted it be printed. It was soon set to music and a whole century later the song that was inspired by Britain's failure to capture Baltimore became America's national anthem.

ABOVE The original star-spangled banner that flew over Fort McHenry. It was made by seamstress Mary Pickersgill with a star for each of the 15 states. It now resides in Washington's Smithsonian Museum.

OPPOSITE Young lawyer and poet Francis Scott Key notices that the Stars and Stripes has survived the night and still flies over the fort. He was inspired to write: "O say, can you see, by the dawn's early light...?"

24

Napoleon's Proclamation of 1 March 1815

This is the proclamation that began one of history's most dramatic episodes. Napoleon's audacious attempt to recreate his imperial power was the last act in a tragedy: one of the greatest military commanders of all time was returning to pursue his final fateful endeavour. It was to end with a humiliating defeat at the Battle of Waterloo on 18 June 1815. "People of France," the document proclaims, "I am back among you to reclaim my rights and yours."

OPPOSITE Napoleon's proclamation to the people of France promising to throw out the unpopular Bourbon king Louis XVIII. He says he has returned to "regain my rights, which are yours".

Five days before he made this forthright proclamation on his return to France, Napoleon Bonaparte was an exile – under British guard on the island of Elba. A year earlier, after 15 years of victories against almost every country in Europe, he had been brought to his knees by a coalition of allied armies and forced to abdicate. He was then packed off to Elba, which is only 240 kilometres (150 miles) south of France, under the remarkably lax supervision of a British officer, Colonel Neil Campbell. At the end of February 1815, Campbell made the mistake of risking a few days off on the Italian mainland to see his doctor (though rumour had it that he was actually visiting his mistress). When he returned on 28 February he was told Napoleon had escaped in a small flotilla led by the brig *Inconstant* painted in British colours. He took with him a force of just over 1,000 French attendants and troops that he had been permitted on the island. Campbell gave chase but he was too late: the French emperor landed at Golfe-Juan near Antibes on the French Riviera on 1 March.

Napoleon was taking a huge risk. France was now back in the hands of the old regime. A French king, Louis XVIII, was restored to the throne, and the country exhausted by war was now enjoying its first year of peace. Louis, however, had done little to show he was ready to learn from the failure of the old Bourbon regime and reform French society. Most importantly, he had made the mistake of disbanding much of the old Grande Armée, which had been devoted to Napoleon. When his former secretary visited him on Elba, Napoleon asked whether his old soldiers still loved him. "Yes, sire," came the reply, "and may I even venture to say, more than ever." This was to be the decisive factor in Napoleon's bold gamble.

The moment he stepped ashore, Napoleon ordered this proclamation distributed as widely as possible. Its wording is clearly intended to appeal mainly to old imperial army veterans. He reminds them of the military victories a year earlier which successfully slowed down the enemy advance on Paris. The first third of the proclamation blames not the army for allowing the enemy to capture Paris in March 1814, but two of his former marshals – the Duke of Castiglione, Marshal Augereau, and the Duke of Ragusa, Marshal Marmont – for their "defection" and "betrayal". Napoleon then reaches out to the French people, claiming that the regime of Louis XVIII is set to restore the old feudal system, meaning peace at home and respect abroad will "be lost for ever". He ends by promising: "It is to you alone and to the brave men of the army that I make, and will always make a glory of all duty."

It is a powerful appeal which must have helped Napoleon's spectacular re-ascent to

PROCLAMATION.

Au Golfe-Juan, le 1.er Mars 1815.

NAPOLÉON,

Par la grace de Dieu et les Constitutions de l'État, Empereur des Français, *etc. etc. etc.*

AU PEUPLE FRANÇAIS.

FRANÇAIS,

La défection du duc de Castiglione livra Lyon sans défense à nos ennemis ; l'armée dont je lui avais confié le commandement était, par le nombre de ses bataillons, la bravoure et le patriotisme des troupes qui la composaient, à même de battre le corps d'armée Autrichien qui lui était opposé, et d'arriver sur les derrières du flanc gauche de l'armée ennemie qui menaçait Paris

Les victoires de Champ-Aubert, de Montmirail, de Château-Thierry, de Vauchamp, de Mormans, de Montereau, de Craone, de Reims, d'Arcy-sur-Aube et de saint-Dizier, l'insurrection des braves paysans de la Lorraine, de la Champagne, de l'Alsace, de la Franche-Comté et de la Bourgogne, et la position que j'avais prise sur les derrières de l'armée ennemie en la séparant de ses magasins, de ses parcs de réserve, de ses convois et de tous ses équipages, l'avaient placée dans une situation désespérée. Les Français ne furent jamais sur le point d'être plus puissans, et l'élite de l'armée ennemie était perdue sans ressource ; elle eût trouvé son tombeau dans ces vastes contrées qu'elle avait si impitoyablement saccagées, lorsque la trahison du duc de Raguse livra la Capitale et désorganisa l'armée. La conduite inattendue de ces deux généraux qui trahirent à la fois leur patrie, leur prince et leur bienfaiteur, changea le destin de la guerre. La situation désastreuse de l'ennemi était telle, qu'à la fin de l'affaire qui eut lieu devant Paris, il était sans munitions, par la séparation de ses parcs de réserve.

Dans ces nouvelles et grandes circonstances, mon cœur fut déchiré : mais mon âme resta inébranlable. Je ne consultai que l'intérêt de la patrie : je m'exilai sur un rocher au milieu des mers : ma vie vous était et devait encore vous être utile, je ne permis pas que le grand nombre de citoyens qui voulaient m'accompagner partageassent mon sort ; je crus leur présence utile à la france, et je n'emmenai avec moi qu'une poignée de braves, nécessaires à ma garde.

Elevé au Trône par votre choix, tout ce qui a été fait sans vous est illégitime. Depuis vingt-cinq ans la France a de nouveaux intérêts, de nouvelles institutions, une nouvelle gloire qui ne peuvent être garantis que par un Gouvernement national et par une dynastie née dans ces nouvelles circonstances. Un prince qui régnerait sur vous, qui serait assis sur mon trône par la force des mêmes armées qui ont ravagé notre territoire, chercherait en vain à s'étayer des principes du droit féodal, il ne pourrait assurer l'honneur et les droits que d'un petit nombre d'individus ennemis du peuple qui depuis vingt-cinq ans les a condamnés dans toutes nos assemblées nationales. Votre tranquilité intérieure et votre considération extérieure seraient perdues à jamais.

Francais ! dans mon exil, j'ai entendu vos plaintes et vos vœux ; vous reclamez ce Gouvernement de votre choix qui seul est légitime. Vous accusiez mon long sommeil, vous me reprochiez de sacrifier à mon repos les grands intérèts de la patrie,

J'ai traversé les mers au milieu des périls de toute espèce ; j'arrive parmi vous, reprendre mes droits qui sont les vôtres. Tout ce que des individus ont fait, écrit ou dit depuis la prise de Paris, je l'ignorerai toujours ; cela n'influera en rien sur le souvenir que je conserve des services importans qu'ils ont rendus, car il est des événemens d'une telle nature qu'ils sont au-dessus de l'organisation humaine.

Français ! Il n'est aucune nation, quelque petite qu'elle soit, qui n'ait eu le droit et ne se soit soustraite au déshonneur d'obéir à un Prince imposé par un ennemi momentanement victorieux. Lorsque Charles VII rentra à Paris et renversa le trône éphémère de Henri VI, il reconnut tenir son trône de la vaillance de ses braves et non d'un prince régent d'Angleterre.

C'est aussi à vous seuls, et aux braves de l'armée, que je fais et ferai toujours gloire de tout devoir.

Signé NAPOLEON.

Par l'Empereur :

Le grand maréchal faisant fonctions de Major-général de la Grande Armée,

***signé*, Comte BERTRAND.**

A VALENCIENNES, chez H. J. PRIGNET, Imprimeur des Administrations, etc. 1815.

supreme power in the days that followed. The French still celebrate his 20-day march from the south coast of France to Paris, calling it the "Route Napoleon". There were abortive attempts by royalists to stop him – the most famous of which was the confrontation that took place near Grenoble, where Napoleon found himself facing a battalion sent with orders to use all means to halt him. When they prepared to fire, Napoleon walked forwards and bared his chest. "If there is one among you who wishes to kill his emperor, let him do so," he cried. Not a shot was fired. As one man, the battalion rushed forwards and embraced him. Even Marshal Ney, who had promised to bring Napoleon to Paris in an iron cage, caved in to the charm of his old comrade-in-arms when they met, and declared for him.

Napoleon was back in Paris on 20 March. He was immediately declared an outlaw at the Congress in Vienna by the allied commanders who had defeated him a year earlier. France was divided about his return, and few doubted that it made war with the allies inevitable. But Napoleon could still rely on the enthusiasm of his old Grande Armée. Their memory of his inspiring leadership in battle helped to mobilize a substantial force of 100,000 men, which headed north to catch the allies before they could fully unite against him. It was a hopeless enterprise. He did indeed surprise the Duke of Wellington and his Prussian ally Marshal Blücher in Belgium and force them to retreat on 16 June, but he was outfought by them two days later at the Battle of Waterloo. Even if he had won Waterloo, he would soon have been massively outnumbered by the armies from Russia and Austria that were hastening from the east.

Within weeks, the man who had escaped so dramatically from Elba on 26 February 1815 surrendered and was sent as a prisoner to St Helena, an island from which he was never to escape. He died six years later, blaming almost everyone but himself for the failure of his last glorious but fatal campaign.

OPPOSITE The Duke of Wellington, on his horse Copenhagen, rallies his troops at a critical moment in the Battle of Waterloo. His infantry in defensive squares held out against a succession of French charges.

BELOW Watched by fascinated British officers on the Royal Navy warship HMS Bellerophon, *Napoleon is carried away to British waters and then to live in exile on the remote island of St Helena.*

25

Brunel's Letter of 12 October 1840

This letter from Isambard Kingdom Brunel, the great British engineer, heralds a revolution in marine technology. Brunel reports that he is persuaded by a recent trial on a ship called the *Archimedes* that a propeller will be more effective than a paddle at driving his new steamship – the *Great Britain*. This decisive moment in 1840 marks the start of the age of the propeller.

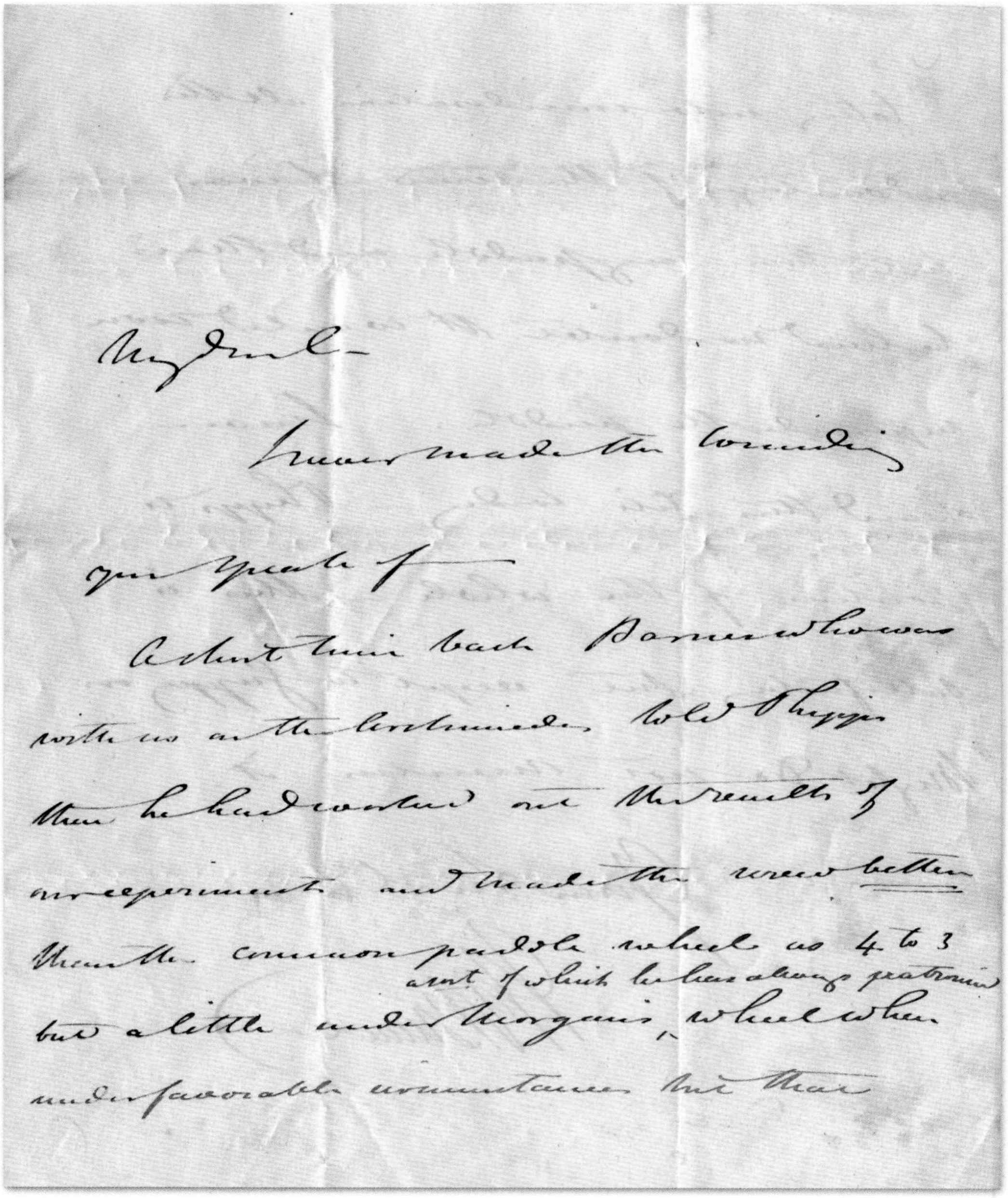

Brunel was a giant of the Industrial Revolution, as large in life as his work was in scale. He was a charming, flamboyant character, brilliant at inspiring others to back his immensely ambitious engineering projects. His pioneering work on the railways transformed popular travel on land, while on sea his three great steamships launched the modern era of oceanic travel.

This letter, written in October 1840, aptly illustrates Brunel's innovative genius. He had already built the record-breaking transatlantic paddle-driven liner, the 2,300-ton SS *Great Western*, the largest passenger ship in the world when she was launched in 1837. She must have been a magnificent sight with her elegant lines, her single funnel and four tall masts. But within a very short time Brunel was aware that another steamship had been launched with a different propulsion system – a propeller instead of a paddle wheel. This was the *Archimedes*, as mentioned in the letter: Brunel says that tests on the *Archimedes* have demonstrated "the advantages of the screw" and that it was now proved to be "better than the common paddle". It was a very exciting development in the history of marine engineering, and for Brunel it came at a critical moment. He was planning a successor

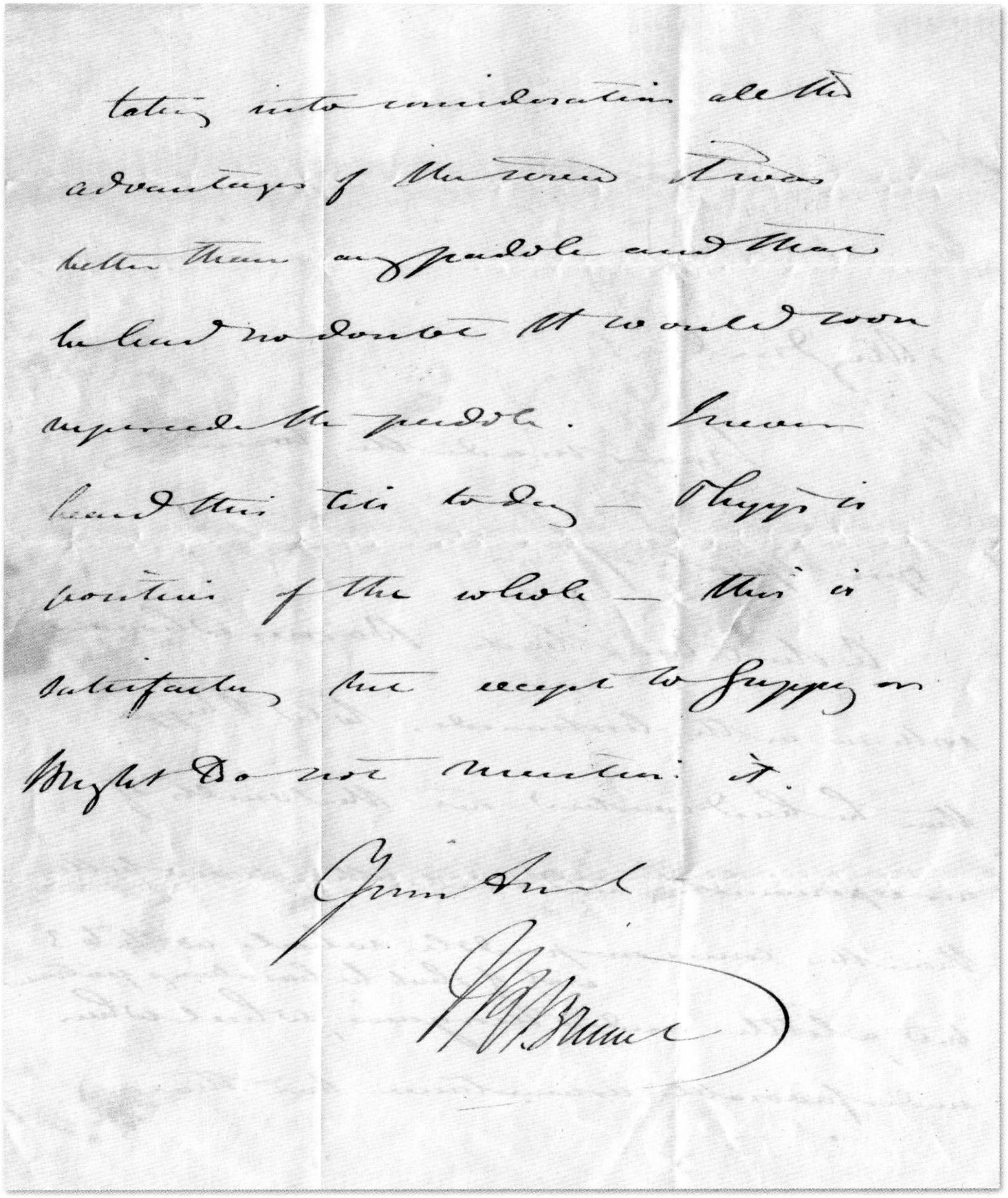

taking into consideration all the advantages of the screw it was better than any paddle and that I believed no doubt it would soon supersede the paddle.

Do not mention it.

Yours truly

I K Brunel

OPPOSITE AND LEFT Brunel's letter confirms his innovative commitment to the propeller as the best means of propulsion. The top of the second page reads: "taking into consideration all the advantages of the screw it was better than any paddle ..."

to the *Great Western*; both the largest steamship in the world and the first to be made entirely of iron. His SS *Great Britain* would be 27 metres (89 feet) longer than the *Great Western*, with a displacement of a further 1,300 tons. The initial plan was to equip her with paddle-wheel propulsion, but the tests had now shown the screw propeller to be better: it was lighter, less obtrusive and – unlike paddle wheels, which could tilt out of the sea if the ship leaned to one side – the screw was securely placed in the centre of the stern well below the water level.

Brunel's problem was that the *Great Britain*'s paddle-driving engine was already well on the way to being produced. These great ships were built with the backing of local financiers, and any delay would be expensive and very unpopular with investors waiting for return on their money. Brunel took the risk. Eighteen months into the build in Bristol, he cancelled the engine order for *Great Britain* and requested that a great propeller with a propeller-shaft engine be designed and installed instead. This was one of many hold-ups that delayed *Great Britain*'s entry into service. Once under way, however, she proved an engineering triumph. Her screw moved her along at up to 11 knots (3 knots faster than the *Great Western*), and she could carry 300 passengers (twice as many as her predecessor) and 120 crew.

Delays meant SS *Great Britain* was not in service until the summer of 1845. She caused quite a stir in New York, where one sceptical scientific magazine remarked that if there was "anything objectionable in the construction or machinery of this noble ship, it is the mode of propelling her by the screw propeller", and that it would not be surprising if it were replaced before long by paddle wheels at the side. The magazine was wrong; Brunel was right. His *Great Britain* had a number of mishaps in her long career plying between Liverpool and New York and later

Australia, but she never used paddle wheels.

Brunel had his failures along with his successes. The tunnel he built with his father Marc Brunel under the Thames was embarrassingly held up by flooding and even fatalities among the workforce. The younger Brunel was himself injured in the course of construction. He built some fine bridges for the Great Western Railway when he was appointed its chief engineer, but his ambitious broad-gauge network proved unsustainable when the rest of the country stuck with its standard gauge. His decision to power the South Devon Railway with "atmospheric" traction, a vacuum pipe system, was tried but failed to function properly and again, to his embarrassment, had to be abandoned.

His pioneering steamships had their problems too. *Great Britain* grounded off Northern Ireland in 1846, a year after her maiden voyage to New York. And by 1886 she was so worn by age and damaged by fire and the weather in the southern ocean that she was abandoned in the Falkland Islands. It was the far-sighted generosity of several benefactors in 1970 that led to her transport on a massive submersible pontoon back to her home port of Bristol. She's now on show there in all her glory, her palatial interior furnishings magnificently restored.

Isambard Kingdom Brunel remains an inspiration to every engineer and the quintessence of creativity to the rest of us. He has left us with many great monuments to the massive risks he took and with the sheer grandeur of his imagination.

OPPOSITE Brunel, aged 51, stands proudly in front of the launching chains of his final steamship, the Great Eastern, *at Millwall dockyard in 1857.*

ABOVE SS Great Britain, *Brunel's propeller-driven steamship, at her exhibition site in Bristol – the drydock in which she was built before being launched in 1843.*

26

The Communist Manifesto

The Communist Manifesto is the most widely read and influential political document of the modern age. Written by radical German philosophers Karl Marx and Friedrich Engels in 1848, its vision of a classless society brought about by a workers' revolution became the basis of a new political movement which changed the course of history.

RIGHT Karl Marx aged 57. Friedrich Engels said this photo showed Marx "in all his serene, confident, Olympian calmness". After Marx's death, Engels ordered more than a thousand copies to be sent to socialists worldwide.

OPPOSITE The only surviving page from the first draft of The Communist Manifesto, *handwritten by Marx. He and Engels wrote the document in just six weeks. It was completed at the end of January 1848 and published one month later.*

The Communist Manifesto was written at a time of great political and economic turbulence in Europe. In what became known as the Revolutions of 1848, uprisings took place in 50 countries, from Germany to the Italian peninsula. There were many reasons for unrest. An industrial slowdown had caused mass unemployment; in Vienna alone, 10,000 workers were laid off. Ireland was crippled by a potato famine, part of a major crop failure that hit the whole of western Europe between 1845 and 1847. Cities were overcrowded, poverty abounded, and the right to vote was largely limited to the upper classes. Middle- and working-class protesters took to the streets to demand new constitutions and governments which gave them a voice. Violent demonstrations in Paris forced King Louis Philippe to abdicate. After riots in London, Queen Victoria was evacuated to the Isle of Wight for her safety. Conditions were ideal for Karl Marx and Friedrich Engels to share the ideals of their fledgling communist movement.

Marx had moved to Paris then Brussels after being exiled from his native Prussia for his revolutionary socialist ideas. Engels, whose wealthy German father owned a factory in Manchester, supported Marx financially as well as intellectually. The two philosophers persuaded fellow members of the newly formed Communist League of London to let them write a pamphlet outlining the philosophy of communism. Many of their ideas had been discussed before, but *The Communist Manifesto* captured them on paper for the first time.

The document, which Marx wrote by hand, is only 23 pages long, but it speaks with great authority about how its authors believed history – and therefore the future – works. "The history of all hitherto existing society is the history of class struggles" is the memorable opening line of the first chapter. It traces those struggles from ancient civilizations with free men and slaves through to the Industrial Revolution with its "bourgeoisie" – capitalist owners of the

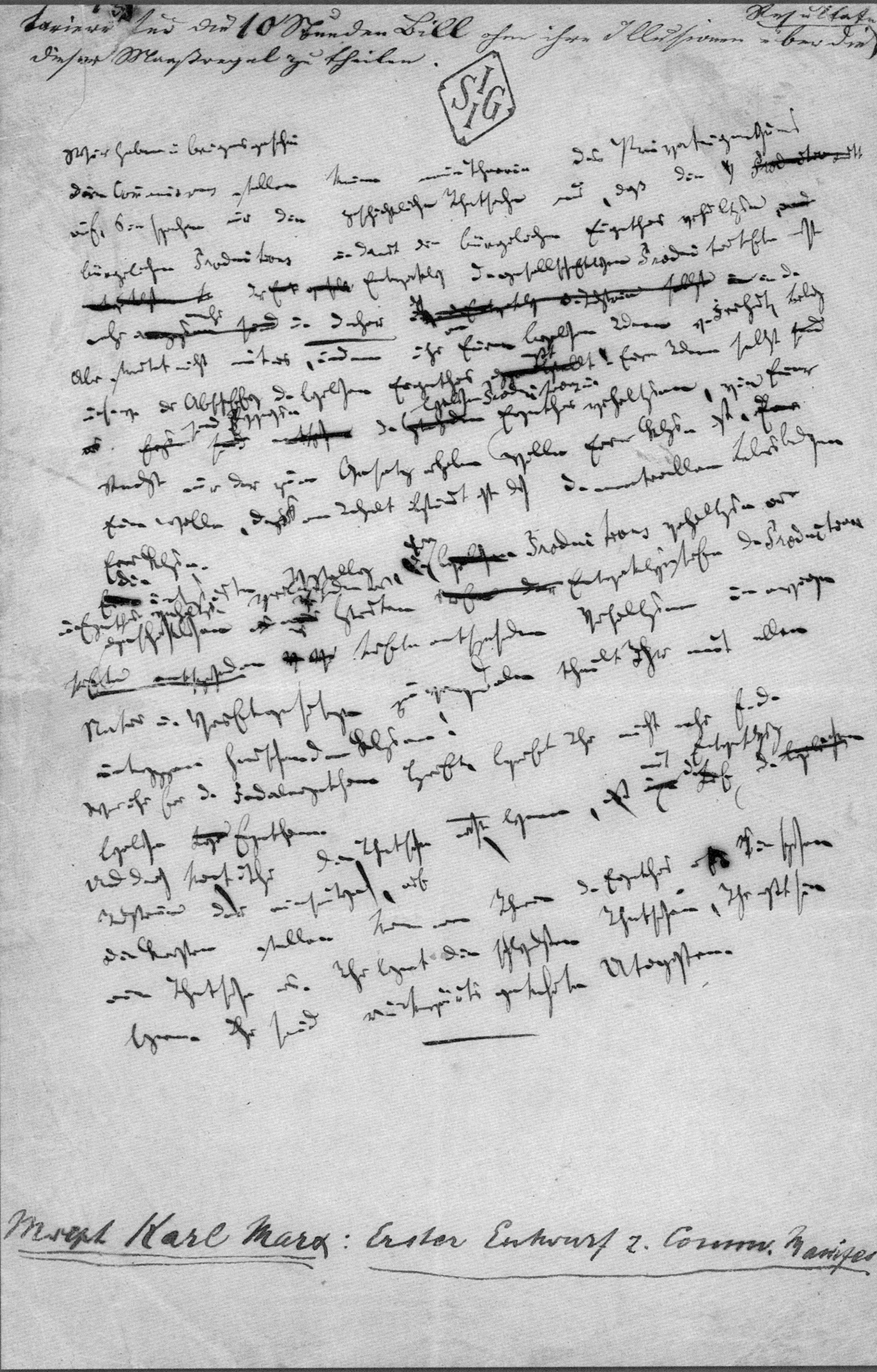
Mscpt. Karl Marx: Erster Entwurf z. Comm. Manifest

LEFT Friedrich Engels, a German socialist philosopher, co-authored The Communist Manifesto. *The son of a wealthy textile manufacturer, he supported Marx and his family financially.*

RIGHT Prussian troops attacking protesters behind a barricade in Berlin's Alexanderplatz on 18 March 1848. Insurgents fired from the windows of nearby buildings and threw paving stones at the king's soldiers.

means of production – and the "proletariat", workers who provided labour. It is unexpectedly complimentary about capitalism, congratulating the bourgeoisie for accomplishing "wonders far surpassing Egyptian pyramids, Roman aqueducts, and Gothic cathedrals". However, the problem with rapid industrialization, Marx and Engels quickly point out, is that by exploiting workers, the bourgeoisie becomes its own "gravedigger": creating an ever-larger class of resentful workers who will recognize their power and stage violent revolutions. They compare the bourgeoisie to a "sorcerer, who is no longer able to control the powers of the nether world whom he has called up by his spells".

The manifesto goes on to describe how workers inspired by communism will join forces to create a classless, equal society. Among other things, it calls for the abolition of private property, an end to child labour, the nationalization of transport systems and free public education – demands that actually sound rather tame today. Marx and Engels claim communism is the true path to follow and dismiss all other forms of socialism as misguided. They confidently predict that the revolution taking place in Germany will produce a widespread proletarian revolution, leading to a world where everyone is equal and living in harmony. Exactly what will replace the status quo is a bit hazy, reflecting the fact that Marx and Engels were theorists who wrote in the abstract and did not offer a blueprint for setting up a communist government. The manifesto ends with words in capital letters that have echoed through the decades: "WORKERS OF THE WORLD, UNITE".

Marx and Engels were wrong about Germany becoming a flag-bearer for communism. None of the 1848 Revolutions succeeded. Some governments introduced reforms; coalitions of middle- and working-class agitators fell apart and security forces backed the establishment. The manifesto was largely neglected for the next two decades, but it received an unexpected boost in 1872 when leaders of Germany's radical Social Democratic Party were accused of treason after agitating against the Franco-Prussian War. During the trial, prosecutors used quotes from the manifesto as evidence. This allowed its legal publication in Germany. Within months, more than nine editions appeared in six languages. As socialism took root over the next 40 years, the number of editions rose into the hundreds.

In 1917, 34 years after Marx died, Vladimir Lenin's Bolshevik Revolution transformed Russia into the world's first socialist state. *The Communist Manifesto* became standard reading for successive generations. At times in the twentieth century, half the people in the world were governed by communist parties. But rather than the state withering away, as Marx had predicted, these regimes were highly authoritarian and hierarchical, which led to communist political systems being discredited. *The Communist Manifesto*, on the other hand, has survived the test of time. Its radical approach to issues such as globalization, economic crises and the growing divide between rich and poor is as relevant today as it was in 1848.

27

The Rules of Football

This nondescript notebook is one of the most significant documents in the history of sport. The 1863 Football Association Minute Book contains the minutes of a series of meetings that drew up the first widely accepted rules for the game of football (soccer). It represents two landmark moments: the launch of what is arguably the most popular game in the world today, and the creation of the Football Association, English football's governing body.

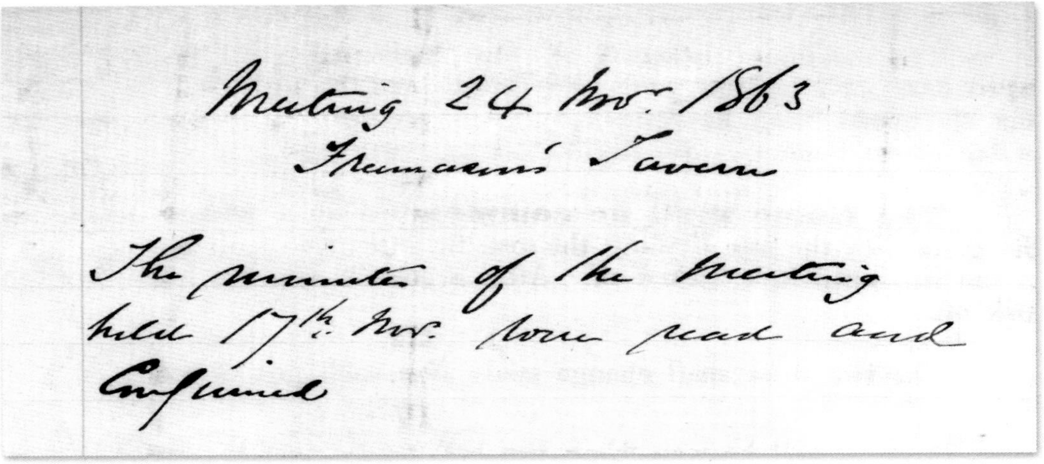
Meeting 24 Nov. 1863
Freemasons' Tavern
The minutes of the meeting held 17th Nov. were read and Confirmed

On 26 October 1863, a group of men gathered at the Freemasons' Tavern near London's Covent Garden. They set out to tackle the greatest sporting conundrum of the age: the inability of football teams to compete with each other because they played by different rules. It took six meetings, and often acrimonious discussion, but on 8 December the group came up with 13 rules which marked the birth of modern football.

Kicking a ball past determined opponents had been part of English life for centuries. The word "footeball" to describe a game first appeared in 1424 in an Act forbidding it. Gangs of men from neighbouring areas played "mass" or "mob" football, battling to kick pigs' bladders from one end of a town to another. It was considered fair game to kick and punch both the bladder and anyone who got in the way. Henry VIII owned a pair of football boots, but that didn't stop him from trying to ban the game in 1540 on the grounds that it incited riots. "Footeballe is nothinge but beastlie furie and extreme violence", wrote one contemporary critic. Records from Cambridge University reveal that a match between students and local townsmen in 1579 descended into a brawl. Students were then forbidden to play football outside college grounds. It was not until the nineteenth century that demands grew for the rules of the game to be standardized. Upper-class boarding schools like Eton and Rugby wanted to play competitive matches, but their games followed different rules. Rugby, for example, allowed extensive

RIGHT The Football Association Minute Book written by Ebenezer Cobb Morley during a series of meetings in autumn 1863. It is now on display at the National Football Museum in Manchester, England.

ABOVE Notes from the 24 Nov meeting.

OPPOSITE A draft of the first 10 (of 13) rules in the Minute Book. Heated debate, particularly about running with the ball and the holding and hacking of players, led to changes in the final version.

I.

The maximum **length of the ground** shall be 200 yards, the maximur **breadth** shall be 100 yards, the length and breadth shall be marked off with flags and the **goal** shall be defined by two upright posts, 8 yards apart, without any tap or bar across them.

II.

The Game shall be commenced by a **place kick** from the centre c the ground by the side winning the toss, the other side shall not approach within 10 yarc of the ball until it is kicked off. After a goal is won the losing side shall be entitled t kick off.

III.

The two sides shall change goals after each goal is won.

IV.

A goal shall be won when the ball passes over the space between the goal pos (at whatever height), not being thrown, knocked on, or carried.

V.

When the ball is in **touch** the first player who touches it shall kick or throw it fro the point on the boundary line where it left the ground, in a direction at right angles wit the boundary line.

VI.

A player shall be **out of play** immediately he is in front of the ball, and mu return behind the ball as soon as possible. If the ball is kicked past a player by his ow side, he shall not touch or kick it or advance until one of the other side has first kicke it or one of his own side on a level with or in front of him has been able to kick it.

VII.

In case the ball goes behind the goal line, if a player on the side to whom tl goal belongs first touches the ball, one of his side shall be entitled to a free kick from tl goal line at the point opposite the place where the ball shall be touched. If a player the opposite side first touches the ball, one of his side shall be entitled to a free kick fro a point 15 yards outside the goal line, opposite the place where the ball is touched.

VIII.

If a player makes a **fair catch** he shall be entitled to a **free kick,** provided l claims it by making a mark with his heel at once; and in order to take such kick he ma go as far back as he pleases, and no player on the opposite side shall advance beyond h mark until he has kicked.

IX.

A player shall be entitled to run with the ball towards his adversaries' goal if l makes a fair catch, or catches the ball on the first bound; but in the case of a fair catch, he makes his mark, he shall not then run.

X.

If any player shall run with the ball towards his adversaries' goal, any player on tl opposite side shall be at liberty to charge, hold, trip, or hack him, or to wrest the ball fro him; but no player shall be held and hacked at the same time.

handling of the ball, while Eton relied more on kicking it. In 1848, five schools met at Cambridge University and drew up a list of common rules (now lost). They applied only to the five schools involved. Similarly, rules laid down by the Sheffield Football Club in 1858 were adopted by just a handful of clubs in northern England.

It was a football-loving lawyer in London who got the ball properly rolling. Ebenezer Cobb Morley lived in the leafy suburb of Barnes, where he'd formed a football club with friends. Frustrated by the difficulty of playing other clubs with different rules, in 1863 he wrote to a popular sporting paper, *Bell's Life*. The game of cricket had standard rules, Morley argued, so why not do the same for football? His letter led to the historic meeting on 26 October at the Freemasons' Tavern. Morley took minutes in a notebook, and his neat handwriting records that representatives of 12 clubs in and around London met "for the purpose of forming an Association with the object of establishing a definite code of rules for the regulation of the game". The group called itself the Football Association, now more commonly known as the FA. Morley's notes reveal that the group based some of its ideas on the rules agreed at Cambridge in 1848. They also record heated debate about two aspects of the game: handling the ball and hacking (kicking an opponent on the shins). The representative from Blackheath Football Club insisted that players be allowed to run with the ball and hack. When that was ruled out, he walked out. Blackheath went on to form a new group: the Rugby Football Union.

Morley's 1863 Football Association Minute

Book lists the 13 rules approved on 8 December. They make fascinating reading, setting the length of the ground at 200 yards long (182.9 metres) and 100 yards (91.4 metres) wide, with goalposts 24 feet (7.3 metres) apart. Players were allowed to catch the ball as long as they did not run with it or throw it. In an obvious attempt to reduce violence on the field, Rule 13 reads: "No player shall wear projecting nails, iron plates, or gutta perca on the soles or heels of his boots."

Over the next few years, the rules were added to and refined. Goal kicks were included in 1869 and corner kicks three years later. Referees first appeared in 1871. Nets and crossbars were added to goalposts. Penalties were not introduced until 1891, largely because football was regarded as a game "played by gentlemen who would never cheat".

The fact that today football (soccer) is played by 200 nations worldwide is testament to the power of the game. It also gives us the chance to use one of our favourite quotes, the incomparable words of footballing legend, and 1970s manager of Liverpool FC, Bill Shankly: "Some people believe football is a matter of life and death. I am very disappointed with that attitude. I can assure you it is much, much more important than that."

OPPOSITE The Freemason's Tavern in central London, where members of the newly formed Football Association met in the autumn of 1863. The laws of football were formally approved here on 8 December.

ABOVE The 1882 English FA final held at Kennington Oval, London, England. Old Etonians beat Blackburn Rovers 1-nil.

28

Darwin's *On the Origin of Species*

Charles Darwin's theory of evolution by natural selection is to us one of the most important ideas in human history. His well-documented examination of the "survival of the fittest" revolutionized the course of science, philosophy and theology. Darwin completed his first draft of *On the Origin of Species* in 1842, but fears of upsetting widespread beliefs that God, not nature, was responsible for all life, meant that he did not publish the book for another 17 years.

ON

THE ORIGIN OF SPECIES

BY MEANS OF NATURAL SELECTION,

OR THE

PRESERVATION OF FAVOURED RACES IN THE STRUGGLE FOR LIFE.

BY CHARLES DARWIN, M.A.,

FELLOW OF THE ROYAL, GEOLOGICAL, LINNÆAN, ETC., SOCIETIES;
AUTHOR OF 'JOURNAL OF RESEARCHES DURING H. M. S. BEAGLE'S VOYAGE ROUND THE WORLD.'

LONDON:
JOHN MURRAY, ALBEMARLE STREET.
1859.

P. D. B.

The right of Translation is reserved.

In 1837, at the age of 28, Charles Darwin sat down and drew a small sketch of a tree which would become a symbol of his revolutionary theory of evolution. Its branches illustrate new species emerging. Some go extinct, a few survive. He drew the tree after returning from a five-year voyage on HMS *Beagle*, a military and scientific expedition which took the eager young naturalist on a voyage around South America and other continents. It was a trip that transformed his understanding of the world.

Darwin was supposed to become a doctor like his father and grandfather, but he hated the sight of blood and left medical school after just one year. He went on to Cambridge University to study for a career in the Anglican Church; however, he proved far more interested in collecting insects and examining their tiny differences than in learning about theology. One of his tutors recommended Darwin join the crew of the *Beagle* as "a gentleman naturalist". He set off in 1831 and, suffering from seasickness, took every opportunity to get off the ship, explore, observe and collect. He was struck by how the fossils of long-extinct animals resembled living species. He observed that characteristics of creatures like the octopus, lizard and bird developed according to the environment in which they lived. He also studied the racial differences of people he met. Everything he saw fed into a growing belief that all creatures had gradually evolved from a single organism.

Back in England, he collated his findings in a series of notebooks and went on gathering evidence to support his ideas. By 1842, six years after returning from his voyage, Darwin had completed an outline of his thesis. For various reasons, he did not publish *On the*

OPPOSITE Title page of the first edition of On the Origin of Species *published in 1859. Darwin produced five more editions adding new arguments.*

ABOVE Darwin wrote the words "I think" at the top of his famous Tree of Life sketch. It shows all creatures have a single origin but evolve into different species.

Origin of Species for another 17 years: his favourite daughter died, as did his father; he wanted more facts to support his beliefs; and, most importantly, he worried about bringing himself and his family into disrepute by challenging the strongly held religious belief that everything in the universe was held together by the hand of God. Darwin knew he was treading on dangerous territory and he confided in a letter to a friend in 1844 that writing about the ability of species to change was "like confessing [to] a murder".

Darwin's relentless pursuit of more evidence might have continued had it not been for the findings of a fellow naturalist, Alfred Russel Wallace. In 1858, Wallace wrote to Darwin outlining his own theory of evolution. It was uncomfortably like Darwin's, and that propelled Darwin to publish his book quickly. He described writing the tract as "living hell", but, determined to reach as wide an audience as possible, he wrote in conversational style, using simple language to develop his straightforward and logical arguments. Interestingly, he does not use the words "evolution" or "survival of the fittest" in the original manuscript. They do not appear until much later editions. Nor does he deny the hand of God in nature, writing, "probably all the organic beings which have ever lived on this earth have descended from some one primordial form – into which life was first breathed by the Creator".

On the Origin of Species by Means of Natural Selection, or the Preservation of Favoured Races in the Struggle for Life (to give its full title) was published on 24 November 1859. All 1,250 copies sold out on the first day. Reaction was mixed. One critic wrote: "When I read the book I laughed out loud." Another called natural selection the "law of higgledy-piggledy".

Darwin was not the first to propose the idea of evolution, but no one else had produced a cohesive and accessible explanation for it. His book attracted worldwide attention and stoked the debate between religion and science which reached a famous climax in 1925 in what became known as the "Scopes Monkey Trial". A US teacher, John Thomas Scopes, was found guilty of violating Tennessee state law by teaching Charles Darwin's theory of evolution. The state had banned the teaching of evolution because it conflicted with the story of creation in the Bible. The law was not repealed until 1967.

As for Darwin, he spent the rest of his life writing new books and updating five editions of his bestselling masterwork. He tinkered constantly with the text, rethinking, revising and responding to criticism. The size of *On the Origin of Species* grew by 25 per cent. It was published in 11 languages, making Darwin a Victorian millionaire. He died in 1882 at Down House, south-east of London, where he had lived and worked for 40 years. Down House has been lovingly preserved in his memory and is well worth a visit. The great man is buried in Westminster Abbey.

ABOVE Down House, where Darwin and his family lived for 40 years. He wrote in the study and came up with ideas while walking on what he called a "thinking path" in the garden.

OPPOSITE This 1868 photograph of Darwin is known as a carte-de-visite. *It was fashionable to send these small photos to friends and, in Darwin's case, to his numerous readers.*

29

The Gettysburg Address

Abraham Lincoln wrote out in his own hand this copy of his famous Gettysburg Address. He had this text in his pocket as he spoke to commemorate the dead after one of the most decisive battles of the Civil War in 1863. The speech has become legendary for its salute to the benefits of democracy.

RIGHT Abraham Lincoln, US President March 1861–April 1865. His greatest achievements were victory for the Union in the Civil War and the abolition of slavery.

OPPOSITE Lincoln's handwritten text of his Gettysburg Speech passed to his secretary John Nicolay. The last sentence reads: "... this nation shall have a new birth of freedom, and that government of the people by the people for the people shall not perish from the earth."

This monumental speech, which reads with all the power, brevity and rhythm of great oratory, was made at a critical moment in American history. It was delivered four and a half months after the most decisive and bloody battle of the US Civil War at the town of Gettysburg in Pennsylvania on 1–3 July 1863. Reaching Gettysburg was the high-water mark of the rebel Confederacy of southern states under their commanding General Robert E. Lee. Flushed with his victory over President Lincoln's Union armies at Chancellorsville, Lee determined to break through the North's defences deeper than ever before. The critical confrontation took place at Gettysburg, where Lee's attacks were conclusively shattered. We have walked through the evocative battle sites and been deeply moved by each with its own memorial and story of the bitter struggle that took place there. There were some 50,000 casualties, the worst slaughter in the savage war that finally ended with the South's defeat in 1865.

Abraham Lincoln had been elected president in 1860, just a year before the southern states declared themselves independent and plunged the United Sates into the Civil War. Lincoln felt he had no choice but to fight, not so much at this early stage to abolish slavery, which was widespread in the South, as to preserve the Union. "My paramount object in this struggle is to save the Union and it is not either to save or destroy slavery," he said in August 1862. "If I could save the Union without freeing any slave I would do it." A few weeks later he was hardening his position and warning that he

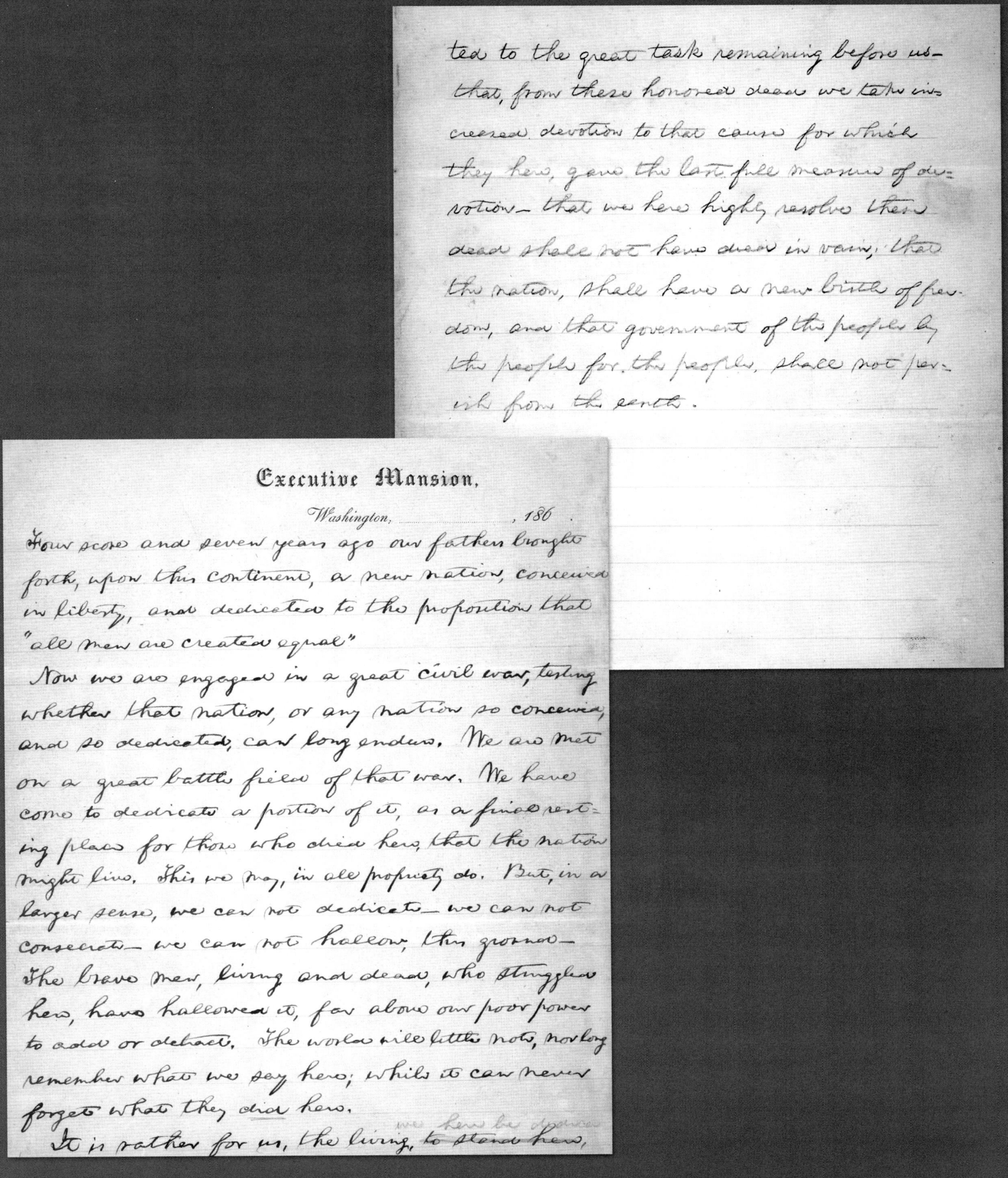

Executive Mansion,

Washington, , 186

Four score and seven years ago our fathers brought forth, upon this continent, a new nation, conceived in liberty, and dedicated to the proposition that "all men are created equal"

Now we are engaged in a great civil war, testing whether that nation, or any nation so conceived, and so dedicated, can long endure. We are met on a great battle field of that war. We have come to dedicate a portion of it, as a final resting place for those who died here, that the nation might live. This we may, in all propriety do. But, in a larger sense, we can not dedicate— we can not consecrate— we can not hallow, this ground— The brave men, living and dead, who struggled here, have hallowed it, far above our poor power to add or detract. The world will little note, nor long remember what we say here; while it can never forget what they did here.

It is rather for us, the living, ~~to stand here,~~ we here be dedica-

ted to the great task remaining before us— that, from these honored dead we take increased devotion to that cause for which they here, gave the last full measure of devotion— that we here highly resolve these dead shall not have died in vain; that the nation, shall have a new birth of freedom, and that government of the people by the people for the people, shall not perish from the earth.

would order the freedom of slaves in any state still in rebellion by January 1863. There seems little doubt that by the time he was invited to attend this consecration of a national cemetery at Gettysburg in November 1863, he was a committed abolitionist.

Lincoln's speech followed a long account of the Battle of Gettysburg by renowned American speech-maker Edward Everett. His oration lasted two hours, Lincoln's just two minutes. Everett later wrote to Lincoln that he wished he had been able to come "as near to the central idea of the occasion in two hours as you did in two minutes".

Lincoln had been invited to Gettysburg to make "some appropriate remarks" after what was clearly intended to be the main address by Everett. Lincoln had this slip of paper with the words of his speech folded up in his pocket, and when he uttered them, there were several bursts of applause.

It is astonishing and uplifting to imagine the impact of what Lincoln said in those two minutes. He began by quoting the words of the 1776 US Declaration of Independence – "All men are created equal". Ironically, the main author of this lofty principle, Thomas Jefferson, was a slave-owner. When Lincoln uttered these same words 87 years later, however, he clearly included slaves. It was not until the thirteenth amendment to the Constitution was approved by Congress and signed off by Lincoln in the year and a half after Gettysburg that slavery was definitively abolished.

Lincoln's striking assertion that this commemoration of the dead at Gettysburg should be the occasion for "increased devotion" to the cause for which they died, the cause of democracy, is the climax of his short speech. He borrowed words from English theologian

John Wycliffe five centuries earlier and from the great Italian revolutionary Giuseppe Mazzini – "government of the people by the people for the people" – and wrapped them in a peroration which led to prolonged applause.

Lincoln's message was addressed to a much wider audience than the group of local politicians and soldiers who stood around him that November day. He was speaking to the millions of Americans who had lost loved ones in the most deadly conflict in their history. It was a challenge to the people of a nation which had won its freedom less than a century earlier that they had to remain united. It was a promise to the rest of the world too: the America which had won its freedom would not easily let it go.

A century after this speech, another renowned American orator, Martin Luther King, stood on the steps of the Lincoln Memorial in Washington to praise the president who had signed the thirteenth amendment outlawing slavery. "This momentous decree", said King, "came as a great beacon light of hope to millions of Negro slaves who had been seared in the flames of withering injustice."

OPPOSITE An artist's impression of Lincoln delivering his speech at the dedication of the Soldiers' National Cemetery at Gettysburg on 19 November 1863.

ABOVE A rare photograph of Lincoln at Gettysburg before he delivered his speech. He is facing the camera in the centre of the picture almost lost in a crush of guards and onlookers.

30

The British North America Act

The British North America Act created the country of Canada. Passed by the British Houses of Parliament in 1867, the Act laid out the structure of the government of the Dominion of Canada and listed the division of powers between the federal government and four provincial governments. One of the most successful constitutional documents of modern times, it remained in London and served, with amendments, as Canada's constitution until Prime Minister Pierre Elliot Trudeau patriated it to Canada in 1982.

OPPOSITE The British North America Act of 29 March 1867, which created the nation of Canada. The Act came into effect on 1 July, uniting British colonies in North America. It was Canada's constitution until 1982.

Among the three million records kept in the Parliamentary Archives at the Palace of Westminster is one very important to all Canadians. Tucked in between the Metropolitan Poor Act and the Dog Licences Act is the British North America Act, 1867. It is an innocuous-looking parchment held together by red ribbon, but this document provided the framework for one of the most successful countries in the world. Under the Act, three British colonies in North America – Canada (as the union of Ontario and Quebec was known at the time), Nova Scotia and New Brunswick – were united as "one Dominion under the name of Canada".

The founding fathers of Canada, local politicians and thinkers, wanted "to take our place among the nations of the world", but the main motive for setting up their own country was fear of their American neighbours. The Civil War in the United States ended in 1865 and some US politicians were talking openly about annexing parts of British North America. In 1866, marauding members of the Fenian Brotherhood, some of whom were Civil War veterans, staged attacks on the colony of Canada to pressure Britain into giving Ireland its independence. That same year the US government ended a lucrative deal which had allowed free trade in natural resources and agricultural products with Britain's North American colonies.

The campaigners wanted to call the new country "the Kingdom of Canada", a title that was refused by the British government. They had to settle for "Dominion", but did get their way on how Canada would be governed, opting for the British parliamentary system with a House of Commons and a Senate. They also borrowed what they believed were the best aspects of the American Constitution. As in the US, there would be a central or federal government and provincial governments but, in Canada's case, the federal government would have general and overriding powers and the provinces limited ones, unlike the American states. According to John A. Macdonald, who became Canada's first prime minister: "We have avoided that great source of weakness which has been the cause of the disruption of the United States." With the graphic example of the US Civil War in mind, he did not want provinces to behave like states, claiming the right to secede. The act clearly spells out the distribution of powers. The federal government is responsible for 29 specific matters, including general taxation, currency, banking and criminal courts. Provincial governments control 16 areas such as education, prisons, hospitals and civil law. All judges above county court level were appointed by the federal government. The British monarch remained head of state. A document of its time, the Act did not mention specific groups like women or indigenous Canadians.

On 12 February 1867, a Bill for the Union of Canada, Nova Scotia and New Brunswick was introduced in the British House of Lords. It allowed Canada to run its own domestic affairs, with Britain remaining responsible for its foreign and defence policy. The Secretary of State for the Colonies, the Earl of Carnarvon, said that it was "laying the foundation of a great State – perhaps one which at a future day may even overshadow this country". The Bill was quickly passed by British politicians eager to see their colonies take more responsibility for spending on matters like defence. They welcomed Canada as a future trading partner

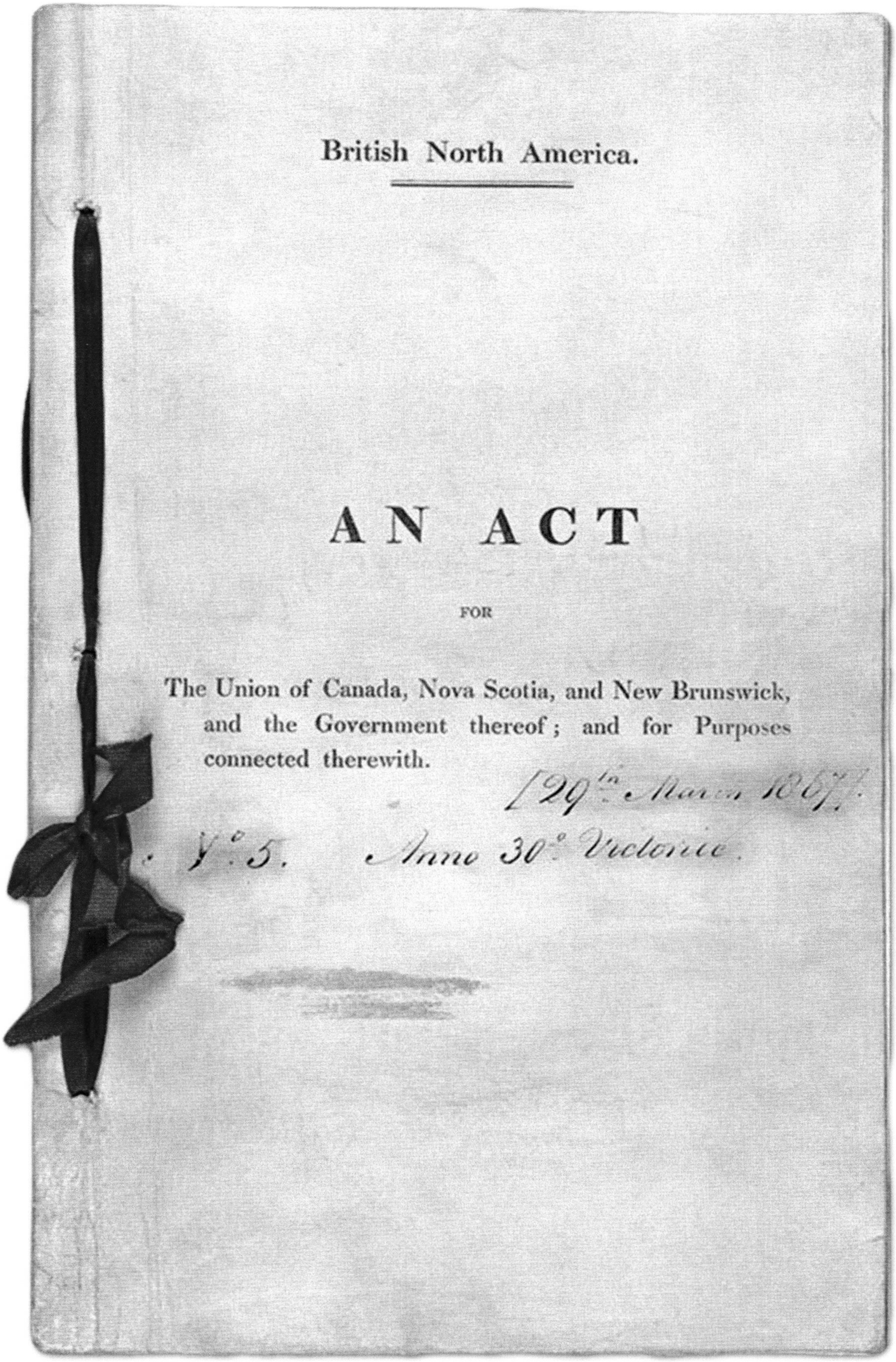

British North America.

AN ACT

FOR

The Union of Canada, Nova Scotia, and New Brunswick, and the Government thereof; and for Purposes connected therewith.

[29th March 1867].

No. 5. Anno 30° Victoriæ.

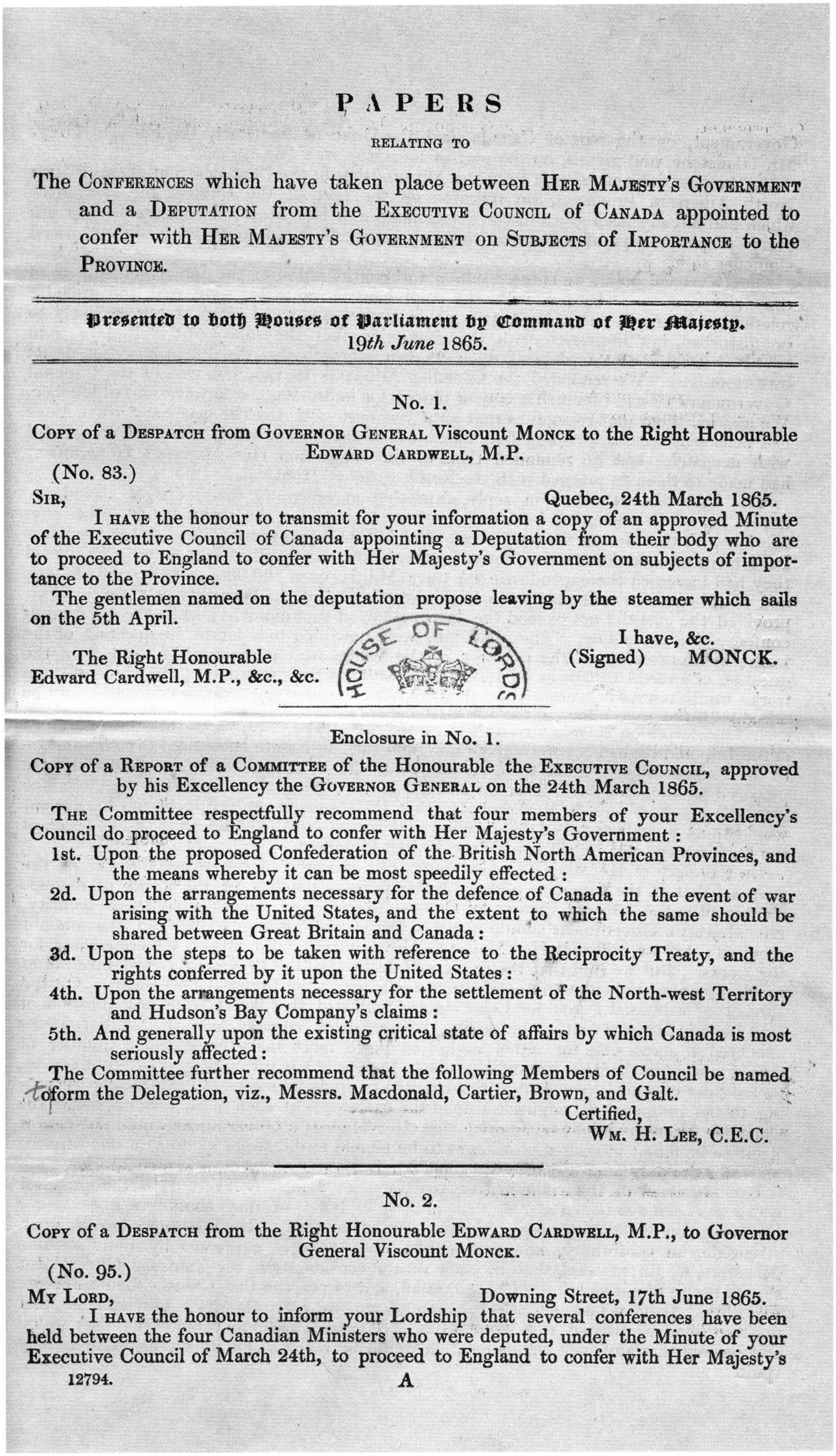

PAPERS

RELATING TO

The CONFERENCES which have taken place between HER MAJESTY'S GOVERNMENT and a DEPUTATION from the EXECUTIVE COUNCIL of CANADA appointed to confer with HER MAJESTY'S GOVERNMENT on SUBJECTS of IMPORTANCE to the PROVINCE.

Presented to both Houses of Parliament by Command of Her Majesty.
19*th June* 1865.

No. 1.

COPY of a DESPATCH from GOVERNOR GENERAL Viscount MONCK to the Right Honourable EDWARD CARDWELL, M.P.

(No. 83.)

SIR, Quebec, 24th March 1865.

I HAVE the honour to transmit for your information a copy of an approved Minute of the Executive Council of Canada appointing a Deputation from their body who are to proceed to England to confer with Her Majesty's Government on subjects of importance to the Province.

The gentlemen named on the deputation propose leaving by the steamer which sails on the 5th April.

I have, &c.
(Signed) MONCK.

The Right Honourable
Edward Cardwell, M.P., &c., &c.

HOUSE OF LORDS

Enclosure in No. 1.

COPY of a REPORT of a COMMITTEE of the Honourable the EXECUTIVE COUNCIL, approved by his Excellency the GOVERNOR GENERAL on the 24th March 1865.

THE Committee respectfully recommend that four members of your Excellency's Council do proceed to England to confer with Her Majesty's Government:

1st. Upon the proposed Confederation of the British North American Provinces, and the means whereby it can be most speedily effected:

2d. Upon the arrangements necessary for the defence of Canada in the event of war arising with the United States, and the extent to which the same should be shared between Great Britain and Canada:

3d. Upon the steps to be taken with reference to the Reciprocity Treaty, and the rights conferred by it upon the United States:

4th. Upon the arrangements necessary for the settlement of the North-west Territory and Hudson's Bay Company's claims:

5th. And generally upon the existing critical state of affairs by which Canada is most seriously affected:

The Committee further recommend that the following Members of Council be named to form the Delegation, viz., Messrs. Macdonald, Cartier, Brown, and Galt.

Certified,
WM. H. LEE, C.E.C.

No. 2.

COPY of a DESPATCH from the Right Honourable EDWARD CARDWELL, M.P., to Governor General Viscount MONCK.

(No. 95.)

MY LORD, Downing Street, 17th June 1865.

I HAVE the honour to inform your Lordship that several conferences have been held between the four Canadian Ministers who were deputed, under the Minute of your Executive Council of March 24th, to proceed to England to confer with Her Majesty's

12794. A

LEFT This document mentions a Canadian delegation to London in the spring of 1865 to discuss confederation. One delegate, John A. Macdonald, became Canada's first prime minister.

OPPOSITE ABOVE Photograph of The Fathers of Confederation, *a painting destroyed in a fire in 1916. Future PM Macdonald stands in the centre reading from a scroll.*

OPPOSITE BELOW Canadian PM Pierre Trudeau and Queen Elizabeth sign the 1982 Constitution Act in Ottawa.

and important member of the British Empire. The British North America Act became law in Canada on 1 July 1867. Confederation was greeted in Ottawa, the new country's capital, with a 101-gun salute. There were fireworks in Toronto, trumpeters in Montreal and a military parade in Halifax.

Passing years saw many amendments to the British North America Act. Since the United Kingdom had full legislative control over Canada, any changes had to be approved by the British Parliament. In 1871, Canada was given the power to establish new provinces and territories. In 1930, newer provinces of British Columbia, Alberta, Manitoba and Saskatchewan gained rights over certain natural resources in federally controlled lands. It was not until 1949 that a British statute gave Canada's Parliament the right to amend the Act – but only where federal powers were involved. Successive federal Canadian governments tried unsuccessfully to get provinces to agree to ask the British to patriate the constitution. Finally, Prime Minister Pierre Elliot Trudeau succeeded. On 29 March 1982, the British Parliament passed the Canada Act, stripping the UK of all law-making powers over Canada. Less than three weeks later, Queen Elizabeth II travelled to Ottawa to sign the new Constitution Act. Today, Canada, with its ten provinces and three territories, owes its stable and democratic society to the British North America Act of 1867.

31

The General Act of the Berlin Conference, 1885

The General Act of the Berlin Conference of February 1885 decided who owned Africa. This was the moment when the European powers – including Britain, France, Portugal and Germany – together with the United States of America agreed to carve up the continent without even a gesture towards the will of the African people.

It is one of the most striking facts about world history that the vast continent of Africa remained largely free of foreign colonial intrusion up to the 1880s. Until then, a scattering of European settlements flourished mainly around the coasts, but most of the rest of it was run by indigenous African rulers. The vast sweep of imperial expansion from 1500 onwards had essentially bypassed Africa. However, in the last few years that led up to the outbreak of the First World War in 1914, a spectacular burst of colonization imposed European rule almost everywhere. It was dubbed the "Scramble for Africa".

Europe's hunger for colonies was driven by an appetite for trade, natural resources and living space for its fast-increasing urban populations enriched by the Industrial Revolution and eager to exploit the opportunities that suddenly opened up. It was a scramble intensified by the competition for territory. The small coastal settlements rapidly absorbed great chunks of the interior, making treaties with and sometimes war on the African tribes and kingdoms whose sovereignty the European colonizers soon appropriated. The imbalance of weaponry made resistance hopeless except in a handful of cases. The Ethiopian Emperor Menelik II's defeat of Italian forces in 1896 was a rare instance of successful African counteraction.

The key European countries competing for a piece of Africa were France in west Africa, Britain in west, south and east Africa, and Portugal mainly in southern Africa. Two relative newcomers were Germany in south-west Africa and Belgium in the central Congo. Germany was enjoying unification under its dynamic Prussian chancellor, Otto von Bismarck, who saw the diplomatic advantage of calling a conference in Berlin to try to agree some rules for exploiting Africa. Anxious to exert his growing influence to balance the African ambitions of Britain, France and Portugal, he persuaded the competing countries to meet and draw up the General Act of February 1885. He was energetically supported in this by King Leopold II of Belgium, who was anxious to win recognition of his acquisition of the Congo as his personal property.

The Berlin Conference was attended by delegates from 14 countries with interests in Africa, including the United States. They met in the grand ballroom of Bismarck's official residence in Berlin. Only two of the delegates had ever been to Africa. Not a single African was present. There are two particularly significant articles in the treaty. Article 8 underlines what the countries wanted the world to believe were their motives in colonizing Africa: "All the Powers exercising sovereign rights or influence ... bind themselves to watch over the preservation of the native tribes, and to care for the improvement of the conditions of their moral and material well-being, and to help in suppressing slavery, and especially the slave trade." There is no mention of any political or human rights for the indigenous people. The powers then go on to stress that they "aim at instructing the natives and bringing home to them the blessings of civilization".

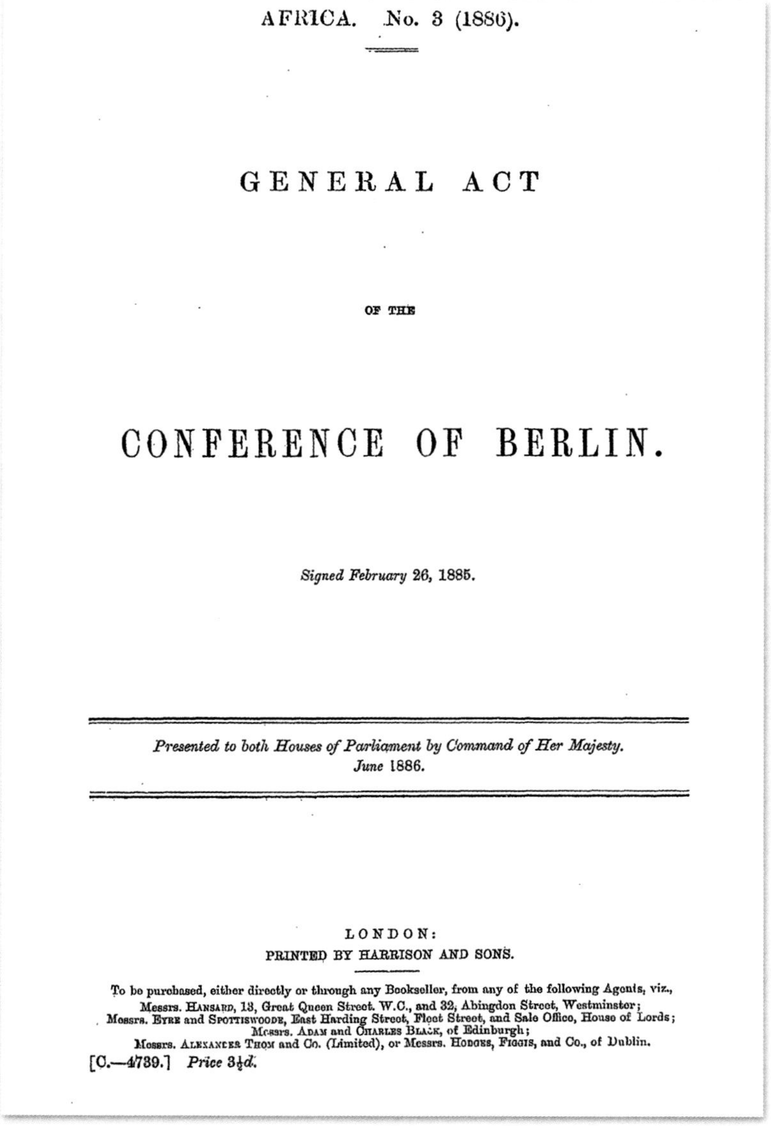

AFRICA. No. 3 (1886).

GENERAL ACT

OF THE

CONFERENCE OF BERLIN.

Signed February 26, 1885.

Presented to both Houses of Parliament by Command of Her Majesty.
June 1886.

LONDON:
PRINTED BY HARRISON AND SONS.

To be purchased, either directly or through any Bookseller, from any of the following Agents, viz.,
Messrs. HANSARD, 13, Great Queen Street. W.C., and 32, Abingdon Street, Westminster;
Messrs. EYRE and SPOTTISWOODE, East Harding Street, Fleet Street, and Sale Office, House of Lords;
Messrs. ADAM and CHARLES BLACK, of Edinburgh;
Messrs. ALEXANDER THOM and Co. (Limited), or Messrs. HODGES, FIGGIS, and Co., of Dublin.

[C.—4739.] *Price 3½d.*

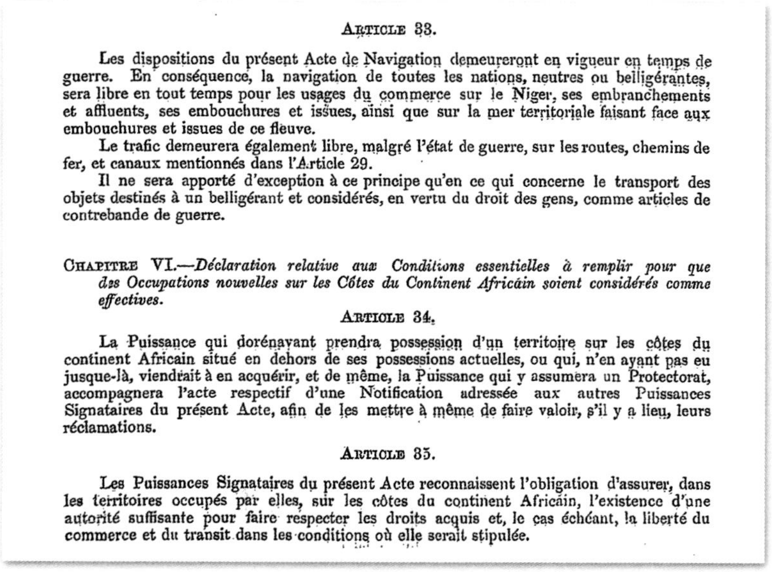

ARTICLE 33.

Les dispositions du présent Acte de Navigation demeureront en vigueur en temps de guerre. En conséquence, la navigation de toutes les nations, neutres ou belligérantes, sera libre en tout temps pour les usages du commerce sur le Niger, ses embranchements et affluents, ses embouchures et issues, ainsi que sur la mer territoriale faisant face aux embouchures et issues de ce fleuve.

Le trafic demeurera également libre, malgré l'état de guerre, sur les routes, chemins de fer, et canaux mentionnés dans l'Article 29.

Il ne sera apporté d'exception à ce principe qu'en ce qui concerne le transport des objets destinés à un belligérant et considérés, en vertu du droit des gens, comme articles de contrebande de guerre.

CHAPITRE VI.—*Déclaration relative aux Conditions essentielles à remplir pour que des Occupations nouvelles sur les Côtes du Continent Africain soient considérés comme effectives.*

ARTICLE 34.

La Puissance qui dorénavant prendra possession d'un territoire sur les côtes du continent Africain situé en dehors de ses possessions actuelles, ou qui, n'en ayant pas eu jusque-là, viendrait à en acquérir, et de même, la Puissance qui y assumera un Protectorat, accompagnera l'acte respectif d'une Notification adressée aux autres Puissances Signataires du présent Acte, afin de les mettre à même de faire valoir, s'il y a lieu, leurs réclamations.

ARTICLE 35.

Les Puissances Signataires du présent Acte reconnaissent l'obligation d'assurer, dans les territoires occupés par elles, sur les côtes du continent Africain, l'existence d'une autorité suffisante pour faire respecter les droits acquis et, le cas échéant, la liberté du commerce et du transit dans les conditions où elle serait stipulée.

OPPOSITE Otto von Bismarck (facing, centre right) chairs the Berlin Conference at his Berlin residence. Note the map of Africa on the wall and the complete absence of any Africans in the room.

LEFT (ABOVE AND BELOW) The text – in French – of the "General Act" of the Berlin Conference. One of the key articles – no. 34 – says that "any European nation that took possession of an African coast, or named themselves as 'protectorate' of one, had to inform the other powers of the Berlin Act of this action."

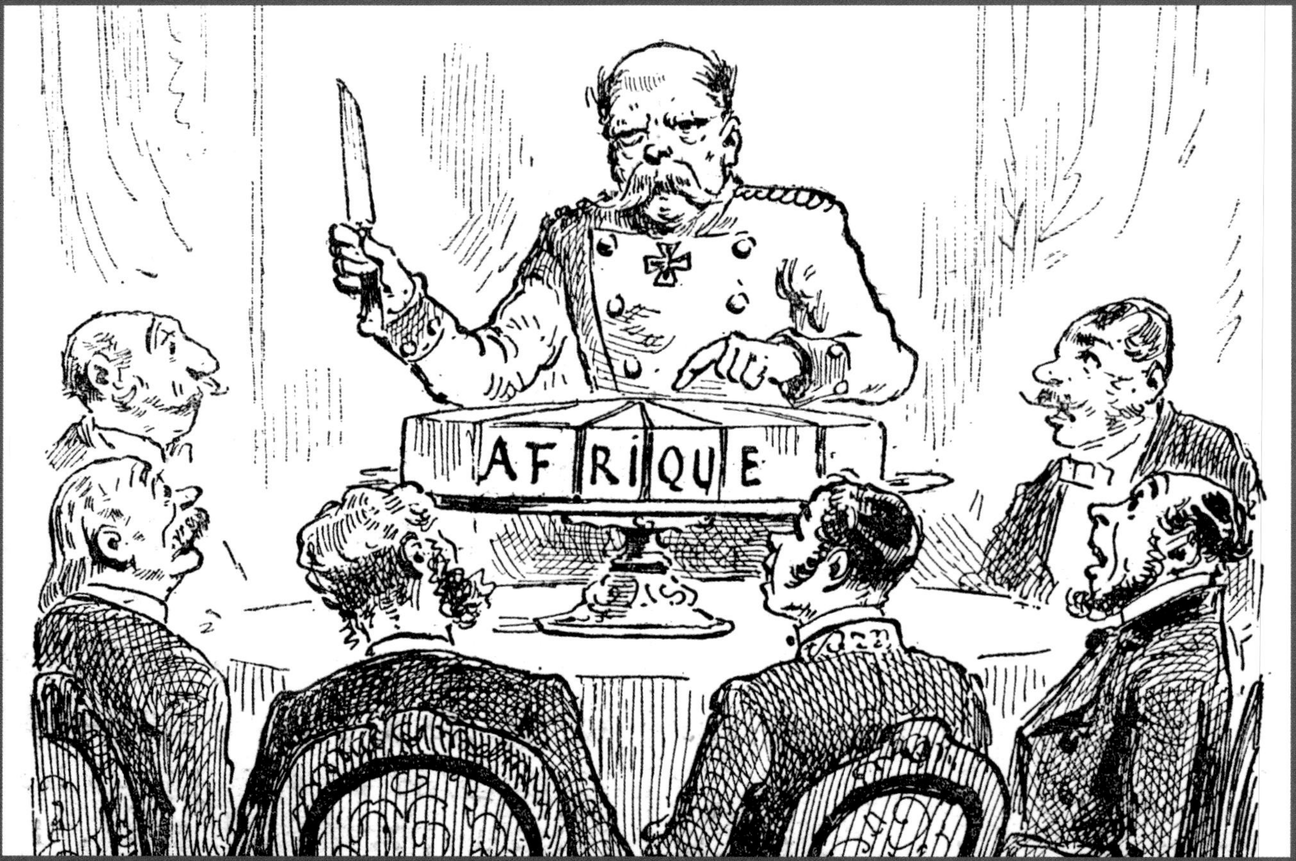
AFRIQUE

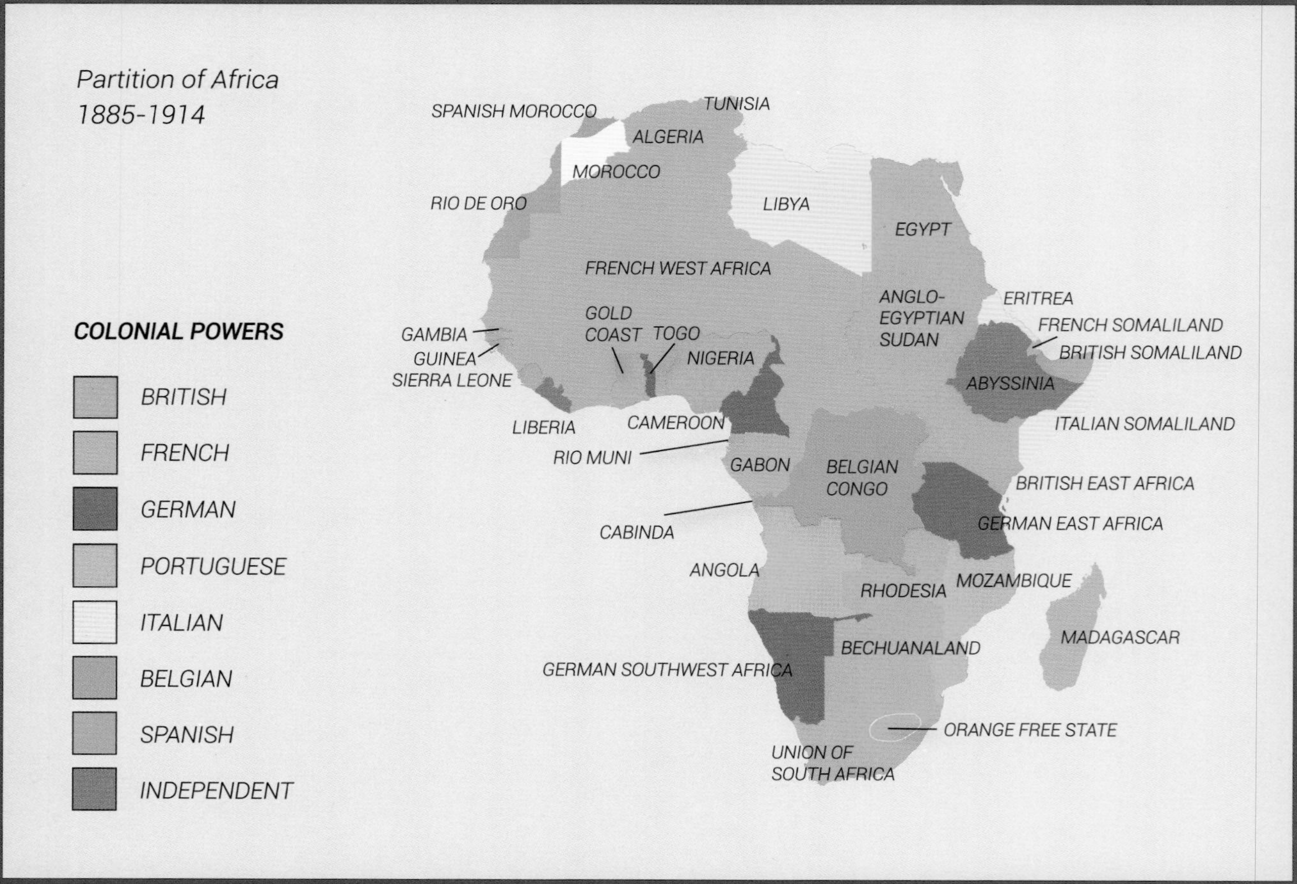
Partition of Africa
1885-1914
COLONIAL POWERS
BRITISH
FRENCH
GERMAN
PORTUGUESE
ITALIAN
BELGIAN
SPANISH
INDEPENDENT
SPANISH MOROCCO
TUNISIA
ALGERIA
MOROCCO
RIO DE ORO
LIBYA
EGYPT
FRENCH WEST AFRICA
ANGLO-
EGYPTIAN
SUDAN
ERITREA
FRENCH SOMALILAND
BRITISH SOMALILAND
GAMBIA
GUINEA
SIERRA LEONE
GOLD
COAST
TOGO
NIGERIA
ABYSSINIA
LIBERIA
CAMEROON
ITALIAN SOMALILAND
RIO MUNI
GABON
BELGIAN
CONGO
BRITISH EAST AFRICA
CABINDA
GERMAN EAST AFRICA
ANGOLA
RHODESIA
MOZAMBIQUE
MADAGASCAR
BECHUANALAND
GERMAN SOUTHWEST AFRICA
ORANGE FREE STATE
UNION OF
SOUTH AFRICA

The other key article in the General Act of Berlin is no. 34, which blithely requests any state that "takes possession of a tract of land" to notify any of the other states what they are doing, to avoid any misunderstanding. Again, there is no recognition of any indigenous African sovereignty.

The main beneficiary to emerge from the platitudes of the Berlin Conference was the Belgian king. Leopold was an imposing figure with an immense beard who had bankrolled the renowned British-American journalist and explorer Henry Morton Stanley. In the years before the Berlin Conference he had instructed Stanley to persuade and cajole countless African tribal leaders to join what Leopold proclaimed was his great philanthropic endeavour: the creation of a state on the Upper Congo River. "There is no question", the king's aides notified Stanley, "of granting the slightest political power to the negroes. That would be absurd." The Berlin Conference effectively recognized Leopold's control of this vast stretch of Africa with its rich resources of rubber and ivory. Immediately after the conference, Leopold called his realm the Congo Free State, and his ruthless exploitation of its people and its riches became an international scandal. It only ended when Leopold was shamed into handing it over to the Belgian government in 1908, a year before he died.

The apparent stamp of respectability that the Berlin Conference bestowed on the European powers lasted much less than a century. By the 1950s and 1960s, nearly all the former African colonies had become free and independent. Some have evolved as democracies, others have been ruled by dictators. The legacy of that short period of European colonization will forever be the subject of bitter controversy.

OPPOSITE ABOVE A French cartoon that says it all. Bismarck presides over the slicing up of a cake marked "Africa".

OPPOSITE BELOW A map illustrating the "Scramble for Africa" from 1885 until 1914. Only two countries, Liberia and Abyssinia (Ethiopia) – marked grey – managed to remain independent.

ABOVE Henry Morton Stanley, the explorer whom Belgian King Leopold sent to manage his Congo empire. Debate goes on as to whether Stanley softened Leopold's orders to impose exclusive white rule.

32

New Zealand Suffrage Petition, 1893

This 270-metre- (886 feet) long petition represents a watershed in the history of women's rights. It was instrumental in making New Zealand the first self-governing country to grant women the right to vote in parliamentary elections and it set a precedent for female suffrage around the world.

While the Electoral Bill that proposed giving women the vote was debated in New Zealand's House of Representatives (Lower House) in 1893, a gigantic petition was rolled out across the chamber floor. It contained the signatures of nearly 32,000 women, a quarter of the European female population of New Zealand. The women's document, consisting of 546 sheets of paper glued together, demanded that "the franchise be extended to them".

New Zealand's female suffrage campaign started in the 1870s, inspired by movements in Europe and North America. The days when women were viewed as second-class citizens, best suited to running the home and bringing up children, were slowly coming to an end. Suffrage bills or amendments were presented to the New Zealand Parliament between 1878 and 1887, but all were defeated. Opponents to votes for women were bluntly outspoken. Suffragettes were dismissed as the "shrieking sisterhood" whose movement

advocated "a leap in the dark", transforming women from "angels of the home to ill-tempered crones".

It took the determined efforts of women like Kate Sheppard to change things. She co-founded the popular Women's Christian Temperance Union, which, like similar organizations around the world, blamed alcohol abuse for social ills from poverty to domestic violence. Sheppard was convinced that if women got the vote, they could transform society. A powerful orator, she complained that women were "tired of having a sphere doled out to us, and of being told that anything outside that sphere is unwomanly". To support her cause, she wrote articles, lobbied politicians and, most crucially, started petitions. Thanks to the recent invention of female-friendly bicycles, her supporters pedalled around the country to gather signatures. In 1891, more than 9,000 women signed. The next year that number doubled.

OPPOSITE In this postcard a young woman on a modern bicycle applauds progressive New Zealand for giving women the vote. Old-fashioned Britain has John Bull riding a penny farthing.

RIGHT The first of 32,000 signatures on New Zealand's Women's Suffrage Petition. It helped make New Zealand the first country in the world to give women the vote.

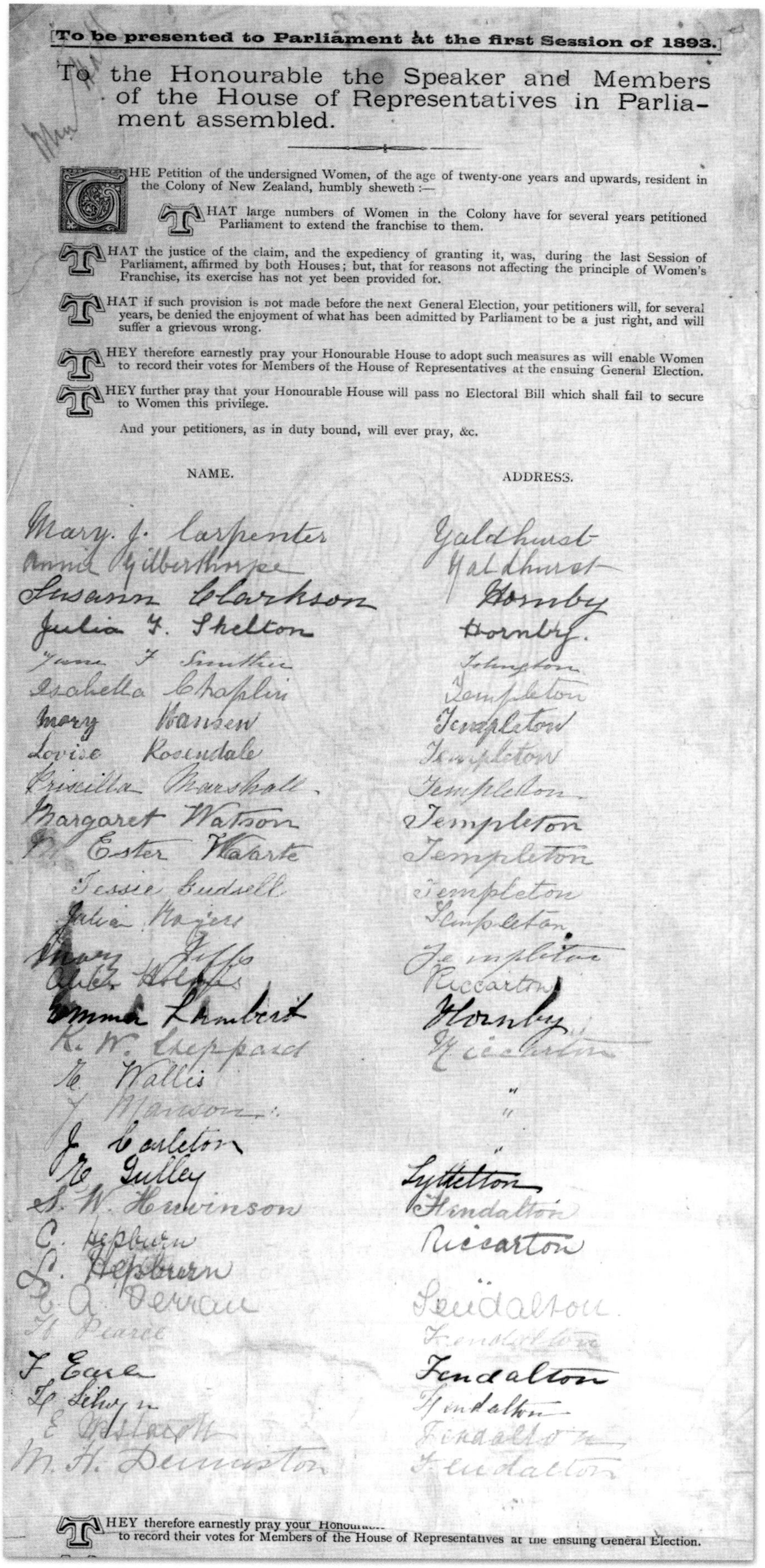
[To be presented to Parliament at the first Session of 1893.]

To the Honourable the Speaker and Members of the House of Representatives in Parliament assembled.

THE Petition of the undersigned Women, of the age of twenty-one years and upwards, resident in the Colony of New Zealand, humbly sheweth :—

THAT large numbers of Women in the Colony have for several years petitioned Parliament to extend the franchise to them.

THAT the justice of the claim, and the expediency of granting it, was, during the last Session of Parliament, affirmed by both Houses; but, that for reasons not affecting the principle of Women's Franchise, its exercise has not yet been provided for.

THAT if such provision is not made before the next General Election, your petitioners will, for several years, be denied the enjoyment of what has been admitted by Parliament to be a just right, and will suffer a grievous wrong.

THEY therefore earnestly pray your Honourable House to adopt such measures as will enable Women to record their votes for Members of the House of Representatives at the ensuing General Election.

THEY further pray that your Honourable House will pass no Electoral Bill which shall fail to secure to Women this privilege.

And your petitioners, as in duty bound, will ever pray, &c.

NAME.	ADDRESS.
Mary J. Carpenter	Yaldhurst
Annie Gilberthorpe	Yaldhurst
Susann Clarkson	Hornby
Julia F. Shelton	Hornby
Jane F Smithie	Templeton
Isabella Chaplin	Templeton
Mary Hansen	Templeton
Louise Rosendale	Templeton
Priscilla Marshall	Templeton
Margaret Watson	Templeton
Ester Waarte	Templeton
Jessie Cudsell	Templeton
[illegible]	Templeton
[illegible]	Templeton
[illegible]	Riccarton
Emma Lambert	Hornby
K. W. Sheppard	Riccarton
M. Wallis	"
J. Manson	"
J. Carleton	"
E. Gulley	Lyttelton
S. W. Hewinson	Fendalton
C. Hepburn	Riccarton
L. Hepburn	
E. A. Ferrau	Fendalton
H. Pearce	Fendalton
F. Eare	Fendalton
[illegible]	Fendalton
E. Mstacott	Fendalton
M. H. Denniston	Fendalton

THEY therefore earnestly pray your Honourable House to adopt such measures as will enable Women to record their votes for Members of the House of Representatives at the ensuing General Election.

The all-important 1893 petition contained close to 32,000 signatures of women from all walks of life. Looking at the document, you can see the elegant penmanship of well-educated women and the "X"s of those who were illiterate.

In 1891 and 1892, New Zealand's Lower House passed Bills which should have enfranchised women, but opponents in the Legislative Council (Upper House) added amendments that sabotaged them. Given that many suffragettes supported a ban on alcohol, politicians who had ties with the liquor industry were particularly vocal adversaries. There was also concern among the ruling Liberal Party that women would vote for the opposition Conservative Party.

In April 1893, yet another Bill supporting votes for women was introduced in the Lower House. It was during this debate that Sheppard's huge petition was dramatically unrolled across the floor of the chamber. Addressed to "The Honourable the Speaker and Members of the House of Representatives in Parliament", the document stated that "large numbers of Women in the Colony have for several years petitioned Parliament" to give them the vote. It said that unless the Bill was passed before an upcoming election, "your petitioners will for several years be denied the enjoyment of what has been admitted by Parliament to be a just right and will suffer a grievous wrong".

The Bill passed easily but it still needed a majority in the deeply divided Upper House. In what became known as the "Battle of the Buttonholes", supporters of the Bill wore white camellias and opponents sported red ones. The premier of New Zealand, Richard Seddon, who was closely aligned to the liquor lobby, was determined to stop the Bill. Knowing that the vote was on a knife-edge, he put pressure on councillors who supported suffrage. He succeeded in getting one to change his mind. This so outraged two opponents of the Bill that they switched sides and voted for it. On 8 September 1893, the Bill passed by 20 votes to 18. Eleven days later, the new Electoral Act became law. All women over the age of 21 who were British subjects or indigenous Maori were entitled to vote. Nearly 80 per cent of New Zealand's eligible female voters used their new mandate in an election just 10 weeks later. There had been warnings that "lady voters" would be hassled by "boorish and half-drunken men". In the event, one New Zealand newspaper reported that the streets on election day "resembled a gay garden party" and "the pretty dresses of the ladies and their smiling faces lighted up the polling booths most wonderfully".

Although some states and territories in the US had allowed European women the vote by 1893, New Zealand became the first self-governing country to permit them to cast ballots in parliamentary elections. Australia followed suit in 1902. Finland was the first European country to enfranchise women in 1906. US women were denied the vote nationwide until 1920 and British females over the age of 21 had to wait until 1928. New Zealand is among the few countries that has had three female heads of government. When we visited, we felt we were in one of the stablest and best-run countries in the world.

RIGHT Women gathering to vote on 28 November 1893. Females were not allowed to stand for Parliament until 1919.

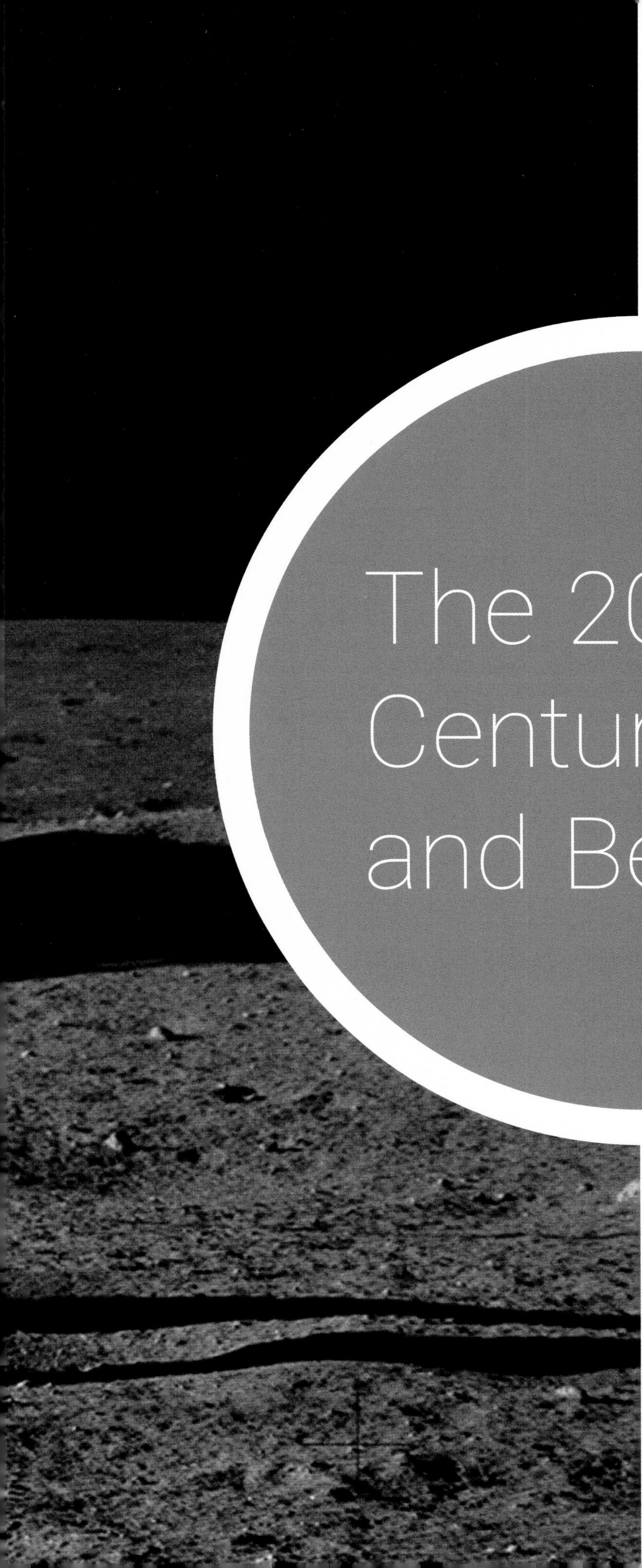

The 20th Century and Beyond

1903–present

33

The Wright Brothers' Telegram

Orville and Wilbur Wright are the world's most famous aviators. They flew the first powered flight on a beach in North Carolina in December 1903. Immediately afterwards, they sent this telegram to their father, Bishop Milton Wright, proudly reporting their achievement. The flight lasted less than a minute but they managed a speed of nearly 50 kilometres (31 miles) per hour.

ABOVE The two aviation pioneers, Wilbur and Orville Wright, on the steps of their house in Dayton, Ohio in 1909.

OPPOSITE ABOVE The telegram sent by Orville Wright to his father on 17 December 1903.

OPPOSITE BELOW The design of the world's first successful aircraft. Two propellers are behind the wing, the elevators in front. The small diagram top left shows the direction of flight aiming downwards.

It was a windy morning on Kitty Hawk beach in North Carolina just a week before Christmas in 1903. Two brothers in their thirties, who owned a bicycle shop back in Ohio, dragged a bizarre-looking contraption to the end of two wooden rails 20 metres (66 feet) long, facing directly into the wind. They anchored it to the ground with a strap and took turns climbing aboard and lying face down on the lower of its two wings. Each wing was made of muslin stretched over a wooden frame with a span of just over 12 metres (39 feet). Projecting in front of the operator's driving position was another flimsy apparatus, an elevator that the flyer could crank up and down with a small hand-lever. By shifting his hips from one side to the other, the wings could be "warped" so that, once in the air, he could bank left or right. Behind was a rudder to control yaw. Mounted beside him was a 12.5 horsepower gasoline engine manufactured in the brothers' bicycle shop. It drove chains that spun two large wooden propellers attached behind the wings. With the engine on full power, the propellers would "push" the primitive aeroplane forward the moment a restraining strap was released.

The two brothers were Orville and Wilbur Wright from Dayton in Ohio. Along with other aviation pioneers, they'd been risking their lives flying gliders for the past few years, but

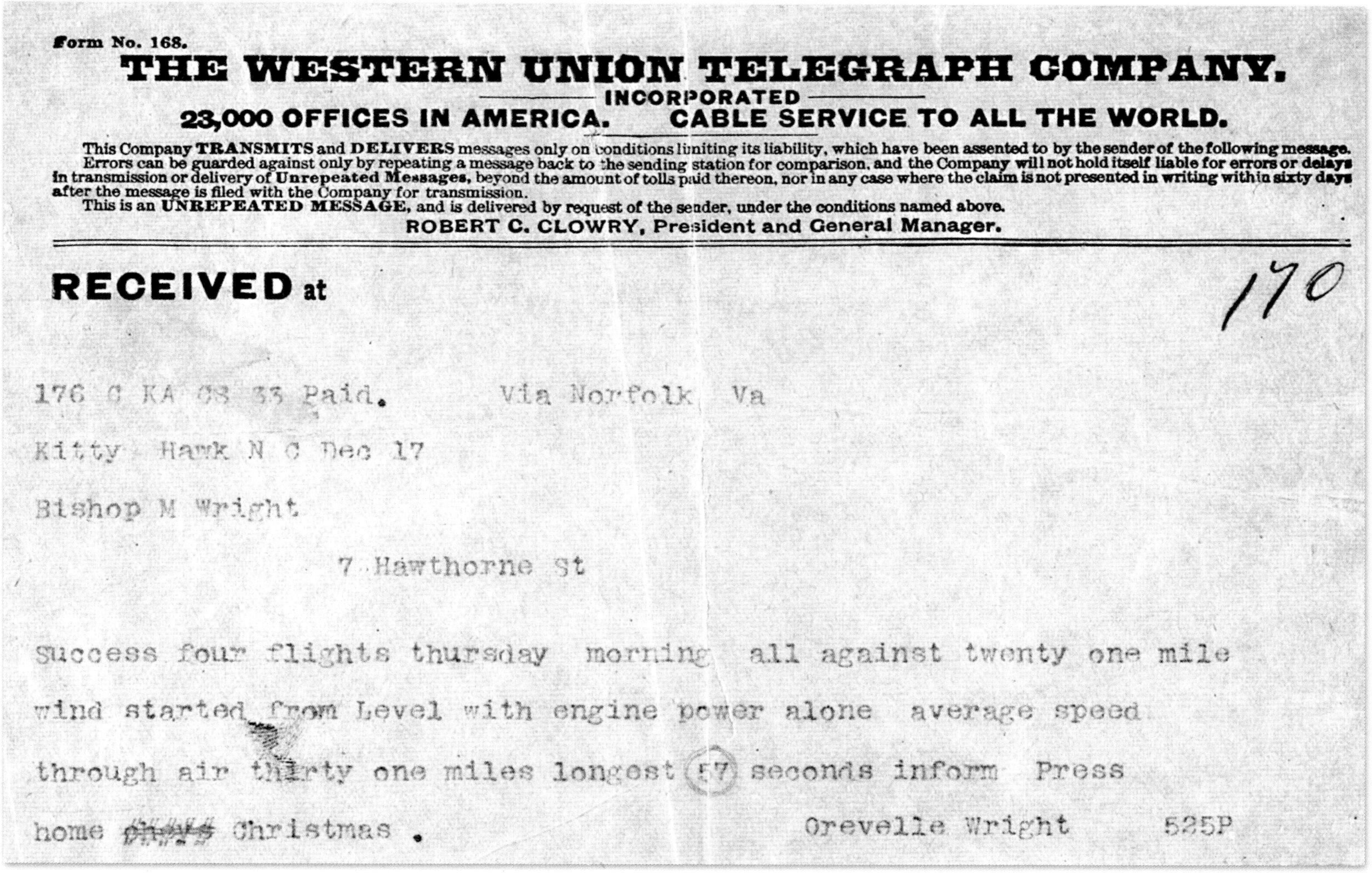

Form No. 168.

THE WESTERN UNION TELEGRAPH COMPANY.

INCORPORATED

23,000 OFFICES IN AMERICA. CABLE SERVICE TO ALL THE WORLD.

This Company **TRANSMITS** and **DELIVERS** messages only on conditions limiting its liability, which have been assented to by the sender of the following message. Errors can be guarded against only by repeating a message back to the sending station for comparison, and the Company will not hold itself liable for errors or delays in transmission or delivery of **Unrepeated Messages**, beyond the amount of tolls paid thereon, nor in any case where the claim is not presented in writing within sixty days after the message is filed with the Company for transmission.

This is an **UNREPEATED MESSAGE**, and is delivered by request of the sender, under the conditions named above.

ROBERT C. CLOWRY, President and General Manager.

RECEIVED at

170

176 C KA CS 33 Paid. Via Norfolk Va

Kitty Hawk N C Dec 17

Bishop M Wright

7 Hawthorne St

Success four flights thursday morning all against twenty one mile wind started from Level with engine power alone average speed through air thirty one miles longest 57 seconds inform Press home ~~[illegible]~~ Christmas .

Orevelle Wright 525P

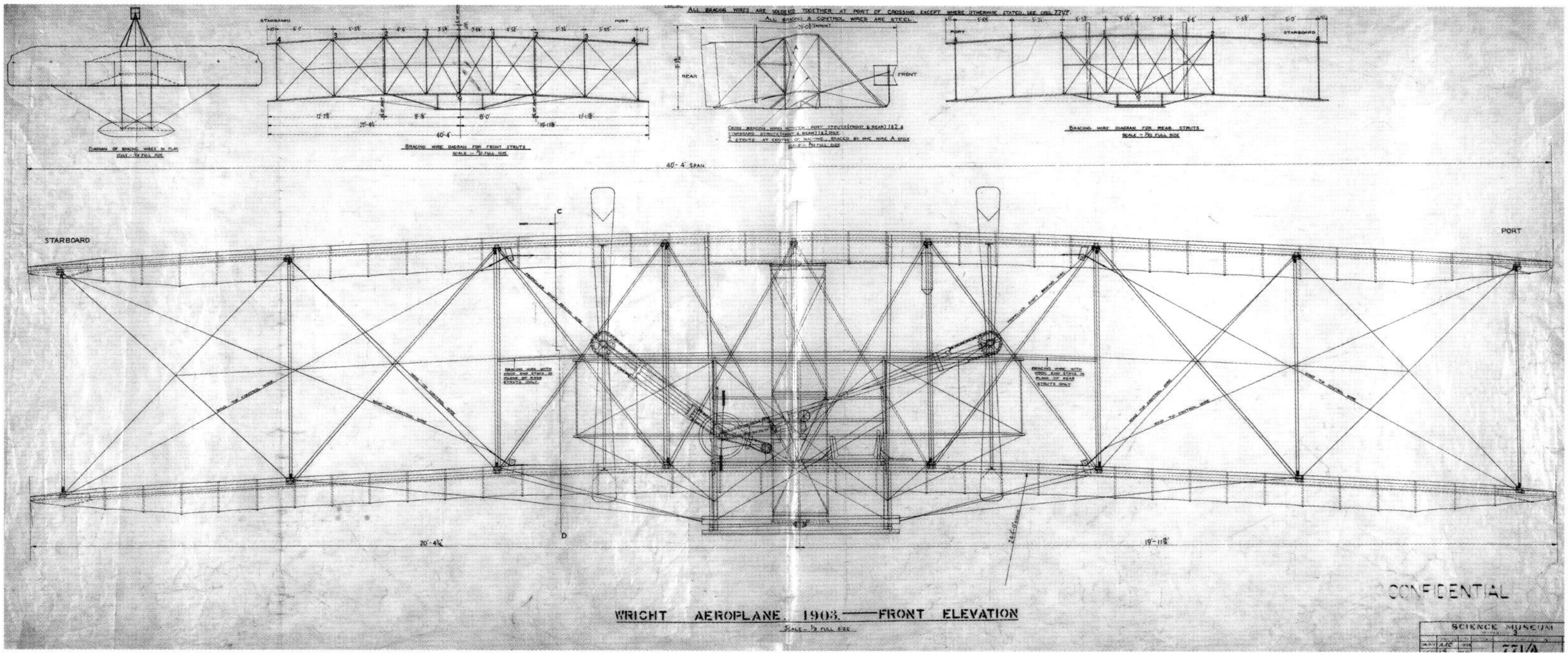

this was their first attempt at powered flight. Each of them had attempted to get airborne for more than a few seconds three times that morning, and it was the elder of the two, Wilbur, whose turn it was to take the controls for the fourth attempt at midday. This would be the flight that made history, the flight that prompted Orville to send the famous telegram to their father, Bishop Milton Wright. Wilbur stayed airborne for 57 seconds and achieved an average speed of nearly 50 kilometres (31 miles) an hour. His flight launched a frenzy of aeronautic competition that would see a pilot breaking through the sound barrier before Orville died in 1948.

Neither of the Wright brothers went to university. They opened a bicycle shop in Dayton in 1892 and their mechanical skill led to a fascination for the challenge of controlled flight. Gliding was dangerous largely because the aircraft – little more than elaborate kites – were very hard to control. Wilbur and Orville built their own wind tunnel and developed various configurations of wings and rudders which they then tried out in practice on their homemade gliders. It was not long before they and their bicycle shop mechanic, Charles Taylor, built an engine out of aluminium and constructed an aircraft light enough to support the engine and one person lying down at the controls.

Remarkably, when the brothers told their local newspaper about the successful flight, it failed to report it. Orville and Wilbur did not become world famous until the summer of 1908, when they took their flying machine to France and captivated a large European audience with a demonstration at a racetrack near Le Mans. Orville went on to make the first flight lasting more than one hour that September in the US. By the summer of 1909, the brothers had been decorated with awards by US President Taft and had sold their new two-seater aeroplane to the US Signals Corps.

Wilbur died in 1912 and Orville went on to take several posts in the aviation industry before he died at the age of 76 in 1948. He told an interviewer, "We dared to hope we had invented something that would bring lasting peace to the earth. But we were wrong." He deplored the destruction caused by aerial bombing in the Second World War but said he didn't have any regrets about his part in the invention of the machine that had done so much useful service to humanity.

Oddly, the country whose two great innovators had invented the powered aeroplane was left starkly behind by Europe as the aviation industry took off after 1910. When the First World War broke out, there was no US air force and the army had no planes, barring a few in the Signal Corps. When the United States joined the war in 1917, it had to rely almost entirely on warplanes provided by the British and French. By the end of the war, US forces in Europe were equipped with 6,384 aircraft, only 1,213 of which were made in the US.

It is one of the miracles of human endeavour that since those early days the development of flight has exceeded all expectations. We can now fly around the world in a day and to the moon in less than a week. Those two men on Kitty Hawk beach began an adventure whose future defies imagination.

RIGHT The Wright brothers' aircraft takes to the air on Kitty Hawk beach in North Carolina. It has just taken off away from camera; the pilot can be seen lying down in the centre and the two propellers turning at the back.

34

Gallipoli Diary of Frederick Tubb

Captain Frederick Tubb VC was a witness to what became a defining moment in Australian military history. His diary records the savage fighting at Lone Pine on the Gallipoli peninsula in 1915. He writes with great modesty about his fight against overwhelming odds when he found himself alone in a trench, with all his comrades dead beside him.

Few military sites on earth are as revered by Australians and New Zealanders as the Gallipoli peninsula in Turkey. The costly operation fought there in the second year of the First World War was the first time these two ex-colonial countries had experienced the full horror of all-out warfare as independent nations. For Australians in particular, one small plateau with a lone pine tree earned itself a special place in history. It was there that a rare successful action in one of the world's most disastrous military campaigns took place between 6 and 9 August 1915. The Australians who fought at the Battle of Lone Pine showed immense courage and resourcefulness. They were awarded no fewer than seven Victoria Crosses, the highest British medal for valour, in that one action alone. Captain Frederick Tubb, from Longwood, Victoria, won one of them. "It would take a book to describe what happened," he wrote in his diary.

We have stood in the cemetery where the battle took place and been stirred by the story of that brutal struggle. Of some 60,000 Australians who fought at Gallipoli, 30,000 were casualties in the eight-month campaign, 2,300 of them in the single action at Lone Pine.

Troops from Australia and New Zealand formed the ANZAC corps in Egypt at the beginning of the First World War and were a convenient source of manpower for Winston

Churchill's plan to seize the Gallipoli peninsula from Turkey in April 1915. Turkey had joined Germany in fighting the British, French and Russians and their allies. Churchill, then First Lord of the Admiralty, prevailed over opponents in the British Cabinet to open a new front in order to threaten Turkey's capital, Constantinople. The Australians and New Zealanders landed at what became known as ANZAC Cove, a few miles up from the tip of the peninsula where a mainly British and French force landed. The Turks, led by German General Liman von Sanders,

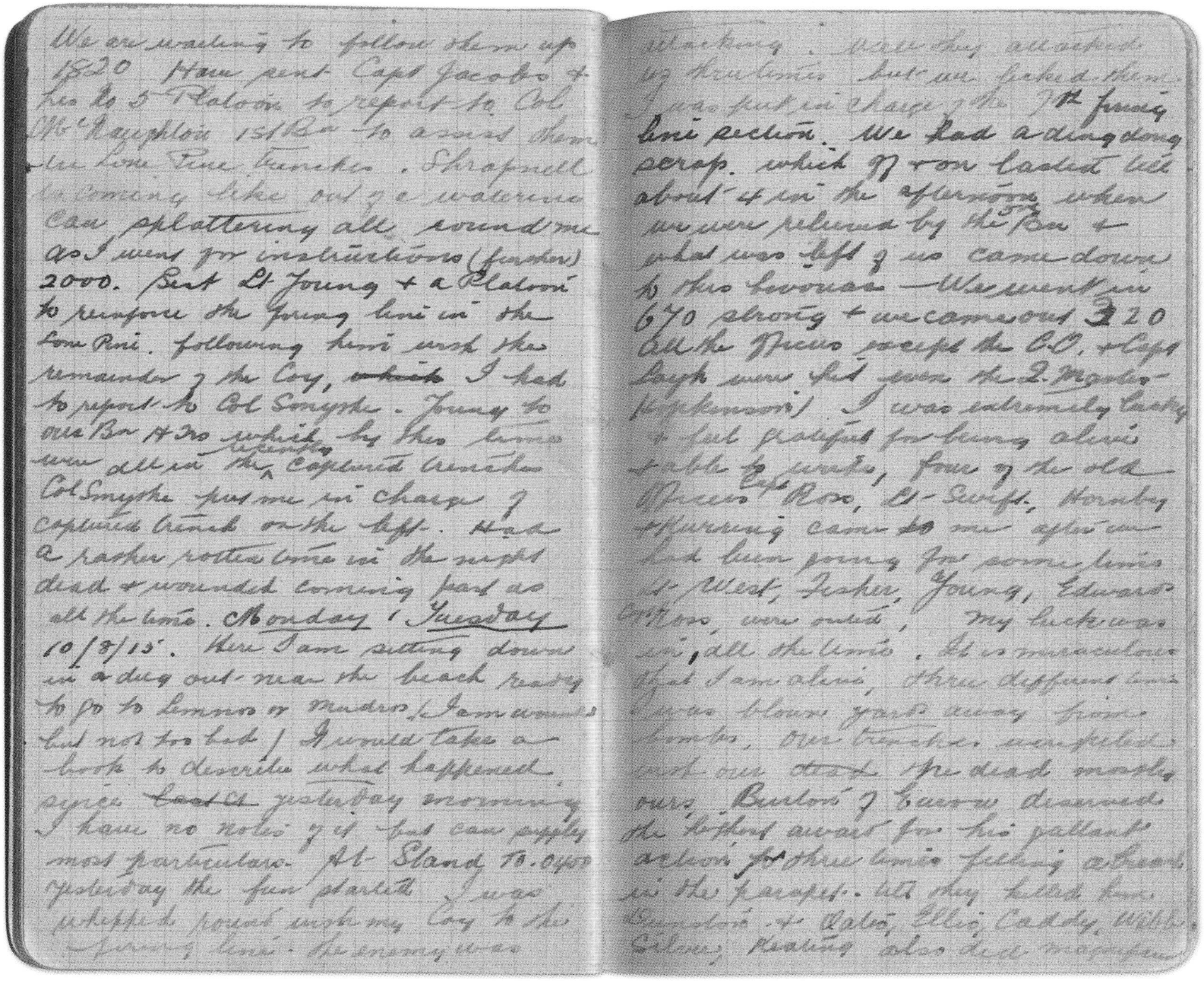

We are waiting to follow them up
1820 Have sent Capt Jacobs &
his No 5 Platoon to report to Col
McNaughton 1st Bn to assist them
in Lone Pine trenches. Shrapnell
is coming like out of a watering
can splattering all around me
as I went for instructions (further)
2000. Sent Lt Young & a Platoon
to reinforce the firing line in the
Lone Pine. following him with the
remainder of the Coy, ~~which~~ I had
to report to Col Smythe. Young to
our Bn H Qrs ~~which~~ by this time
were all in the recently captured trenches
Col Smythe put me in charge of
captured trench on the left. Had
a rather rotten time in the night
dead & wounded coming past us
all the time. Monday & Tuesday
10/8/15. Here I am sitting down
in a dug out near the beach ready
to go to Lemnos or Mudros, I am wounded
but not too bad / It would take a
book to describe what happened
since ~~last...~~ yesterday morning
I have no notes yet but can supply
most particulars. At Stand To. 0400
yesterday the fun started. I was
whipped round with my Coy to the
firing line. the enemy was

attacking. Well they attacked
us three times but we licked them.
I was put in charge of the 7th firing
line section. We had a ding dong
scrap, which off & on lasted till
about 4 in the afternoon when
we were relieved by the 5th Bn &
what was left of us came down
to this bivouac — We went in
670 strong & we came out 320
All the officers except the C.O. & Capt
Leigh were hit even the 2. Major
Hopkinson) I was extremely lucky
& feel grateful for being alive
& able to write, four of the old
officers Capt Rose, Lt Swift, Hornby
& Hurring came to me after we
had been going for some time
Lt West, Fisher, Young, Edwards
Capt Ross, were outed, My luck was
in, all the time. It is miraculous
that I am alive, three different times
I was blown yards away from
bombs, Our trenches were filled
with our dead the dead mostly
ours, Burton of Euroa deserved
the highest award for his gallant
action for three times filling a breach
in the parapet. till they killed him.
Dunstan & Oates, Ellis, Caddy, Webb
Silver, Keating also did magnificent

fought courageously, and successfully held the invaders back. Poor leadership on the Allied side and the failure to exploit a number of tactical opportunities led the British government to a final humiliating withdrawal in December 1915 and January 1916.

The Battle of Lone Pine was one striking exception to this tale of woe. ANZAC troops had been corralled in their tight bridgehead all through a long hot summer. Plagued by lice, short of water and struggling to survive on a poor diet of bully beef and biscuits, they were called upon one last time on 6 August to expand their perimeter. In support of a thrust by the New Zealanders to their left, the Australian 1st Brigade was launched across the plateau at the Turkish trenches only a few metres away. They were ordered past the site of the lone pine tree sketched by their commander three months earlier and since destroyed by shellfire. A massive artillery barrage from Royal Navy ships offshore had the Turks cowering in their dugouts. At 5.30 p.m. when the big guns stopped, the Australians leapt up and charged into lethal fire from Turkish riflemen and machine-gunners. Enough Australians survived the carnage to swarm into the first line of Turkish trenches and engage in a frantic

OPPOSITE Captain Frederick Tubb, one of Australia's heroes at Gallipoli. He won the Victoria Cross for his action in 1915.

ABOVE Tubb's diary of 10 August 1915 describes (right-hand page) how, the day before, "we had a ding dong scrap, which off and on lasted till about 4 in the afternoon ..." Further on he writes: "I was extremely lucky and feel grateful for being alive ..."

hand-to-hand struggle which eventually forced the Turks back to their second line. First round to the Australians, but for the next three days they were under ferocious counterattack.

Frederick Tubb was in charge of one captured trench, clogged with dead and wounded, and under constant bombardment. He ordered his men to pile up barricades to protect their newly won trenches and rebuild them when the Turks burst through, again and again flinging their hand-bombs around corners and over any obstructions. "We had a ding dong scrap," he wrote. "We yelled and yelled at the black devils and we knocked them out like rabbits." He told his comrades to throw blankets on the Turkish grenade-like bombs or lob them back at the enemy, but, one by one, Tubb's comrades died in the chaos: "Many of our brave boys were blown to pieces." One of his men picked up a Turkish bomb to throw back but it exploded in his face. "All our bomb throwers were killed, so were the volunteers to replace them." Tubb found himself alone when the Turks blew up a barricade and poured through. He fought them back and held his position single-handed until help arrived. "I was extremely lucky. I was wounded three times," he wrote after he was evacuated, badly wounded: "All but me of our good old 7th section are gone." Tubb was awarded the Victoria Cross for his gallantry. He was killed at Ypres by a German sniper in 1917.

Somehow the Australians hung on at Lone Pine for another harrowing four months, and today a dawn service is held annually to commemorate this and other gruesome battles in the ANZAC sector at Gallipoli.

ABOVE Australian troops charge the Turks at Lone Pine. It was one of the fiercest battles of the Gallipoli campaign. More than 2,300 Australians died.

OPPOSITE Australian soldiers in trenches at Lone Pine, August 1915. This picture became a popular Australian postage stamp that year.

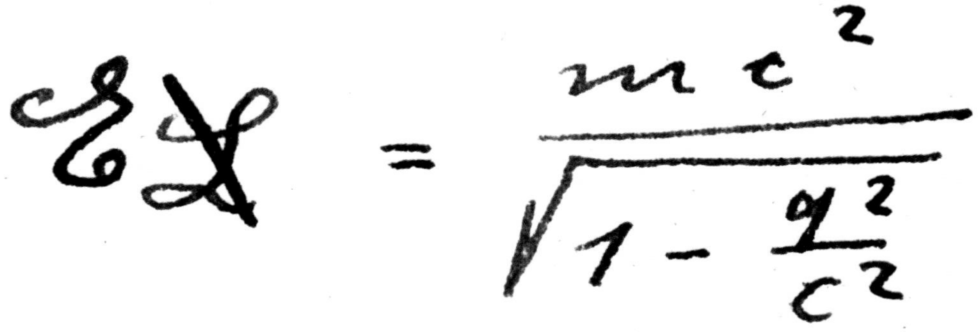

35

The General Theory of Relativity

Albert Einstein's General Theory of Relativity gave us an astonishingly new understanding of the interplay of space, time, matter, energy and gravity. It is considered the most important breakthrough in modern physics. The impact of his theory was so all-embracing that it's not surprising *Time* magazine named Einstein "the person of the century" on 31 December 1999.

ABOVE In this equation Einstein replaces "L" (light energy) with "E" (for energy in general). He later rearranged the variables to form his famous E=mc².

OPPOSITE A handwritten draft page from the General Theory of Relativity, published by Einstein on 11 May 1916. A version of Einstein's most famous equation can be seen near the top.

In 1905, an unknown 26-year-old technician working in a Swiss patent office submitted four papers to a scientific journal. They led to young Albert Einstein being hailed as a genius. One of them revealed his Special Theory of Relativity, which ripped apart accepted notions of space and time as separate and absolute. On the contrary, proclaimed Einstein, for the laws of physics to remain the same for all observers, then both lengths and times vary depending on where you're looking from. He came to this stunning conclusion with the help of what he called "thought experiments" – taking real-life scenarios to explain the laws of science. For example, he imagined one person on a fast-moving train and another on a station platform. Lightning hits both ends of the train as its middle passes the person on the platform. That person must see the lightning strikes happen at the same time. However, the person on the train must see the front struck before the back, because the train is moving forwards, so the flash has less far to travel. The same events – lightning striking the train's ends – are viewed as simultaneous from the platform but not from the train. Therefore things happening at the same time is a relative concept! This suggested to Einstein that time and space are intertwined in a single continuum known as "spacetime". He also postulated that nothing can travel faster than the speed of light (299,792 kilometres or 186,000 miles a second). He invented what became the world's most famous equation, $E = mc^2$ (E is energy, m is mass and c is the speed of light), demonstrating that there is a deep equivalence between mass and energy. Because the speed of light is such a big number, even a small mass can be converted to a huge amount of energy.

But something was missing from his theory: gravity. Sir Isaac Newton's Law of Gravitation in 1687 states that gravity is an invisible force that attracts two objects together, decreasing in strength as they get further apart. Einstein shattered that view yet made his discovery sound simple: "I was sitting on a chair in my patent office in Bern. Suddenly a thought struck me: if a man falls freely, he would not feel his weight. I was taken aback. This led me to the theory of gravity." The image of a falling man travelling inside an elevator falling at the same speed, weightless and unable to tell if he was falling or in deep space, convinced Einstein that acceleration and gravity are equivalent. He later called it "the happiest thought in my life".

Einstein published these further findings in 1916 as the General Theory of Relativity. Among many other things, it recognized that all massive objects cause a distortion – a curving – in spacetime, which is felt as gravity. An example commonly used to explain this complex idea is to take a rubber sheet and place a heavy ball on it. The weight of the ball causes a dip in the sheet, so when a lighter marble is rolled across the sheet it doesn't roll in a straight line but curves around the ball. The

Nach diesen Vorbereitungen kehren wir zu unserem physikalischen Problem zurück. Solange der physikalische Zustand der von uns betrachteten Platte (z. B. deren Energieinhalt) inbezug auf einen mitbewegten Beobachter ungeändert bleibt, und wir ausschliesslich fortschreitende Bewegung der ~~ganzen~~ Platte ~~ins~~ als Ganzes ins Auge fassen, können wir dieselbe sicherlich als materiellen Punkt von einer gewissen Masse M ansehen. Man erhält dann für die Energie E der Platte inbezug auf Σ unter Berücksichtigung des Umstandes, dass dieselbe inbezug auf Σ' sich in Ruhe befindet, gemäss (28) den Ausdruck

$$E = \frac{Mc^2}{\sqrt{1-\frac{v^2}{c^2}}}$$

Diese Gleichung gelte für den Zustand der Platte vor Aussendung der beiden Licht-wellenzüge. Nach Aussendung der Wellenzüge hat die Energie der Platte inbezug auf Σ' um $-2\eta' = \Delta E'$, inbezug auf Σ um $-(\eta_1 + \eta_2) = \Delta E$ zugenommen. Zwischen beiden besteht wegen (29) die Gleichung

$$\Delta E = \frac{\Delta E'}{\sqrt{1-\frac{v^2}{c^2}}}$$

~~Nach diesen zwei Gleichungen ist die Energie~~ $E+\Delta E$ ~~der Platte nach der~~ Aussendung der Wellenzüge gegeben durch

$$(E+\Delta E) = \frac{\left(M + \frac{\Delta E'}{c^2}\right)}{\sqrt{1-\frac{v^2}{c^2}}}$$

Dieser Ausdruck ist nach (28) gleichlautend wie der Ausdruck der Energie einer mit der Geschwindigkeit v bewegten Platte von der Masse $\left(M + \frac{\Delta E'}{c^2}\right)$; die träge Masse der Platte nimmt also um $\frac{\Delta E'}{c^2}$ zu, wenn ~~sich~~ deren Ruh-Energie (Energie für einen mitbewegten Beobachter) eine Änderung um $\Delta E'$ erfährt.

Wir müssen noch zeigen, dass aus dem Impulssatz das nämliche Resultat folgt. Vor der Aussendung der Wellenzüge ist die Bewegungsgrösse B der Platte inbezug auf Σ ~~nach~~ (27) gegeben durch

$$B = Mv$$

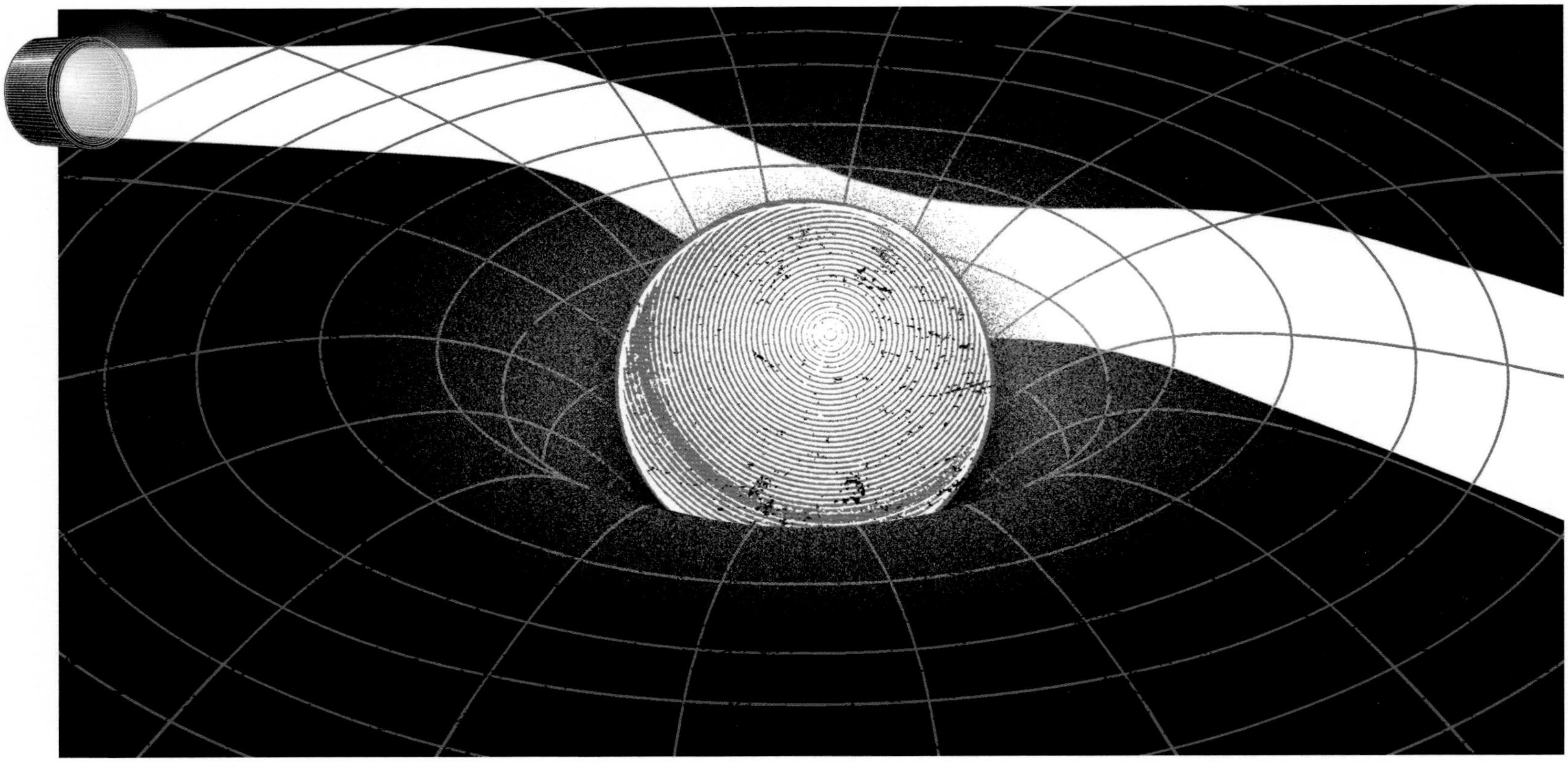

marble travelling along a surface warped by the ball looks as if it is attracted by a gravitational force, just as the Earth looks as if it is attracted to the sun. Einstein argued that beams of light from distant stars must also travel along curved trajectories as they pass around the warped spacetime near the sun. After his calculations were confirmed by scientists observing a solar eclipse in 1919, he was asked what would have happened if he'd been proved wrong. "I would have been sorry for the Dear Lord because the theory is correct", was his no-nonsense reply.

Another of Einstein's counterintuitive realizations was that time is also affected by the influence of huge masses. The nearer you are to a massive object like the Earth, the slower time passes. So clocks on mountaintops tick ever so slightly quicker than those at sea level, meaning that people effectively live a tiny fraction less long the higher the place they live.

Einstein's theory was quickly hailed as brilliant and he became a scientific hero. When his young son asked why he was so famous, Einstein used a thought experiment to explain how he discovered that gravity was the curving of the fabric of spacetime. He said a blind beetle does not notice the curve when it walks over a curved branch; "I was lucky enough to notice what the beetle didn't."

The General Theory of Relativity has given us a new, large-scale understanding of the universe. It explains phenomena from the origin of stars to black holes. It has been used in the creation of nuclear weapons and power plants and to identify the mass of distant galaxies. Our cars and phones guide us to locations because, thanks to Einstein, GPS takes account of the earth's gravitational field in order to work out our destination with pinpoint accuracy.

There is so much more to Einstein's findings than non-scientists like us have either the time or ability to explain but we believe it is less important to understand his theory than to marvel at what it makes possible.

OPPOSITE ABOVE In order to illustrate the effect that mass has on the curvature of spacetime, a heavy ball is placed on a rubber sheet.

OPPOSITE BELOW In a "mind experiment", Einstein imagined two people watching lightning strike both ends of a train. He realized that time moves differently depending on whether someone is moving or stationary.

ABOVE Einstein lecturing in Vienna in 1921, the year that he was awarded the Nobel Prize. Oddly, he won it not for his Theory of Relativity but for his "discovery of the law of the photoelectric effect".

36

Woodrow Wilson's 14 Points

Woodrow Wilson, President of the United States from 1913 to 1921, jotted down the first draft of his visionary 14-point plan for peace in shorthand before the end of the First World War. He delivered his famous speech on the peace plan to Congress in January 1918 and took his proposals to the Paris Peace Conference which followed a year later in Versailles. He hoped they would create a new, fairer and more peaceful world.

Woodrow Wilson, whose country came late into the First World War but had a decisive impact, played a key role in the peace conference that followed it. The US president, a Democrat, a fine-looking upright fellow with a priestly demeanour, combined idealism and stubborn arrogance. He committed the United States to joining the war against Germany in the spring of 1917, but was against imposing punishing peace terms. In January 1918, ten months before the war ended, Wilson presented to the US Congress a 14-point peace formula which avoided mentioning harsh demands on Germany in the event of its defeat. He was a passionate liberal internationalist and his 14 points included a commitment to transparent peace arrangements with no secret deals, absolute freedom of navigation and trade where possible, and German evacuation of territory occupied during the war. He went on to reject any vindictive retribution against Germany: "We do not wish to block or injure in any way her legitimate influence or power." He just wanted Germany to accept a position of peace and equality rather than mastery. He also proclaimed his plan for a League of Nations, the precursor of the United Nations (see page 186). Its council would make decisions only by unanimous vote. Russia and for a time Germany would be excluded. History shows much of Wilson's dream was too ambitious, but he pursued it with resolute persistence.

The US president's aspirations won a mixed reception from other governments and from prominent Americans. Former Republican President Theodore Roosevelt dismissed Wilson's 14 points as "meaningless ... one more scrap for the diplomatic waste paper basket". To defeated Germany, there was an attraction in the prospect of peace based on Wilson's principles. To some of Europe's hard-headed victors, particularly the French, whose country had been devastated by the war, Wilson's ideas were dangerously feeble. France's old warhorse, Prime Minister Georges Clemenceau, so hated Germany he told his heirs to bury him standing up, defiantly facing the German frontier. He viewed Wilson's conciliatory attitude to Germany as appallingly saint-like. "Talking to Wilson is like talking to Jesus Christ," he said. David Lloyd George, another of the Versailles peacemakers, found Wilson kindly and straightforward but

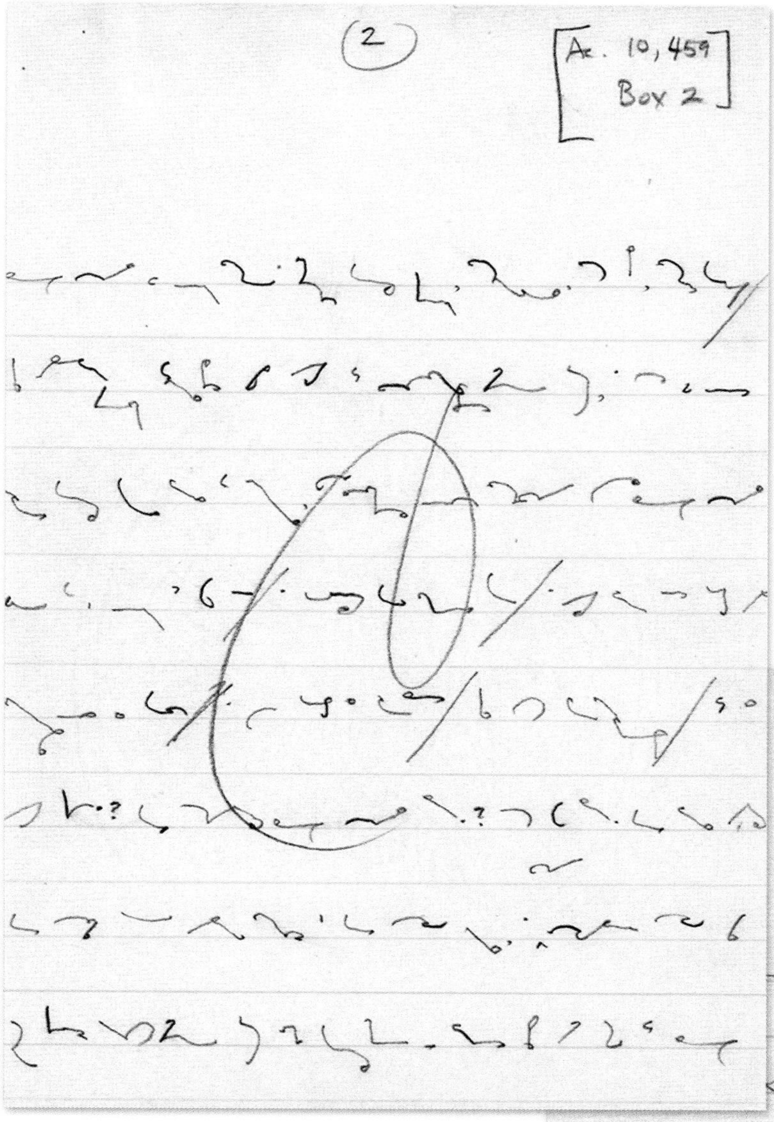

OPPOSITE Woodrow Wilson addresses the US Congress in January 1918 laying out his plan for peace with Germany and a new League of Nations.

LEFT AND BELOW Wilson's original shorthand notes for his speech detailing his 14-point plan for peace. He learned shorthand because he found it difficult to write in longhand.

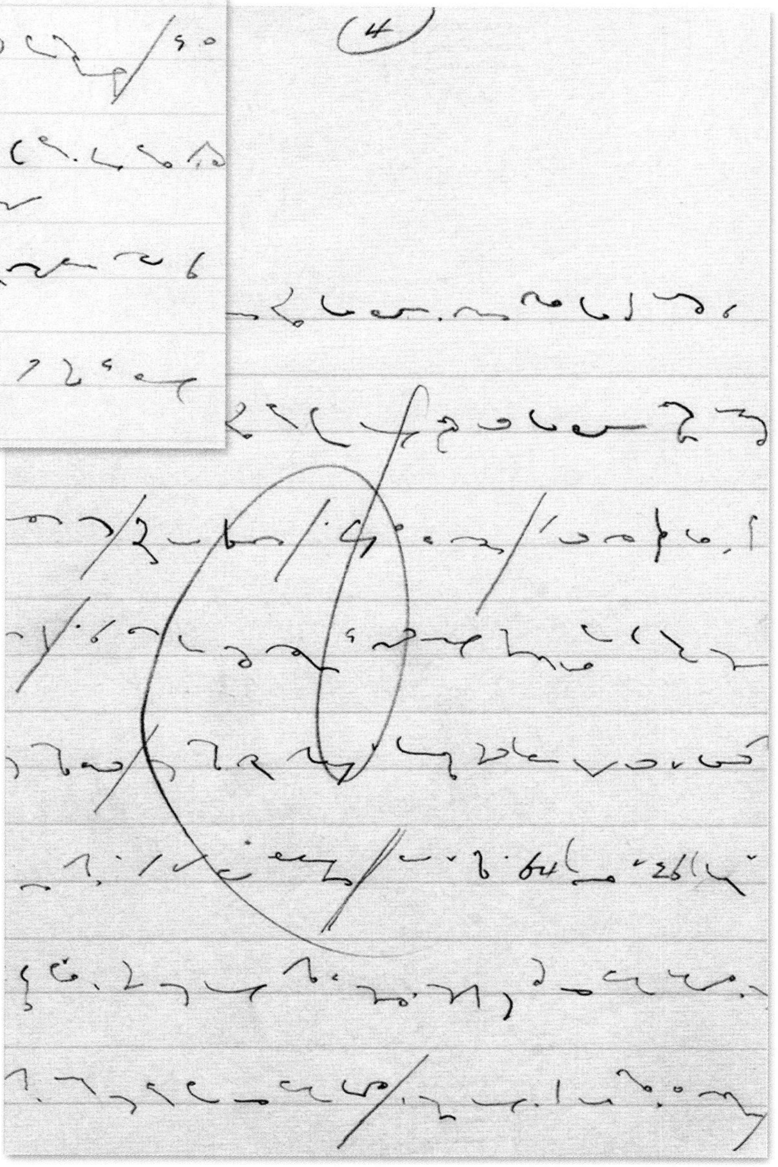

also "tactless, obstinate and vain". Even so, both Lloyd George and Clemenceau endorsed Wilson's League of Nations.

Whatever the other peacemakers thought of Wilson's 14 points, none doubted America's right to take a leading place at the table. The US lost 53,000 dead in the First World War, far fewer than France's one million and Britain's 750,000, but the US military and financial contribution to victory was widely recognized. Wilson was given a huge popular welcome when he arrived in Europe on 13 December 1918, a month after the Armistice. When he joined the other three key peace negotiators – Lloyd George, Clemenceau and Italy's prime minister, Vittorio Orlando – in Paris for the beginning of the formal talks in January 1919, Wilson, as a head

LE ROY
GOUVERNE

of state, was given a seat a few inches higher than the others.

As they settled down to what amounted to five months of often-rancorous discussion, differences soon emerged. The British and Americans haggled over how large navies should be and what to do about all the confiscated German warships cooped up in Scapa Flow off Scotland. The tension was conveniently relaxed when the fleet's German crews scuttled the lot a week before the peace was signed. Wilson was firmly opposed to the scale of the financial reparations France and Britain were demanding of Germany. He believed the French demand for £44 billion ($220 billion at the time) was ten times too much. Wilson's 14 points made clear that he was unhappy about stripping Germany of territory, but Clemenceau wanted France to remain in the Rhineland and the Saar coalfields. It was an issue that at one stage made the French prime minister so furious that he walked out of the room. In the end, both Wilson and Clemenceau compromised on the main issues. Only part of the Rhineland was to remain occupied for 15 years, and the population of the Saarland – mainly German-speaking – would be allowed to vote on the issue in 1935. In the event, they chose overwhelmingly to be part of Germany.

Wilson's most lasting contribution to the peace settlement, his plan for a League of Nations, was accepted with little enthusiasm by Lloyd George and Clemenceau, but generally welcomed in Europe and beyond. It was to have a short life. The League conspicuously failed to keep the peace in Manchuria in 1931, in Ethiopia in 1935, and was unable to prevent the Second World War. It was finally abandoned in 1946 and replaced by the United Nations.

Ironically the United States was one of the few countries that refused to join the League. In spite of Wilson's tireless propagation of its virtues, it failed to pass in the Senate. Wilson suffered a debilitating stroke in October, only three months after he returned from Paris, and died in 1924. Like all the other peacemakers at Versailles, Wilson had done his best, and it is hardly fair to blame him or the other peacemakers for the catastrophe of the Second World War that followed 20 years later. But his spirit lives on and his 14 points deserve their secure place in the history of peacemaking.

OPPOSITE The Treaty of Versailles is signed in the Hall of Mirrors on 28 June 1919. Seated L to R: Italian PM Vittorio Orlando, US President Woodrow Wilson, French PM Georges Clemenceau and UK PM David Lloyd George.

ABOVE The four top Allied leaders in Paris sign the treaty: (L to R) Lloyd George, Orlando, Clemenceau and Wilson.

37

Coco Chanel Sketch

Coco Chanel rewrote the book on fashion and revolutionized the way women dressed in modern times. Her trademark little black dress, classic collarless suit and handbag with innovative shoulder strap were all about simplicity, comfort and elegance. Her undisputed talent, rags-to-riches story and extraordinary love life made her an icon of the twentieth century.

ABOVE This sketch of Chanel's little black dress was featured in US Vogue magazine, October 1926. Editors named it the "Ford dress", predicting it would have the same mass appeal as the Model T car.

OPPOSITE Chanel in 1936, when her couture business employed 4,000 people. At the start of the Second World War three years later, she closed her business down, saying, "This is not a time for fashion."

"I don't do fashion, I am fashion." Coco Chanel was as forthright as she was gifted. She also had a talent for exaggeration. Born in 1883, she claimed to be ten years younger. After her mother died when she was 12, her impoverished French father placed Chanel and her sisters in an orphanage. She later recounted those tough times as an idyllic period spent living with two doting aunts. It was in the orphanage that Gabrielle Bonheur Chanel learned to embroider, sew and iron – skills which helped her to emerge as one of the most celebrated fashion designers in history.

Chanel had wanted to be an actress and started off in cabarets, where she gained the nickname Coco. Happily for us, she couldn't sing, so when a rich British lover, Arthur "Boy" Capel, offered to set her up in business in 1913, she opened a hat shop in the fashionable seaside town of Deauville. Her hats were soon joined by sweaters, suits and dresses made of jersey, a machine-knit material traditionally used for men's underwear. Her flowing, practical designs were seen as a welcome escape from the tight-fitting female corsets and complicated petticoats fashionable at

the time. Chanel's slogan of "luxury must be comfortable" became the mantra of women who wanted well-tailored clothes that would allow them to look great and move freely in their daily activities. Fashion magazines like *Harper's Bazaar* took note: "The woman who hasn't at least one Chanel is hopelessly out of fashion," it proclaimed.

By 1919, Chanel had established a *maison de couture* in Paris. Here she created the classic tweed suit, her chic and still-popular quilted bag, and what *Vogue* dubbed "the little black dress". According to the magazine, "the frock that all the world will wear" was to fashion what the Model T Ford was to transport. Coco Chanel had well and truly liberated the female silhouette and given women modern clothes and accessories they loved to wear. She also became the first designer to market her own perfume in an eye-catching bottle.

Somehow amid her hectic business life, Chanel found time for passionate and very public affairs. Her lovers included Pablo Picasso, Igor Stravinsky, Grand Duke Dmitri Pavlovich of Russia and the Duke of Westminster. When the duke asked her to marry him, it's said she turned him down with the imperious reply, "There have been several duchesses of Westminster. There is only one Chanel."

However, it was an affair with German diplomat Baron Hans Günther von Dincklage in Paris during the Second World War that nearly destroyed Chanel's reputation and her business empire. The war had forced her to close her shops and she moved into the Ritz Hotel, also home to top-ranking German military officers. French intelligence documents reveal that Chanel worked with von Dincklage to spy for the Germans. The documents describe her as

OPPOSITE Chanel day dress, 1919. She said that her rule of thumb when designing dresses was: "Would I wear that myself? If the answer is no, I don't do it."

RIGHT Chanel with Winston Churchill and his son Randolph at a hunt in 1928. She met Churchill through the Duke of Westminster, with whom she had a ten-year affair.

"a vicious anti-Semite" who praised Hitler. They chart her involvement in Operation Model Hat, a plan to have Chanel meet British Prime Minister Winston Churchill in 1944. She knew Churchill from her time as the Duke of Westminster's lover and was tasked with persuading him to negotiate peace with Germany. The meeting never happened and after the war Chanel denied collaborating with the Germans and quickly left France to live in Switzerland.

In 1954, Chanel, now in her seventies, returned to Paris and reopened her fashion house because, she told a friend, she was "dying of boredom". The French press did not give her a warm reception. Her reputation was still tainted by her close associations with Germans during the war, but fashion editors from the rest of the world welcomed the reappearance of Chanel with open arms. As soon as they saw the updated version of her classic suit with its beautifully trimmed collarless jacket and elegant flared skirt, the accolades started pouring in. Coco Chanel was once more the undisputed First Lady of fashion.

In early 1971, at the age of 87, Chanel was still hard at work preparing for her spring collection. On 10 January, after a walk with a friend, she died in her bed in the Ritz Hotel. Her last words to her maid were, "You see, this is how you die."

The life of Coco Chanel has been immortalized in plays, movies and books. Katharine Hepburn starred in the Broadway production of the musical *Coco*. Perhaps the greatest legacy of the woman who delighted in describing herself as "a simple little dressmaker" is the continuing success of her fashion label and the other products that bear her name.

38

Anne Frank's Diary

Anne Frank has been described as one voice which speaks for the estimated six million Jews who perished in the Holocaust. Her teenage diary, written while hiding from the Nazis from 1942 to 1944, speaks to us all. One of the most famous documents of the twentieth century, it has been translated into 70 languages and sold more than 30 million copies.

ABOVE Anne Frank in 1941 aged 12. After the Germans invaded the Netherlands, Jews were not permitted to attend non-Jewish schools. She attended the Jewish Lyceum in Amsterdam.

OPPOSITE ABOVE Anne's October 1942 diary pages. She includes letters, photos and news about Jewish friends "being taken away in droves. The Gestapo is treating them very roughly and transporting them in cattle trucks ..."

OPPOSITE BELOW The Anne Frank House in Amsterdam is now a museum. The family hid in a secret annexe at the back of the building.

The first thing that struck us when we visited the Anne Frank House in Amsterdam was there was no furniture. It was removed along with all other valuables by the Gestapo who discovered Anne and her family hiding in a secret annexe in August 1944. Only a few searing reminders of their concealed life remain: a wall chart where Anne's father recorded the heights of his growing daughters, photographs of movie stars pasted to the wall of Anne's room and a mirror in which she could see the night sky reflected. Carefully protected in a glass case is the diary that Anne wrote while hiding from the Nazis. To anyone who has read her work, the house feels agonizingly familiar.

Anne received the red and white diary as a thirteenth birthday present on 12 June 1942. The first few entries are full of cheerful schoolgirl gossip, but on 8 July she writes: "the whole world has suddenly turned upside down". Her Jewish parents were taking Anne and her sister Margot into hiding to avoid being sent to concentration camps.

The Franks had moved to Amsterdam from Germany in 1933 after Hitler came to power. Otto Frank set up successful businesses, but when Germany invaded the Netherlands in 1940, he became the victim of tough new anti-Jewish laws. To avoid having his companies confiscated, he transferred ownership of them to non-Jewish friends. From 9 July 1942 to 4 August 1944, these friends provided food and kept the Frank family safe in a 46 square metre (500 square foot) space above a building from which Otto had run his business.

Anne's diary entries give us a very detailed account of life in the cramped rooms concealed behind a swinging bookcase. Three members of the van Pels family joined the Franks in their hideout, followed by Fritz Pfeffer, a dentist, who shared Anne's room. He brought distressing news about Jews being rounded up and transported to death camps: "... the stories he had to tell us were so gruesome and dreadful that we can't get them out of our minds." She recounts the tensions of being cooped up in a confined place. "The house is still trembling from the after effects of our

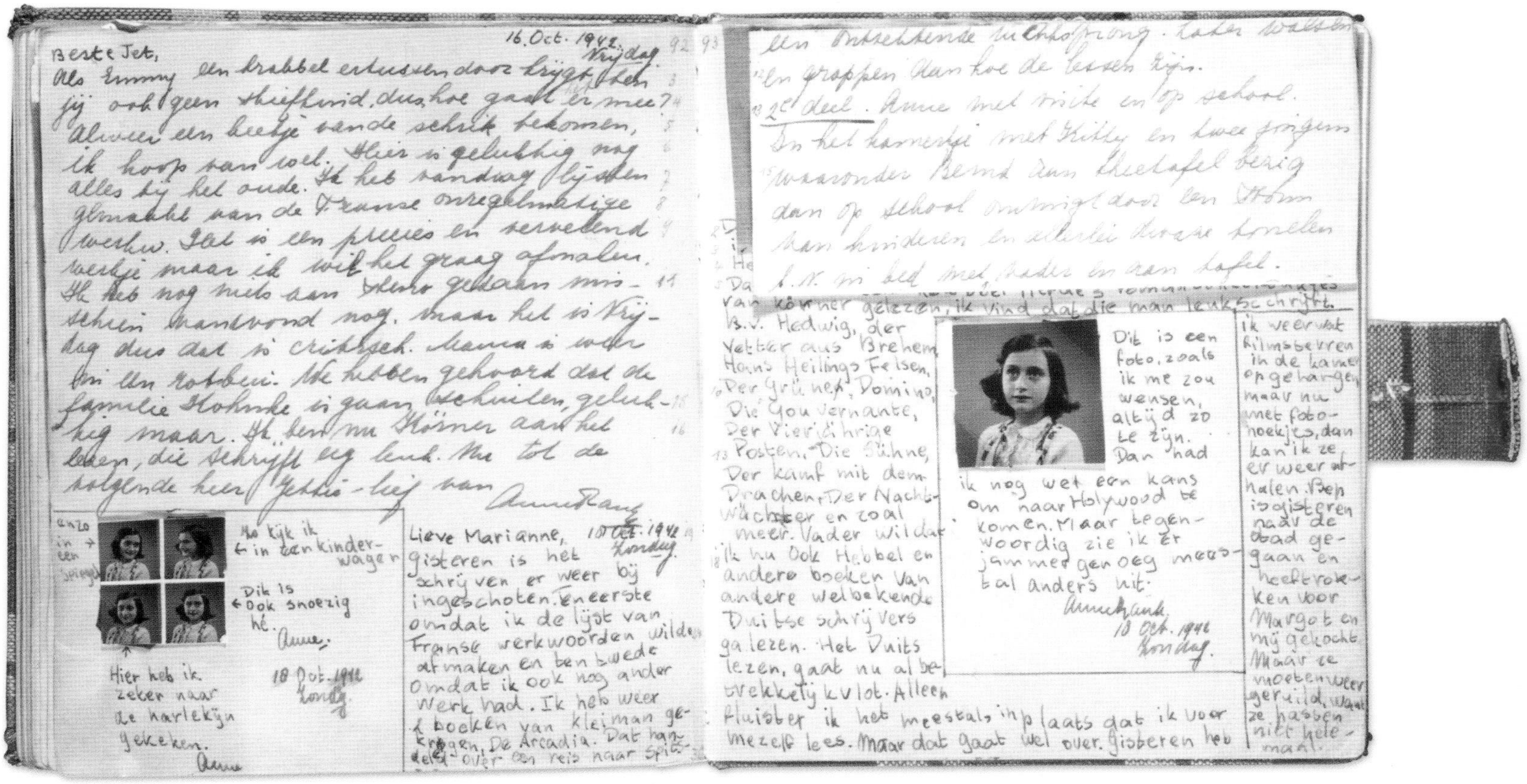

Beste Jet, 16. Oct. 1942. Vrijdag

Lieve Marianne, 18 Oct. 1942 Zondag

gisteren is het schrijven er weer bij ingeschoten. Ten eerste omdat ik de lijst van Franse werkwoorden wilde afmaken en ten tweede omdat ik ook nog ander werk had. Ik heb weer 4 boeken van Kleiman gekregen, De Arcadia.

Hier heb ik zeker naar de harlekijn gekeken. Anne

Dit is een foto, zoals ik me zou wensen, altijd zo te zijn. Dan had ik nog wel een kans om naar Holywood te komen. Maar tegenwoordig zie ik er jammer genoeg meestal anders uit. Anne Frank 18 Oct. 1942 Zondag

van Körner gelezen, ik vind dat die man leuk schrijft. B.v. Hedwig, der Vetter aus Bremen, Hans Heilings Felsen, Der grüne Domino, Die Gouvernante, Der vierjährige Posten, Die Sühne, Der Kampf mit dem Drachen, Der Nachtwächter en zo al meer. Vader wil dat ik nu ook Hebbel en andere boeken van andere welbekende Duitse schrijvers ga lezen. Het Duits lezen, gaat nu al betrekkelijk vlot. Alleen fluister ik het meestal, in plaats dat ik voor mezelf lees. Maar dat gaat wel over. Gisteren heb

ik veel van filmsterren in de kamer opgehangen ... Margot en mij gekocht.

quarrels." She complains of seeing the outside world only "through dusty curtains, tacked over dirt-caked windows", but, "When I think about our lives here, I usually come to the conclusion that we live in a paradise compared to the Jews who aren't in hiding." On 6 June 1944 she describes the joy of hearing about D-Day on the BBC: "The invasion has begun. A huge commotion in the Annexe. Is this really the long-awaited liberation? The liberation we've all talked so much about. It fills us with fresh courage and makes us strong ... Those awful Germans have oppressed and threatened us so long that the thought of friends and salvation means everything to us! ... Maybe, Margot says, I can even go back to school in September or October."

As well as offering a fascinating commentary on everyday life in hiding, Anne shares her secrets. None is more poignant than her growing fondness for Peter van Pels. On 22 August 1942 she describes her fellow teenager as "hypersensitive and lazy". By 3 March 1943, "Peter is a darling" and on 16 April 1944, after they exchange a first kiss, Anne is "too happy for words".

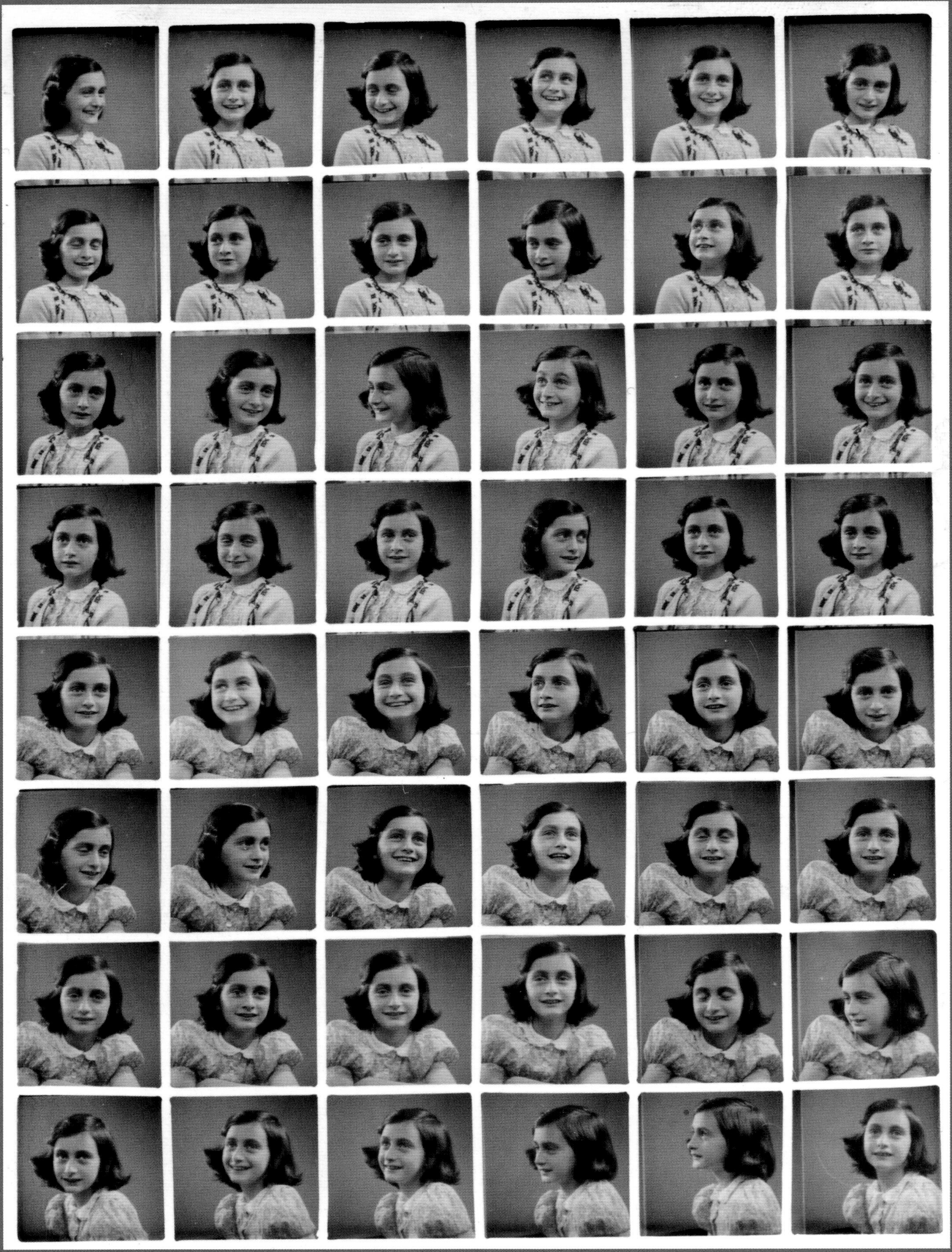

The budding romance and Anne's diary end abruptly on 4 August 1944. That's when a Gestapo officer and members of the Dutch security police raided the annexe after what was probably a tip-off. All eight fugitives were taken to a prison in Amsterdam and then to Westerbork transit camp. On 3 September they departed with more than 1,000 others on what turned out to be the last transport to leave Westerbork for Auschwitz in Poland. Anne's mother Edith died there of starvation. In October 1944, Anne and her sister were moved to Bergen-Belsen in Germany. Both perished there, probably from typhus, just weeks before British soldiers liberated the camp on 15 April 1945.

Otto Frank was the only member of the family to survive the Holocaust. After the war he returned to Amsterdam and was handed Anne's diary and a bundle of notes by one of the loyal friends who had looked after the family in hiding. She had found the documents scattered on the floor of their annexe after the raid. It took Otto two years to find a publisher for what became one of the world's bestselling books.

Anne's diary entry on 5 April 1943 reads, "When I write, I shake off all my cares. My sorrow disappears, my spirits are revived ... will I ever be able to write something great?" The answer to that question turned out to be a resounding yes.

OPPOSITE Anne's passport photos. Before going into hiding her father applied for American immigration visas. His applications were destroyed when the Germans bombed the US consulate building in Rotterdam in 1940.

ABOVE The Frank family on a day out in 1941. One year later they were hiding from the Nazis.

RIGHT The hinged bookcase which hid the opening to the secret annexe. Trusted former employees of Otto Frank supplied food and brought news from the outside world.

39

Albert Einstein's Manhattan Project Letter

A month before the Second World War began, Albert Einstein, the world-renowned physicist, wrote this letter to US President Franklin Roosevelt, urging him to consider the development of an atomic bomb. It points out that Germany was aware of the potential of such a weapon. This letter prompted the launch of the Manhattan Project, which built the weapon that destroyed the Japanese cities of Hiroshima and Nagasaki and ended the war.

More than anything else that has overshadowed the future of world peace is the threat of its destruction by nuclear weapons. One man who played an important role in their invention was Albert Einstein. He was not instrumental in the team that designed the first atomic bomb in America, but it was this letter warning President Roosevelt of the likely power of the weapon that prompted its development.

The nuclear project began in the decade after Einstein's great contribution to science with his General Theory of Relativity (see page 158). In 1911 Ernest Rutherford revealed that an atom consisted of much smaller particles. Rutherford's successors went on to discover that the core of the atom was the nucleus, comprising a number of protons and neutrons. The more protons and neutrons a nucleus contained, the heavier its atomic weight, and one of the heaviest elements of all turned out to be a very unstable one: uranium. By 1939 scientists realized that splitting the nucleus of uranium – an action called nuclear fission – would start a chain reaction that generated

ABOVE The Manhattan project's official seal circled by a mushroom cloud.

RIGHT The gaseous diffusion plant at Oak Ridge, Tennessee, where radioactive material was produced for the first atomic bomb dropped on Hiroshima.

OPPOSITE Einstein's letter telling Roosevelt that recent nuclear research has made great strides and that "extremely powerful bombs of a new type may thus be constructed". In the last paragraph he warns that the Germans are engaging in the same kind of research.

Albert Einstein
Old Grove Rd.
Nassau Point
Peconic, Long Island

August 2nd, 1939

F.D. Roosevelt,
President of the United States,
White House
Washington, D.C.

Sir:

Some recent work by E.Fermi and L. Szilard, which has been communicated to me in manuscript, leads me to expect that the element uranium may be turned into a new and important source of energy in the immediate future. Certain aspects of the situation which has arisen seem to call for watchfulness and, if necessary, quick action on the part of the Administration. I believe therefore that it is my duty to bring to your attention the following facts and recommendations:

In the course of the last four months it has been made probable - through the work of Joliot in France as well as Fermi and Szilard in America - that it may become possible to set up a nuclear chain reaction in a large mass of uranium,by which vast amounts of power and large quantities of new radium-like elements would be generated. Now it appears almost certain that this could be achieved in the immediate future.

This new phenomenon would also lead to the construction of bombs, and it is conceivable - though much less certain - that extremely powerful bombs of a new type may thus be constructed. A single bomb of this type, carried by boat and exploded in a port, might very well destroy the whole port together with some of the surrounding territory. However, such bombs might very well prove to be too heavy for transportation by air.

r ores of uranium in moderate
nada and the former Czechoslovakia,
um is Belgian Congo.
think it desirable to have some
Administration and the group
s in America. One possible way
trust with this task a person
rhaps serve in an inofficial
llowing:
nts, keep them informed of the
ommendations for Government action,
em of securing a supply of uran-

rk,which is at present being car-
of University laboratories, by
ed, through his contacts with
contributions for this cause,
and perhaps also by obtaining the co-operation of industrial laboratories which have the necessary equipment.

I understand that Germany has actually stopped the sale of uranium from the Czechoslovakian mines which she has taken over. That she should have taken such early action might perhaps be understood on the ground that the son of the German Under-Secretary of State, von Weizsäcker, is attached to the Kaiser-Wilhelm-Institut in Berlin where some of the American work on uranium is now being repeated.

Yours very truly,
A. Einstein
(Albert Einstein)

OPPOSITE The atomic cloud over Hiroshima on 6 August 1945. The US bomb had the explosive power of 15,000 tons of TNT.

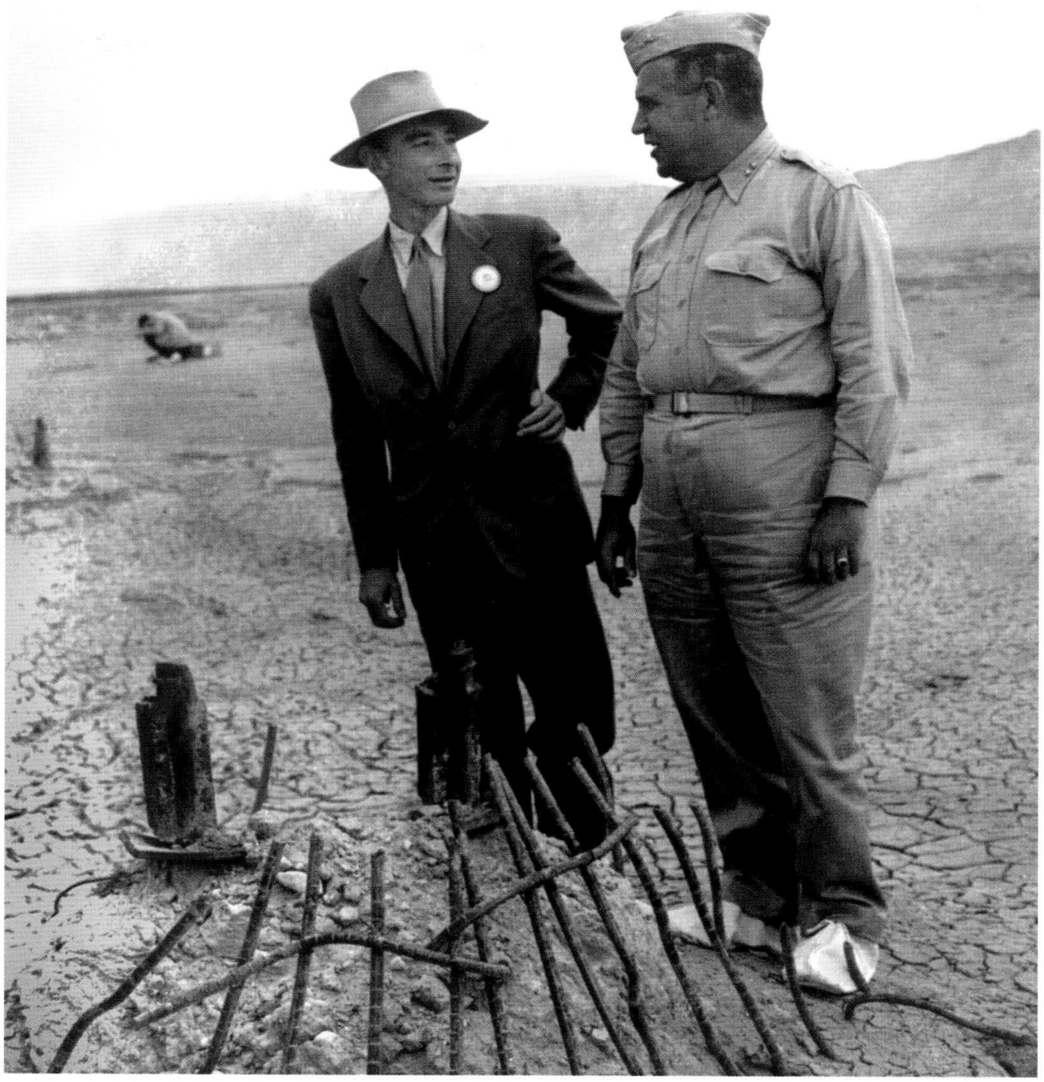

RIGHT Professor Oppenheimer, head of the secret Los Alamos laboratory, and Manhattan project director General Groves examine the remains of the first atomic bomb's test tower in 1945.

energy previously undreamed of, enough to power a bomb thousands of times more destructive than any yet produced.

Two of the scientists deep into this research at the USA's Columbia University were Hungarian Leo Szilard and Italian Enrico Fermi. They were concerned that scientists in Hitler's increasingly aggressive Nazi Germany might also be within reach of this breakthrough and they decided to bring this to the attention of the US government. Who better, they reckoned, than Albert Einstein to sign a letter to the US president? Einstein agreed and Szilard drafted it for him to sign on 2 August 1939. They decided that the best way to be sure Franklin Roosevelt would read the document was to ask a member of the president's staff to hand it to him. Alexander Sachs, one of Roosevelt's economic advisers, agreed to deliver it. Because of the outbreak of war, Sachs had to wait two months to get access to the president. On 11 October, Roosevelt asked Sachs to read him the letter in the Oval Office. The president's reaction was immediate; he wrote back to Einstein saying that the letter had led him to set up a committee "to thoroughly investigate the possibilities of your suggestion regarding the element of uranium".

Roosevelt's enthusiasm for the project boosted the momentum of scientific research, and in the summer of 1942 the president transferred control to the US Army, which created the Manhattan Engineer District, also known as the Manhattan Project, in New York City. The project was boosted by the Maud Report, top-secret findings which British scientists shared with their American allies. These findings indicated that a critical mass of uranium 235 weighing just 10 kilograms (22 pounds) would produce an immense explosion and could be packed into a bomb light enough to be carried on an aircraft. The race was on to produce the weapon that could win the war. Money was no object; what mattered was time. From the winter of 1942, when Hitler was at the height of his power, the United States committed $2 billion to the Manhattan Project. Under the scientific control of Robert Oppenheimer and the military command of Colonel Leslie Groves, massive production facilities were built at Oak Ridge, Tennessee, and Hanford in Washington State. A test site was constructed at Los Alamos in New Mexico.

The first successful test of an atomic bomb was carried out in July 1945. On 6 August and 9 August 1945, two bombs were dropped on Hiroshima and Nagasaki, ending the war with Japan. The scale of the devastation and the loss of human life transformed the perception of war. For the rest of the century and into the twenty-first, other states joined the rush to create nuclear weapons. And while the nuclear threat has done much to deter countries from risking a major war, the danger of some government or group triggering a catastrophic exchange has grown more and more alarming.

Before Einstein died in 1955, he forecast the dangers of nuclear weapons. He condemned their use against Japan and regretted his letter to President Roosevelt, saying: "Had I known that the Germans would not succeed in developing an atomic bomb, I would not have lifted a finger."

40

D-Day Map

D-Day was the crowning triumph for the Western Allies in the Second World War. This map of the Allied assault was prepared by the British Geographical Section of the General Staff (GSGS). It names the units that were the first to land on the five beaches in Normandy and shows (in blue) the approach corridors in the sea cleared of mines and (in red) the positions of the main bombarding Allied warships.

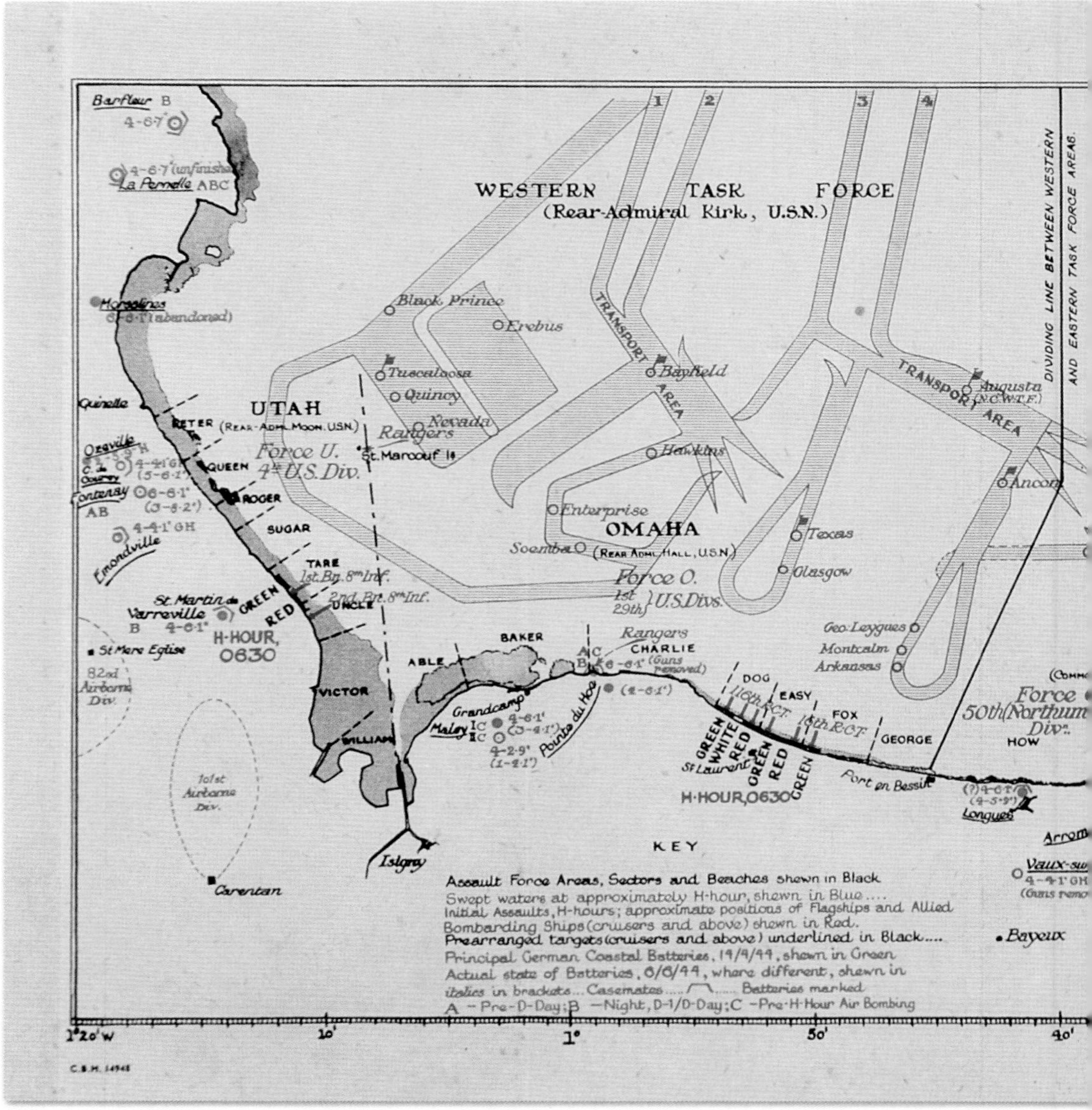

ABOVE *This overall map of the D-Day assault was prepared by the British Geographical Section of the General Staff (GSGS). German coastal batteries are marked in green. Channels swept clear of mines, through which landing craft could pass, are indicated in blue. The units to land on each beach are indicated in red, from the US 4th Division at Utah Beach on the west of the landing zone to the British 3rd Infantry Division at Sword Beach to the east.*

The success of the immense D-Day landing meant that victory over Hitler's Nazi Germany was changing from a probability to a certainty.

The plan to land the largest amphibious force in history to attack Hitler from the west was a massive gamble. On 4 June 1944, a vast force of some 150,000 men and 6,000 vessels waited on the south coast of England for the signal to steam across the English Channel to the coast of German-occupied France. The weather was stormy with only a brief lull promised for 6 June. Previous amphibious operations had resulted in heavy losses. Churchill feared 20,000 could die in the first hours, and his chief of staff, Field Marshal Alan Brooke, was "uneasy about the whole operation". Among the many unknowns was whether the Allies' massive deception scheme – Operation Fortitude – had worked. It was designed to persuade the Germans that the invasion would take place in the north-east corner of France around Calais rather than on the beaches of Normandy much further away to the west and south.

General Dwight Eisenhower, the Supreme Allied Commander, faced a grim choice: risk that relatively favourable weather window on the 6th or postpone for up to two weeks? At 4 a.m. on 5 June he decided. He told his huge force of US, Canadian and British troops that they would go the next day. "We will accept nothing less", he told them, "than full victory."

That night, 24,000 airborne troops landed in Normandy by parachute and glider, the US

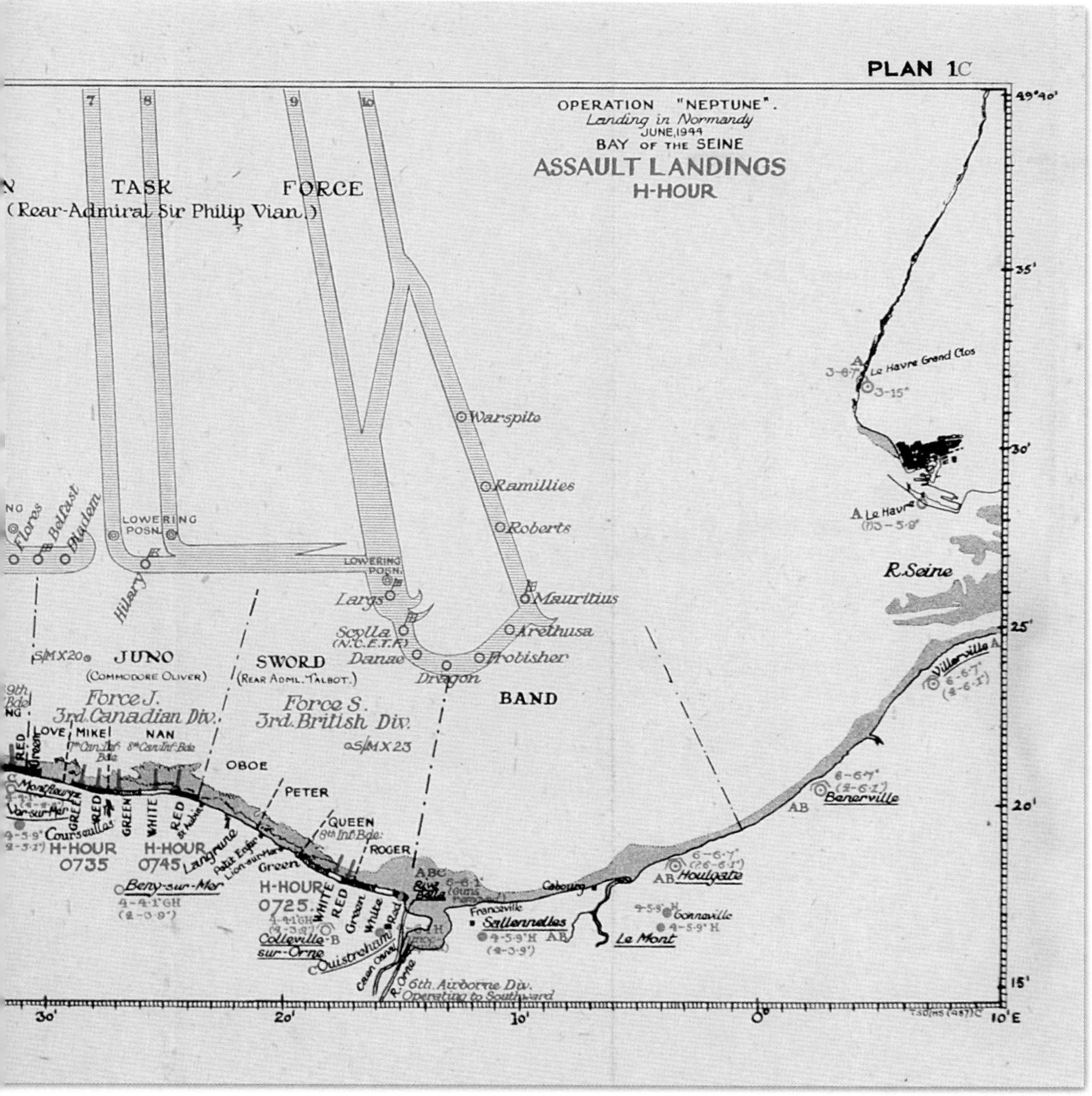

TOP RIGHT 68-year-old Field Marshal Karl Rudolf Gerd von Rundstedt, Supreme Commander of the German forces in the west.

ABOVE RIGHT Field Marshal Erwin Rommel. Known as the Desert Fox in North Africa, he did less well as the commander of Army Group B, which failed to counter the Allied assault on the Normandy beaches.

RIGHT Air Chief Marshal Tedder of the RAF, General Eisenhower and General Montgomery plan the D-Day invasion in 1944. Montgomery and Tedder later fell out over how to pursue the campaign after D-Day.

LEFT US landing craft disembark men and vehicles as barrage balloons fly overhead to guard against counterattack from the German air force. There were 7,000 US casualties on D-Day, most of them in the heavy fighting on Omaha Beach.

forces on the Cherbourg peninsula to the west and the British near Ouistreham at the eastern end of the 80-kilometre (50-mile) front. Many went astray in poor visibility, but the Americans captured the key town of Sainte-Mère Eglise and the British seized two vital bridges across the river and canal that marked the eastern flank of the Allied landing zone. There are countless stories of gallant action by the airborne forces at both edges of the battlefield.

By the early hours of 6 June, the fleet of nearly 200 warships together with 1,500 troop and supply ships and 4,000 landing craft was well on its way. "It was almost like Piccadilly Circus," said an officer on HMS *Glasgow*. It was at times near chaos. The choppy water caused widespread seasickness. As they neared the coast, several tank crews drowned when their specially designed canvas flotation cradles failed to float in deep water. For the tens of thousands of foot soldiers who scrambled down the ramps, survival was a matter of luck as much as tactical skill as they splashed their way up the exposed beaches. On the western flank, the Americans landed 23,000 men successfully on Utah Beach with 210 casualties. Eight kilometres (5 miles) to the east, on Omaha Beach, the slaughter from enemy fire was for a time almost unimaginable. The US 1st Division lost more than 2,000 men killed and many more wounded. Omaha saw the most effective and lethal German defence, but by the end of the day 34,000 US troops had established a bridgehead well beyond the shore.

The British and Canadians landed on Gold, Juno and Sword beaches, seen on the east of the map. The British suffered 3,000 casualties, the Canadians 1,000, from German fire that varied in strength from place to place. One Canadian company commander watched in horror as a Canadian tank, dodging enemy fire, ran over his dead and wounded men. He only managed to halt the tank by shattering its track with a hand grenade.

The success or failure of the landing now depended on the strength of any counterattack. The first 24 hours would be critical, and the Allies were helped by three massive German failures. The commander of the German 7th Army on this coast, Erwin Rommel, one of Hitler's most formidable field marshals, was celebrating his wife's birthday back home in Germany. Hitler himself was asleep for half the morning and his staff did not wake him because they were convinced the landings were a diversionary attack. Most German troops and tanks were still massed nearer Calais where they anticipated the main Allied assault would come. Even when Hitler was finally woken, he refused to shift his forces further west or to commit any substantial force of armour which could have crushed the Allies. The tanks of the crack 21st Panzer Division did stage a counterattack, but it was too little too late.

The objectives of the first day of the offensive proved too ambitious. Few of them were achieved. It took the Allies until July to reach the town of Caen 10 kilometres (6 miles) inland. But the bridgeheads secured on 6 June were an impressive beginning to what turned into an unstoppable advance across Nazi-occupied France that saw Paris liberated on 25 August. The Allies reached the Rhine by February 1945. The courage, determination and skilled planning of D-Day made it the Western Allies' single most significant stride to victory. Coupled with Soviet victories in Eastern Europe, they led to the defeat of Hitler in May 1945.

41

Churchill-Stalin Percentages Agreement

In October 1944, as the Second World War neared its end, Winston Churchill, the British prime minister, passed this piece of paper to Soviet leader Joseph Stalin at a meeting in Moscow. Stalin eyed it and indicated his agreement with a large tick in the top right of the note. It was a stroke of diplomacy as brisk and shocking as any in world history. The two men had carved up between them a great swathe of Eastern Europe as Nazi Germany retreated.

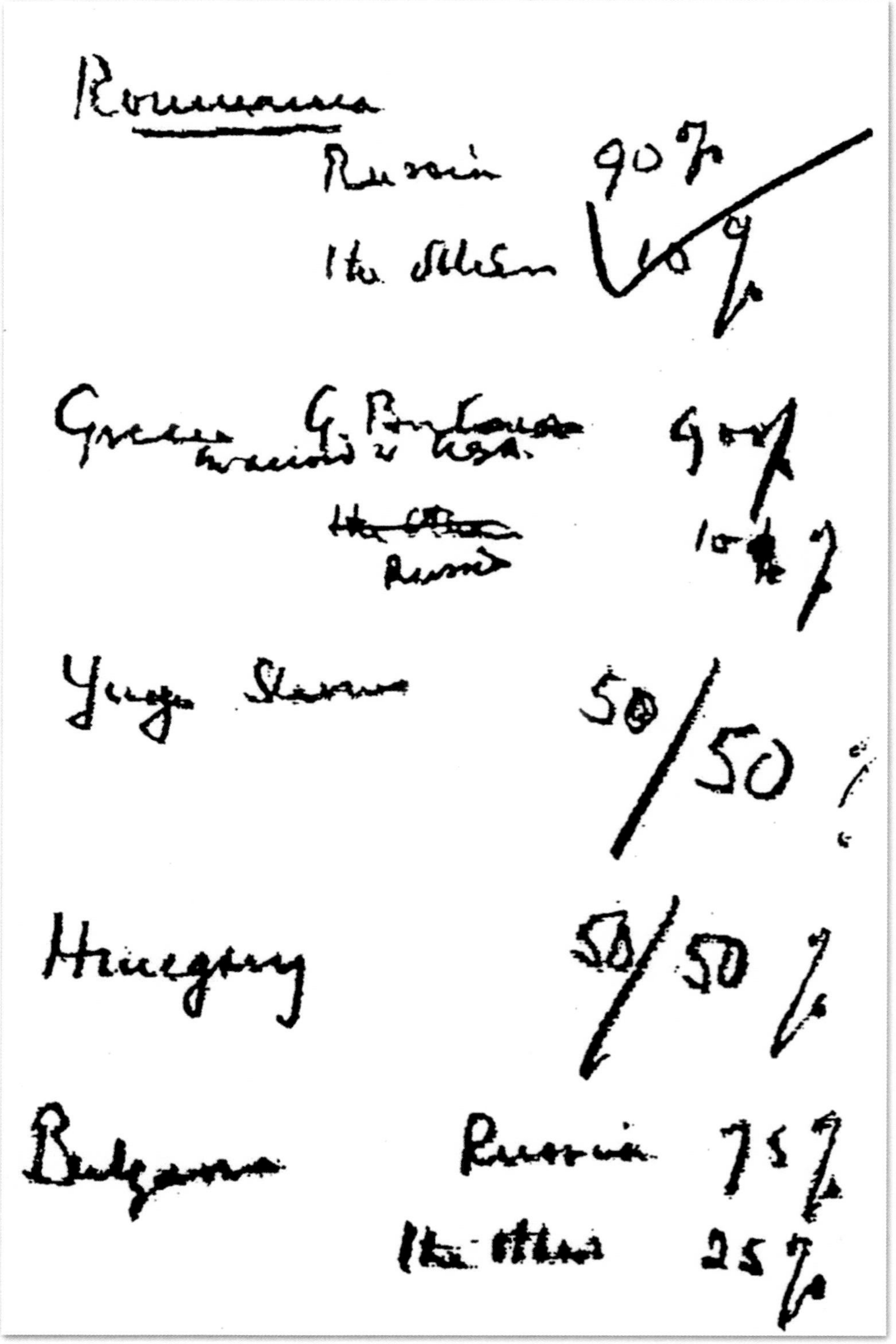

RIGHT The briskly scrawled note suggesting a rough percentage breakdown of post-war Balkan control that Churchill passed to Stalin in Moscow. The British PM later described it as his "naughty document".

OPPOSITE Winston Churchill, Joseph Stalin and British Foreign Secretary Anthony Eden at their October 1944 meeting in Moscow.

Churchill met Stalin in the autumn of 1944, just four months after the Western Allies began their liberation of France. In the east, the Soviets were already three years into their costly struggle to push Hitler's armies back to Berlin. Stalin's forces had occupied Romania in August, Bulgaria in September and were poised to invade Hungary. No one now doubted that Hitler faced defeat: all eyes were on of the future of liberated Europe.

Churchill knew that he and his US allies were not in a strong position to demand decisive influence in countries already occupied by Stalin. But he was anxious to preserve Britain's say in the future of Greece, which its armies had fought to save from Hitler, and to protect Greece from a communist takeover. There had also been contact with the government of the devious Miklós Horthy in Hungary and with the partisan leader Josip Tito in Yugoslavia about Western interest in these countries' post-war direction. All this was high on Churchill's agenda as he sat down with Stalin in the Kremlin on 9 October. Churchill writes in his memoirs that he suggested to Stalin (no doubt after a glass or two of whisky): "Let us settle about our affairs in the Balkans. ... How would it do for you to have 90 per cent predominance in Romania, for us to have 90 per cent of the say in Greece and go 50/50 about Yugoslavia?" He pushed across the table to Stalin what he later referred to as his "naughty document". It prescribed the percentage of influence he thought each side should maintain in the five Balkan countries.

It also suggested a 50/50 split in Hungary and a 75/25 split in favour of the Soviets in Bulgaria. After Stalin's tick appeared to signify his acceptance of Churchill's carve-up plan, Churchill recalls there was a long silence. "At length I said, 'Might it not be thought rather cynical if it seemed we had disposed of these issues, so fateful to millions of people, in such an offhand manner? Let us burn the paper.' 'No, you keep it,' said Stalin."

So embarrassed was Churchill about the chutzpa of doing this deal with Stalin that he described it only in the vaguest terms to US President Roosevelt. He simply assured the president that "nothing will be settled except preliminary agreements between Britain and Russia, subject to further discussion". The British prime minister was well aware of two new geopolitical realities: the Soviets were now well on the way to imposing communist regimes in Eastern Europe; and Britain's global strength was fast becoming second to the USA's. His best opportunity lay with getting a deal on Greece.

Churchill and his foreign secretary Anthony Eden spent another week and a half in Moscow, and in the end Stalin and his foreign minister Vyacheslav Molotov did more than pocket the percentages Churchill had conceded. They swung the balance even more in their favour. Soviet predominance in Hungary and Bulgaria which had been offered as 50/50 and 75/25 respectively was boosted to 80/20 in each case. The British had little choice but to recognize the reality of Soviet influence in those countries, but Churchill managed to maintain Britain's bid for 90/10 for Greece. Remarkably, Stalin stuck to the deal. Whether honouring this agreement or swayed by other factors, he gave no support from then on to communist revolutionaries in Greece or to their backers in bordering countries like Yugoslavia.

Churchill could claim a measure of success in constraining Stalin in the Balkans, but neither he nor Roosevelt were to have any success in curbing Soviet ambitions in Poland, the largest of the East European countries Stalin's armies were liberating. During the meetings in Moscow, Churchill persuaded Stalin to meet the leader of the Polish government in exile, Stanisław Mikołajczyk. It was a failure. Stalin insisted that any post-war Polish government would have to accept giving up a sizeable slice of its eastern territory to the Soviet Union. Mikołajczyk refused. Stalin made no further effort to accommodate him. He was already in close touch with a group of Polish communists called the Lublin Committee, the Kremlin's choice as the next government of Poland. With Soviet armies rolling across Poland towards Berlin, there was little that Roosevelt or Churchill could do to secure compromise.

The outcome of the Second World War and of the peace conference that followed resulted in total Soviet domination of Eastern Europe – 100 per cent and nothing less. As Churchill himself remarked in 1946, "from Stettin in the Baltic to Trieste and the Adriatic, an iron curtain has descended across the Continent". That scrap of paper jotted with percentages, now held in Britain's National Archives, earned itself an intriguing place in history.

RIGHT Soviet tanks drive through Poland in the last months of the Second World War. Soviet domination of Eastern Europe lasted four and a half decades. There was little that the Western Allies were willing or able to do to prevent it.

42

The Charter of the United Nations

The Charter of the United Nations makes the most ambitious promises in international history. Designed to preserve peace and security in a world ravaged by two world wars, the document also pledges to promote human, political and social rights. US President Harry Truman called it "a solid structure upon which we can build a better world".

ABOVE US Secretary of State Edward Stettinius addresses a meeting of the "Steering Committee" at the San Francisco Conference. Heads of delegations attending the conference are seated around the table.

OPPOSITE The preamble to the Charter of the United Nations. It took 400 committee meetings over two months for representatives of 50 nations to agree on the Charter.

The opening words of the Charter of the United Nations powerfully sum up its noble intentions: "to save succeeding generations from the scourge of war, which twice in our lifetime has brought untold sorrow to mankind, and to reaffirm faith in fundamental human rights, in the dignity and worth of the human person, in the equal rights of men and women and of nations large and small."

Plans for an effective organization to preserve world peace and security emerged during the Second World War. It would replace the League of Nations, which had failed in its goal to keep the peace after the First World War. In 1941, US President Franklin Roosevelt and British Prime Minister Winston Churchill signed the Atlantic Treaty, proposing a new international organization. It was endorsed in 1942 by the United Nations, the name given to 26 allied countries fighting Germany, Italy and Japan. The United States, United Kingdom and Soviet Union were instrumental in structuring the new organization, with input from China. In August 1944, representatives from those four countries met at Washington's Dumbarton Oaks estate to work out a blueprint. They agreed on two main decision-making bodies: the General Assembly of all member nations, which would not have legislative powers, and the Security Council, whose resolutions would be binding on all UN members. There were disagreements about issues such as membership and voting rules, but they were smoothed over at the Yalta Conference in February 1945.

Two months later, with war in the Pacific still raging, delegates from 50 countries gathered at the United Nations Conference on International Organization in San Francisco to hammer out details of the UN Charter. They endorsed the broad framework already agreed but there was particularly heated debate about the powers and composition of the Security Council, the core peacekeeping organ. Chapter 6 of the document allows the Security Council to settle international disputes by "negotiation, enquiry, mediation, conciliation, arbitration, [and] judicial settlement ..." If that fails, Chapter 7 gives it permission to resort to military action such as "blockade, and other operations by air, sea, or land forces of members of the United Nations".

The Security Council was to have five permanent members – the United States, United Kingdom, France, Soviet Union (reduced to Russia in 1991) and Nationalist China (replaced

CHARTER OF THE UNITED NATIONS

WE THE PEOPLES OF THE UNITED NATIONS
DETERMINED

to save succeeding generations from the scourge of war, which twice in our lifetime has brought untold sorrow to mankind, and

to reaffirm faith in fundamental human rights, in the dignity and worth of the human person, in the equal rights of men and women and of nations large and small, and

to establish conditions under which justice and respect for the obligations arising from treaties and other sources of international law can be maintained, and

to promote social progress and better standards of life in larger freedom,

AND FOR THESE ENDS

to practice tolerance and live together in peace with one another as good neighbors, and

to unite our strength to maintain international peace and security, and

to ensure, by the acceptance of principles and the institution of methods, that armed force shall not be used, save in the common interest, and

to employ international machinery for the promotion of the economic and social advancement of all peoples,

HAVE RESOLVED TO COMBINE OUR EFFORTS
TO ACCOMPLISH THESE AIMS.

Accordingly, our respective Governments, through representatives assembled in the city of San Francisco, who have exhibited their full powers found to be in good and due form, have agreed to the present Charter of the United Nations and do hereby establish an international organization to be known as the United Nations.

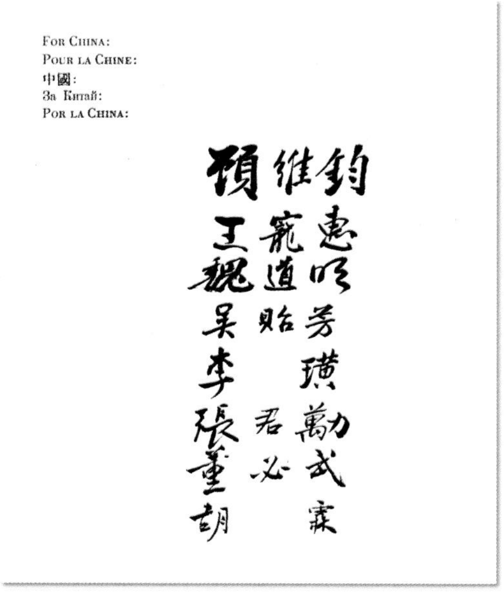
For China:
Pour la Chine:
中國:
За Китай:
Por la China:

For the Union of Soviet Socialist Republics:
Pour l'Union des Républiques Soviétiques Socialistes:
蘇維埃社會主義共和國聯邦:
За Союз Советских Социалистических Республик:
Por la Unión de Repúblicas Socialistas Soviéticas:

by Communist China in 1971) – and six non-permanent members (later increased to ten). The five permanent members of the Security Council could veto any resolution, which alarmed smaller nations. They feared that if one of the "Big Five" threatened another country, it could use its veto to stop the Security Council recommending action against it. Attempts to have the veto power reduced were finally abandoned in the interests of world peace.

Delegates also agreed on other main bodies, including the Economic and Social Council, which would direct international action on social and economic matters, and the International Court of Justice, designed to settle legal disputes between nations.

The final draft of the Charter was put to a vote in San Francisco's Opera House on 25 June 1945. Traditionally such decisions were taken by a show of hands. On this occasion delegates were asked to stand if they accepted the draft. Every delegate rose, along with their staff, members of the press and 3,000 visitors. There was a huge cheer as the Charter was passed unanimously.

The UN, born in great hope, has become the object of severe scrutiny. The Security Council's power of veto is particularly criticized for hindering its effectiveness. Russia, for example, vetoed attempts to impose sanctions on Syria during that country's civil war. The United States repeatedly used its veto on resolutions condemning Israel. The Security Council has also been accused of indecision – notably when it failed to take action during the genocides in Rwanda in 1994 and in Darfur nine years later.

On the positive side, the Security Council successfully passed resolutions condemning North Korea's invasion of South Korea in 1950, providing the basis for the intervention of UN forces in the Korean War. It condemned Saddam Hussein's 1990 invasion of Kuwait, which also made international action possible. And there is a long list of the UN's achievements in other fields. They include peacekeeping operations, post-conflict resolution and reconstruction, war criminal prosecutions, protecting human rights, helping women and children, assisting refugees and disaster victims, fighting hunger and seeking solutions to climate change.

Today we are less likely to die during armed combat than at any time in history. The fear of nuclear war and mutually assured destruction certainly has played its part in that, but the United Nations has also had a major role. The horrors of conflicts in Vietnam, Syria and elsewhere have discredited the Charter's pledge "to save future generations from the scourge of war", but we have no doubt that the UN and its agencies make the world a safer and better place.

OPPOSITE President Harry Truman addresses the closing session of the United Nations Conference in San Francisco on 26 June 1945.

ABOVE The signatures of Chinese and Soviet delegates on the UN Charter. China had the honour of signing first because it was the first victim of aggression by an Axis power: Japan.

43

A Structure for DNA

The final draft of biophysicists James Watson and Francis Crick's 1953 article about the structure of DNA is one of the seminal scientific papers of the twentieth century. This document unlocked the genetic code which determines the characteristics of all living organisms. The groundbreaking discovery of how life works reshaped the study of biology and led to major advances such as DNA profiling, the mapping of the human genome and the biotechnology industry.

ABOVE James Watson (left) and Francis Crick pose with their model of a DNA molecule.

OPPOSITE The final draft of Watson's and Crick's 1953 article on the structure of deoxyribonucleic acid, which appeared on 25 April 1953 in the scientific journal Nature.

On 28 February 1953, patrons of the Eagle pub in Cambridge, England, were settling down to lunch when two men rushed in and exclaimed that they had "found the secret of life". That's how James Watson recalls the way he broke the news that he and Francis Crick had finally cracked the elusive structure of DNA. They had been trying to come up with a model of this master molecule of life for 18 months, and at last they had it! The single-page article containing their findings was published in the journal *Nature* two months later, accompanied by an elegant drawing of a DNA molecule by Crick's artist wife Odile. The order in which the men's names appeared on the document was decided by the toss of a coin.

Other researchers had made important findings about the existence and composition of deoxyribonucleic acid (DNA), but it took the intuition and determination of Watson and Crick to gather these findings into a coherent theory. A Swiss doctor, Friedrich Miescher, first discovered the substance DNA in 1869 on pus from a bandage. In the 1940s, DNA was identified as "the transforming principle" which could confer new characteristics in bacteria ("transforming" them) when passed between cells. Scientists believed DNA contained instructions for the growth and development of most of the cells in a living body, but it was not known how it passed information about traits like eye colour and blood group from one generation to the next. Watson and Crick set out to solve the mystery by finding out what DNA looked like and exactly how it could encode information.

Two contemporary discoveries had a crucial impact on their research. American chemist Linus Pauling's pioneering work on building physical models of the structure of proteins was adapted by Watson and Crick to great effect. But perhaps their luckiest break was seeing an X-ray image of a DNA fibre which suggested it consisted of two strands coiled into a double helix, corkscrew-like shape. The image was taken by British scientists Rosalind Franklin and Maurice Wilkins. Wilkins showed the photo to Watson and Crick without Franklin's knowledge, which led to accusations that Franklin's contribution to the discovery of DNA was not properly recognized. The minute Watson saw the image he realized its significance: "My mouth fell open and my pulse began to race."

Once they knew the general shape was a double helix, Watson and Crick were able to

final version

~~8 Scroop~~
9 Portugal Place
11 pt

A STRUCTURE FOR D.N.A.

We wish to suggest a structure for the salt of deoxyribose nucleic acid (D.N.A.). This structure has novel features which are of considerable biological interest.

A structure for nucleic acid has already been proposed by Pauling and Corey.[1] They kindly made their manuscript available to us in advance of publication. Their model consists of three intertwined chains, with the phosphates near the fibre axis, and the bases on the outside. In our opinion this structure is unsatisfactory for two reasons:

1. We believe that the material which gives the X-ray diagrams is the salt, not the free acid. Without the acidic hydrogen atoms it is not clear what forces would hold the structure together, especially as the negatively charged phosphates near the axis will repel each other.

2. Some of the van der Waals distances appear to be too small.

Another three-chain structure has recently been suggested by Fraser.[9] In his model the phosphates are on the outside, and the bases on the inside, ~~It is stated that the bases can be~~ linked together by hydrogen bonds. This structure as described is ~~vague and~~ rather ill-defined, and for this reason we shall not comment on it.

We wish to put forward a radically different structure for the salt of deoxyribose nucleic acid. This structure has two helical chains each coiled round the same axis (see figure). We have made the usual chemical assumptions, namely that each chain consists of phosphate di-ester groups joining β-D-deoxyribo-

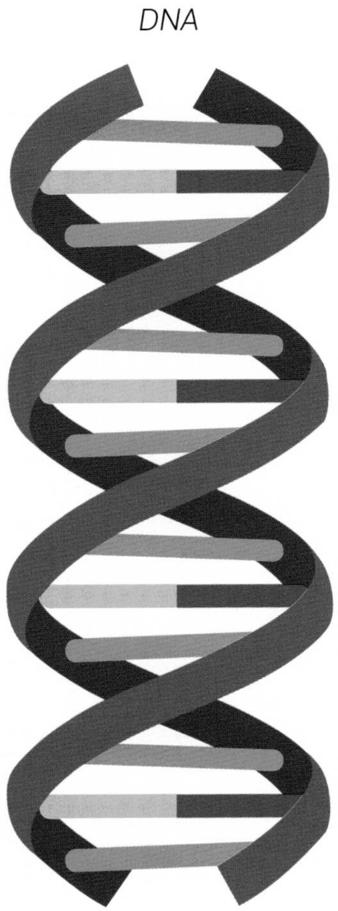

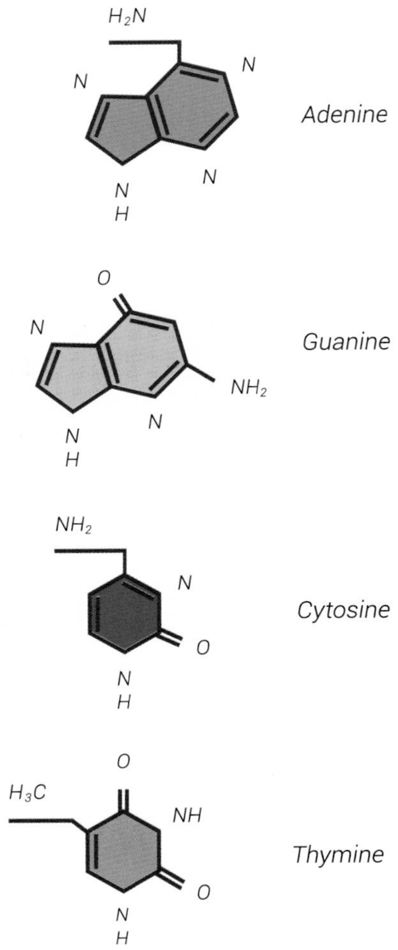

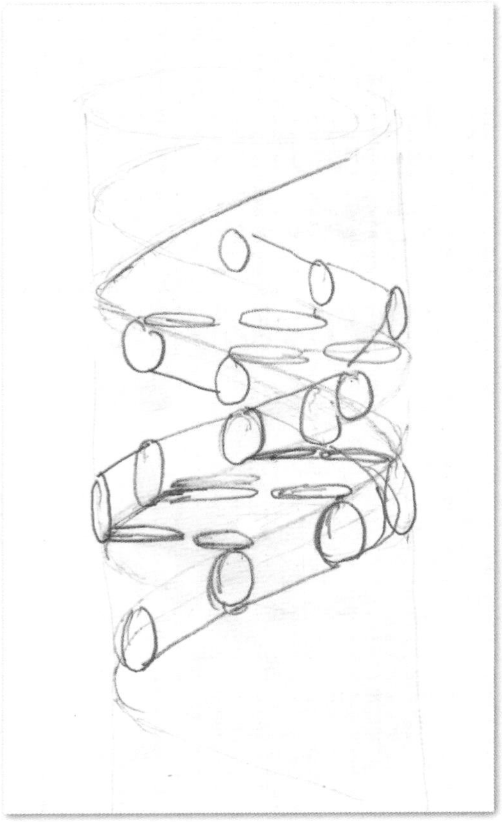

build a detailed model of the structure. They made cardboard cutouts of the chemical components of DNA and moved them around their desktops, trying to make them fit together. After several failed attempts they finally produced a model which showed that DNA is made up of a spiral "ladder". Phosphate and sugar molecules are on the outside, with the rungs consisting of four paired nitrogen-containing bases: adenine (A) with thymine (T) and guanine (G) with cytosine (C) (see diagram above). The sequence of billions of just these four bases contains the information which determines the characteristics of living organisms. Sections of DNA are known as genes and each one creates a specific protein, made up of complex chemicals that dictate how the body works. For example, haemoglobin is a red protein in blood, and keratin is a protein in hair, skin and nails. The Human Genome Project reported in 2003 that human bodies have more than 20,000 genes.They are contained in long strands of DNA coiled tightly inside the 23 pairs of chromosomes found in the nuclei of most cells in our bodies.

James Watson and Francis Crick were awarded the Nobel Prize in Physiology or Medicine in 1962 along with Maurice Wilkins, who had provided the pair with the X-ray of DNA. The contribution of Wilkins' colleague Rosalind Franklin was not acknowledged. She had died of cancer four years earlier and the Nobel Prize honours only those alive at the time of nomination.

The legacy of Watson's and Crick's discovery is jawdropping. DNA profiling has transformed forensic science. Minute samples of blood, semen, skin, saliva or hair can link an individual to a crime scene. It determines paternity and tells us who our ancestors are. Samples taken from dead organisms dating back to Neanderthal times can be used to reveal evolutionary history. Genetic modification has revolutionized agriculture, biotechnology, reseach and medicine. Now that we know there are genetic factors in human diseases such as cancer and Alzheimer's, new preventive strategies are being developed, including gene therapy – the alteration of genes to treat or stop disease.

The modern world of DNA seems a very long way from the two men who moved bits of cardboard around their desks. When Francis Crick went home on the night of their breakthrough on 28 February 1953, he told his wife, "We seem to have made a big discovery." Years later she told him, "You were always coming home and saying things like that, so naturally I thought nothing of it."

ABOVE LEFT The DNA spiral "ladder" with rungs consisting of four paired nitrogen-containing bases: adenine (blue) with thymine (light purple) and guanine (yellow) with cytosine (dark purple).

ABOVE RIGHT This pencil sketch of a DNA double helix was drawn by Odile Crick, the artist wife of Francis. It accompanied the article on the structure of DNA which appeared in Nature.

OPPOSITE Watson and Crick used these aluminium templates in their model of DNA. They represent four nitrogen-containing bases: A is for adenine, T for thymine, C for cytosine and G for guanine.

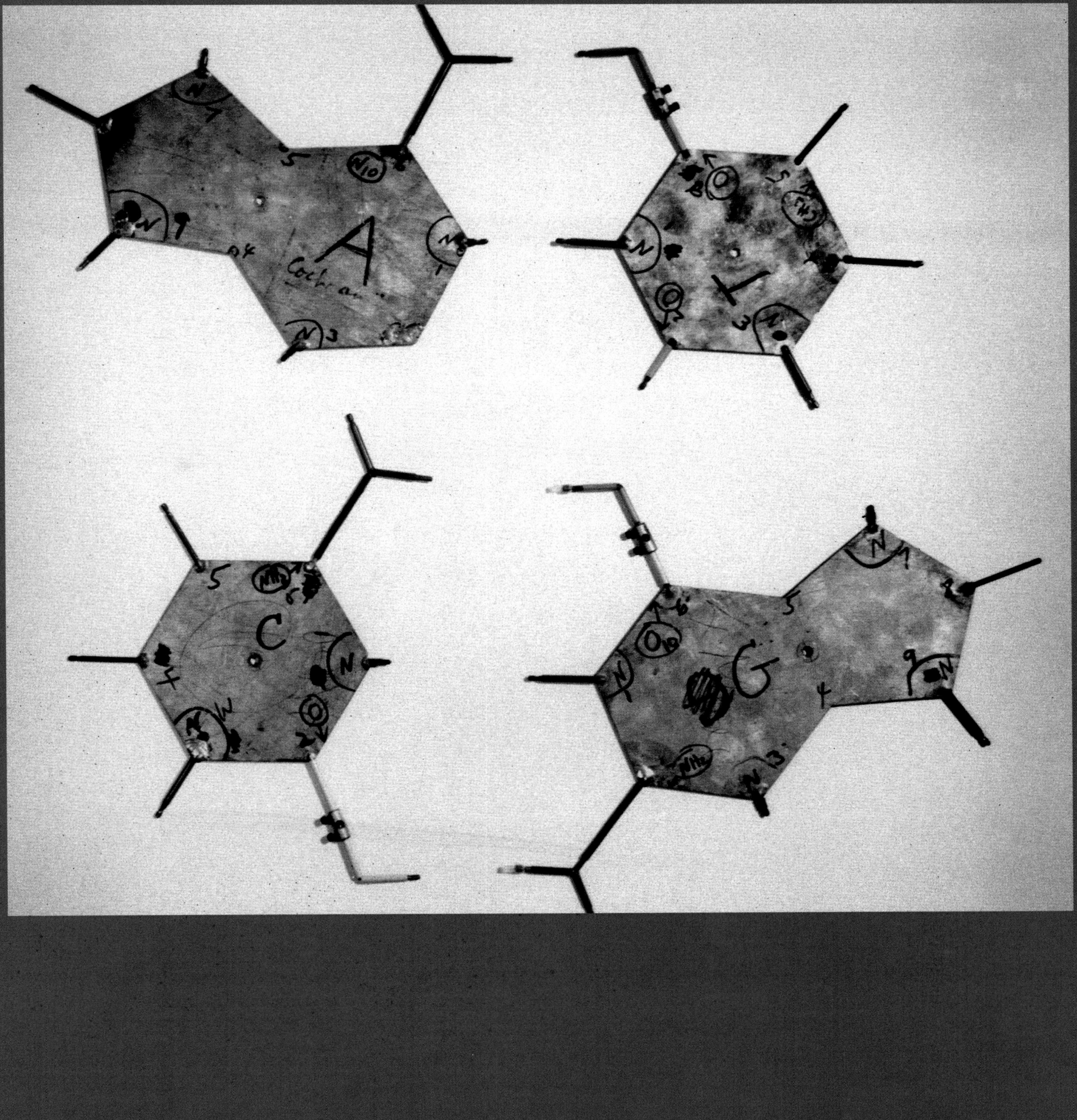
A
T
C
G

44

The Treaty of Rome

The Treaty of Rome, which established the European Economic Community, was signed on 25 March 1957. The leaders who put their names to it launched the first successful peaceful unification of a continent in history. Within 60 years the European Union had become the world's largest trading bloc and the second most productive economy after the United States.

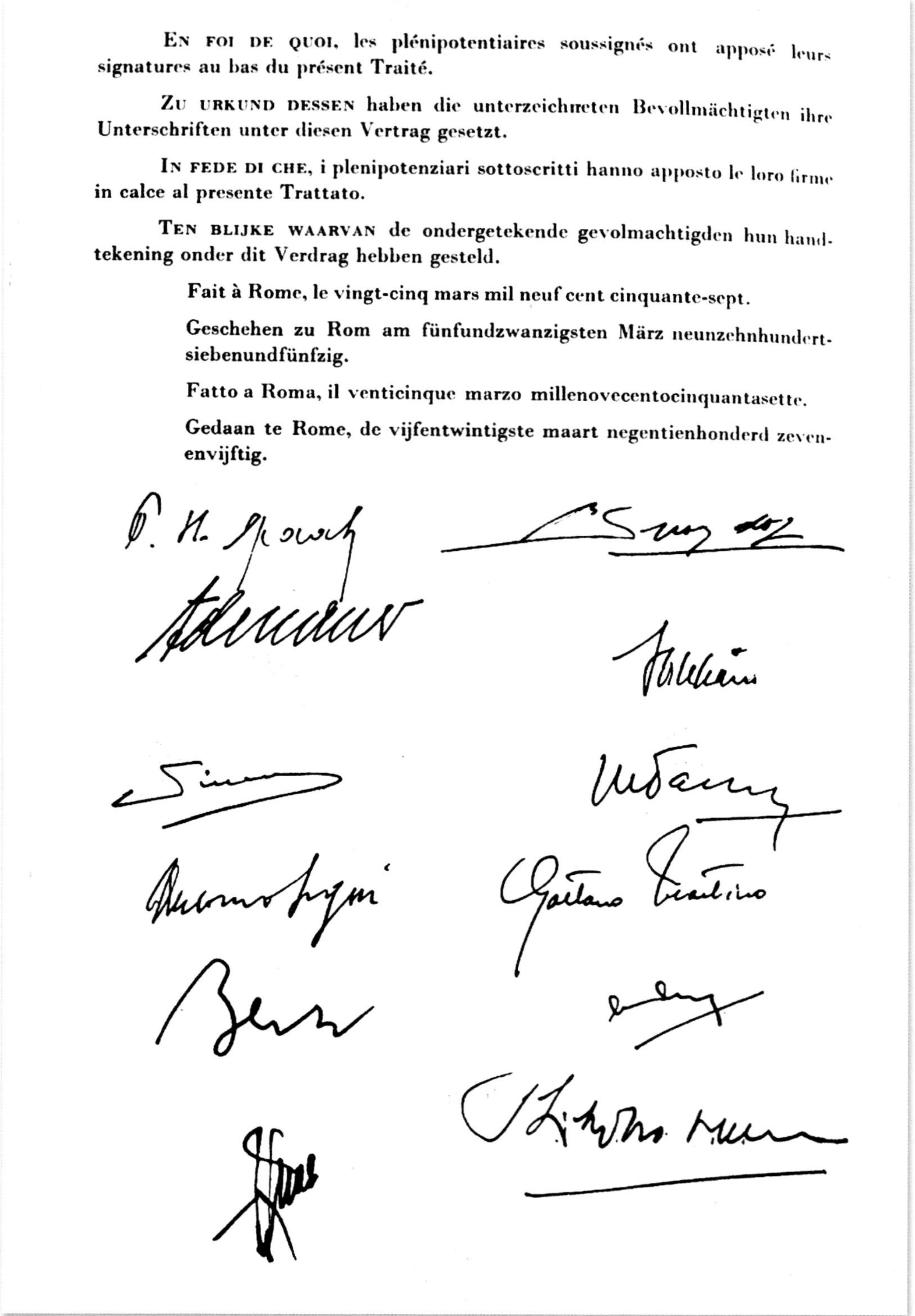

EN FOI DE QUOI, les plénipotentiaires soussignés ont apposé leurs signatures au bas du présent Traité.

ZU URKUND DESSEN haben die unterzeichneten Bevollmächtigten ihre Unterschriften unter diesen Vertrag gesetzt.

IN FEDE DI CHE, i plenipotenziari sottoscritti hanno apposto le loro firme in calce al presente Trattato.

TEN BLIJKE WAARVAN de ondergetekende gevolmachtigden hun handtekening onder dit Verdrag hebben gesteld.

Fait à Rome, le vingt-cinq mars mil neuf cent cinquante-sept.

Geschehen zu Rom am fünfundzwanzigsten März neunzehnhundertsiebenundfünfzig.

Fatto a Roma, il venticinque marzo millenovecentocinquantasette.

Gedaan te Rome, de vijfentwintigste maart negentienhonderd zevenenvijftig.

ABOVE Signatures of 12 ministers from the six founding countries on the Treaty of Rome. The first two in the left-hand column are German Chancellor Adenauer's and former Belgian Premier Paul-Henri Spaak's. Clearly legible four down is the signature of the Italian PM Antonio Segni.

OPPOSITE The signing of the Treaty of Rome in the Palazzo dei Conservatori on 25 March 1957. German Chancellor Adenauer sits fifth from the left in the front row.

The Second World War shattered Europe. Only a handful of countries escaped devastation. All vowed that such a conflict must never be allowed to happen again. Even Winston Churchill, who had led Britain to victory, called for a United States of Europe in 1946. But Britain was noticeably absent from the great endeavour that began four years later. Inspired by the declaration of French Foreign Minister Robert Schuman in 1950 to "make war not only unthinkable but materially impossible", a particularly gifted group of European leaders got to work.

Their first enterprise in 1951 was the European Coal and Steel Community (ECSC). Six countries – Belgium, France, Italy, Luxembourg, the Netherlands and West Germany – signed up to regulate their industrial production under a centralized supranational authority. This began the process of pooling national sovereignty that led to the European Economic Community (EEC) six years later. Encouraged by European visionaries such as France's Jean Monnet, the political economist who was the first leader of the ECSC, Belgium's former prime minister Paul-Henri Spaak and German academic and diplomat Walter Hallstein, the six countries moved on to draw up the Treaty of Rome.

It was signed in a grand ceremony on 25 March 1957 at Palazzo dei Conservatori on Rome's Capitoline Hill. The signatures of member countries' leaders included those of Spaak and the German Chancellor Conrad Adenauer (the top two on the left-hand side of the document). The Italians had been so rushed with preparations that they had failed to print all but the first and last pages of the voluminous document. Right at the top were the words that proclaimed the leaders' determination to "lay the foundations of an ever-closer union among the peoples of Europe". They also resolved to "ensure the economic and social progress of

their countries by common action to eliminate the barriers which divide Europe ... pooling their resources to preserve and strengthen peace and liberty, and calling upon the other peoples of Europe who share their ideal to join in their efforts".

The substance of the treaty was the customs union which abolished all tariff barriers. To run the new Community, the treaty established three new bodies: the Council of the European Community (composed of leaders of the six countries) would make the big decisions; the Commission would run the European Community from day to day and make recommendations to the Council; and the European Parliament, elected by popular vote in the member countries, would have limited legislative powers. There was a growing chorus of opposition to the new system from a wide group of critics. They claimed that there was a blatant democratic deficit, particularly in the structure of the Commission, whose members were appointed by the six governments and not elected.

Politics aside, the economic benefits of the new construct soon became clear. The EEC's common market prospered and other countries clamoured to join. In spite of initial French reluctance, the United Kingdom, Denmark and Ireland became members in 1973. They were followed by Greece in 1981, Spain and Portugal in 1986, Austria, Finland and Sweden in 1995, 10 more in 2004, Bulgaria and Romania in 2007, and the twenty-eighth member, Croatia, joined in 2013. The community, now called the European Union (EU), is at the time of writing the world's largest trading bloc and its second biggest producer.

Since the signing of the Treaty of Rome, the Community has taken huge strides towards further integration. In 1993, it launched the single market, which provided for free movement of goods, capital, services and labour. Most European countries adopted a common currency, the euro. Twenty-two of the 28 members removed border controls and there has been a gradual increase in majority voting in the Council of Ministers.

All these measures in the spirit of promoting "ever-closer union" mentioned in the Treaty of Rome have prompted concerns in some countries about loss of national sovereignty. In Britain, opposition to the increasing scope of the union led to a referendum in June 2016. A majority voted to leave the EU. The two main concerns in Britain and other sceptical countries are immigration and democracy. Critics complain that the free movement of workers allows migrants from poorer EU members to undercut wages in richer countries. They also worry about too much control being exercised by "unelected bureaucrats" in the European Commission in Brussels.

The European Union has developed into a single market of 500 million people. Some of them may now take a dim view of Churchill's starry-eyed prophecy that in a united Europe "there would be no limit to the happiness, prosperity and glory which its people would enjoy". But few can deny that this unique experiment in inter-state governance and cooperation has brought stability and peace to a continent with a deeply troubled past.

ABOVE Jean Monnet, political economist, one of the founding fathers of the Treaty of Rome.

Map showing the 28 members of the European Union in February 2020. The 6 original members are in red, the other 22 which joined later (from Britain, Ireland and Denmark in 1973 to Croatia in 2013) in brown. The UK is currently in the process of withdrawal.

45

The Beatles Itinerary

This list of American cities scrawled on an envelope by Beatles manager Brian Epstein set Liverpool's Fab Four on the path to becoming the bestselling band in history. The itinerary was drawn up in advance of the group's first North American tour in 1964. Their 32 concerts in just 33 days catapulted John Lennon, Paul McCartney, George Harrison and Ringo Starr from "Merseyside mopheads" to international superstars.

ABOVE George Harrison, Paul McCartney, Ringo Starr and John Lennon with manager Brian Epstein at Heathrow Airport on 22 September 1964 returning from the Beatles' triumphant North American tour.

OPPOSITE The used envelope on which Brian Epstein scrawled dates and names of cities for the Beatles' first North American tour. Note the date on the postmark: 25 March 1964, just weeks after the group appeared on The Ed Sullivan Show.

Beatlemania had well and truly arrived in Britain by 1963, but the four lads from Liverpool remained relatively unknown in North America. While songs like "Love Me Do", "Please Please Me" and "From Me to You" shot to the top of the British hit parade, the group's music was scarcely heard across the pond. Capitol Records, the American company which had rights to the Beatles' recordings, turned them down at first because "British acts don't have an audience in America". The company changed its tune in December 1963 after a disc jockey in Washington DC asked a British Airways flight attendant to bring him the group's latest single, "I Want to Hold Your Hand". When he played it on air, the audience response was overwhelmingly positive, so it was hurriedly released in the US. The disc became a number-one hit and sold a million copies, but the American media remained sceptical. The Beatles made no secret of the fact that they were heavily influenced by American artists such as Elvis, Little Richard, Buddy Holly and Carl Perkins, but most US journalists chose to ignore that. Articles focused instead on their hair, matching suits and Beatle boots. Journalists played on the word "beetle" and suggested an "infestation" had hit the UK. Reports dismissed the band as "Britain's new madness" and "a novelty act".

Most negative coverage ended abruptly after the group appeared live on *The Ed Sullivan Show* on 9 February 1964. A record 73 million viewers (40 per cent of the population) tuned in to watch John, Paul, George and Ringo perform five songs, including "All My Loving", "She Loves You", and "I Saw Her Standing There". After what was later described as the most important moment in the history of rock and roll, North America went crazy for the Beatles. The band's manager Brian Epstein made plans for an ambitious tour which would take the

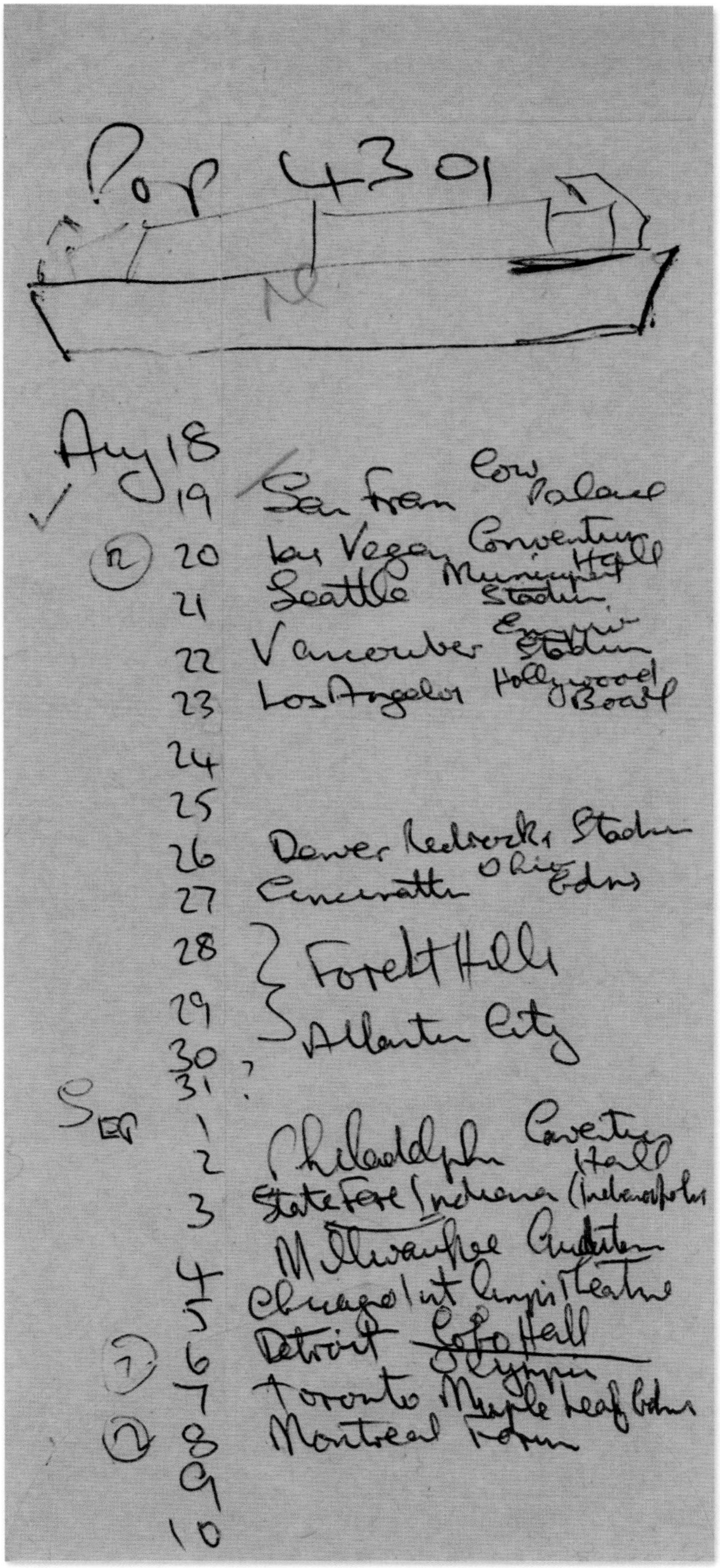
Pop 4301
Aug 18
19 San Fran Cow Palace
20 Las Vegas Convention Hall
21 Seattle Municipal Stadium
22 Vancouver Empire Stadium
23 Los Angeles Hollywood Bowl
24
25
26 Denver Red Rocks Stadium
27 Cincinnati Ohio Gdns
28 Forest Hills
29 Atlantic City
30
31
Sep 1
2 Philadelphia Convention Hall
3 State Fair Indiana (Indianapolis
Milwaukee Auditorium
4 Chicago Int Amphi Theatre
5 Detroit Olympia
6
7 Toronto Maple Leaf Gdns
8 Montreal Forum
9
10

11 Jacksonville Florida
12 Montgomery Alabama
13 Baltimore
14
15 Charlotte N. Carolina Municipal Stadium
16 New Orleans
17
18 Dallas Texas Trade Mart
19 Houston Texas
20 Palace
GREAT BRITAIN
POSTAGE
3d
LONDON
25MAR
1964
E.C.4.
THE INDEPENDENT NEWSPAPER
DAILY EXPRESS
7 Toronto
6 or 8 Montreal
9 Springfield Massachusetts
$2000
67

LEFT Screaming teenagers in San Francisco welcome the Beatles at the start of their American tour on 18 August 1964. Dozens of police stopped fans breaking through special barriers.

OPPOSITE ABOVE Police prevent fans from rushing on stage as the Beatles play at the Las Vegas Convention Hall on 20 August. Both shows that day were sold out.

OPPOSITE BELOW After this performance in the Seattle Centre Coliseum on 21 August, police helped by US sailors in the audience formed a human barrier so the Beatles could get to their dressing room.

band across the US and Canada, playing 32 shows in 24 cities in just 33 days.

Epstein had become manager of the Beatles after hearing them play at Liverpool's Cavern Club in 1961. The group had gone through a range of names (the Quarrymen, Johnny and the Moondogs, Silver Beetles) before settling on the Beatles. They played to small but growing audiences in their hometown of Liverpool and in Hamburg, Germany. John, Paul and George made up the original Beatles with drummer Pete Best. Ringo Starr replaced Best in 1962. Epstein first took the band to Decca Records, which turned them down. They then auditioned for Electrical and Musical Industries (EMI) and landed a recording contract. A year later they had a string of hits in Britain and were national heroes. Now Epstein wanted to make them an international phenomenon.

The Beatles arrived in the United States at a tumultuous time. President Kennedy had been assassinated nine months earlier, the Vietnam War was raging and summer race riots had shocked the nation. The Beatles offered an escape from these grim realities with their upbeat music, catchy lyrics and ability to connect with audiences in an unprecedented way. They played their first concert in San Francisco on 19 August 1964 surrounded by a sea of screaming fans. Nineteen girls fainted, 50 fans tried to invade the stage, and another 50 were injured in the crush. The group had to be taken back to their hotel in an ambulance after their limousine was besieged. In New York fans rioted, in Atlantic City the Beatles dodged frantic admirers by jumping into a seafood truck. The sold-out concerts earned the band more than one million dollars, beating records set by Frank Sinatra and Judy Garland. They got a congratulatory telegram from Elvis, and the great Bob Dylan gave his seal of approval: "Everybody else thought they were for the teenyboppers ... but it was obvious to me that they had staying power". There was criticism, particularly from the older generation, but that didn't bother the band. When informed that a noted psychiatrist had called them "a menace to society", George Harrison replied, "Psychiatrists are a menace, too."

The Beatles continued touring all over the world. However, by 1966 they'd had enough. John complained, "People aren't listening to the music." Paul dreaded waiting for the armoured car journey back to a guarded hotel room: "I sit there and say to myself, 'I really don't want to go through this any longer. We have the money. Let's take off for Brighton!'" The touring stopped and the band continued recording amid growing internal discord. Their eleventh and last album, *Abbey Road*, was released in September 1969. The group officially announced its break-up just months later. The Beatles were only together for nine years, but their music, which personified the transformational youth culture of the 1960s, continues to resonate with generation after generation.

THE
BEATLES

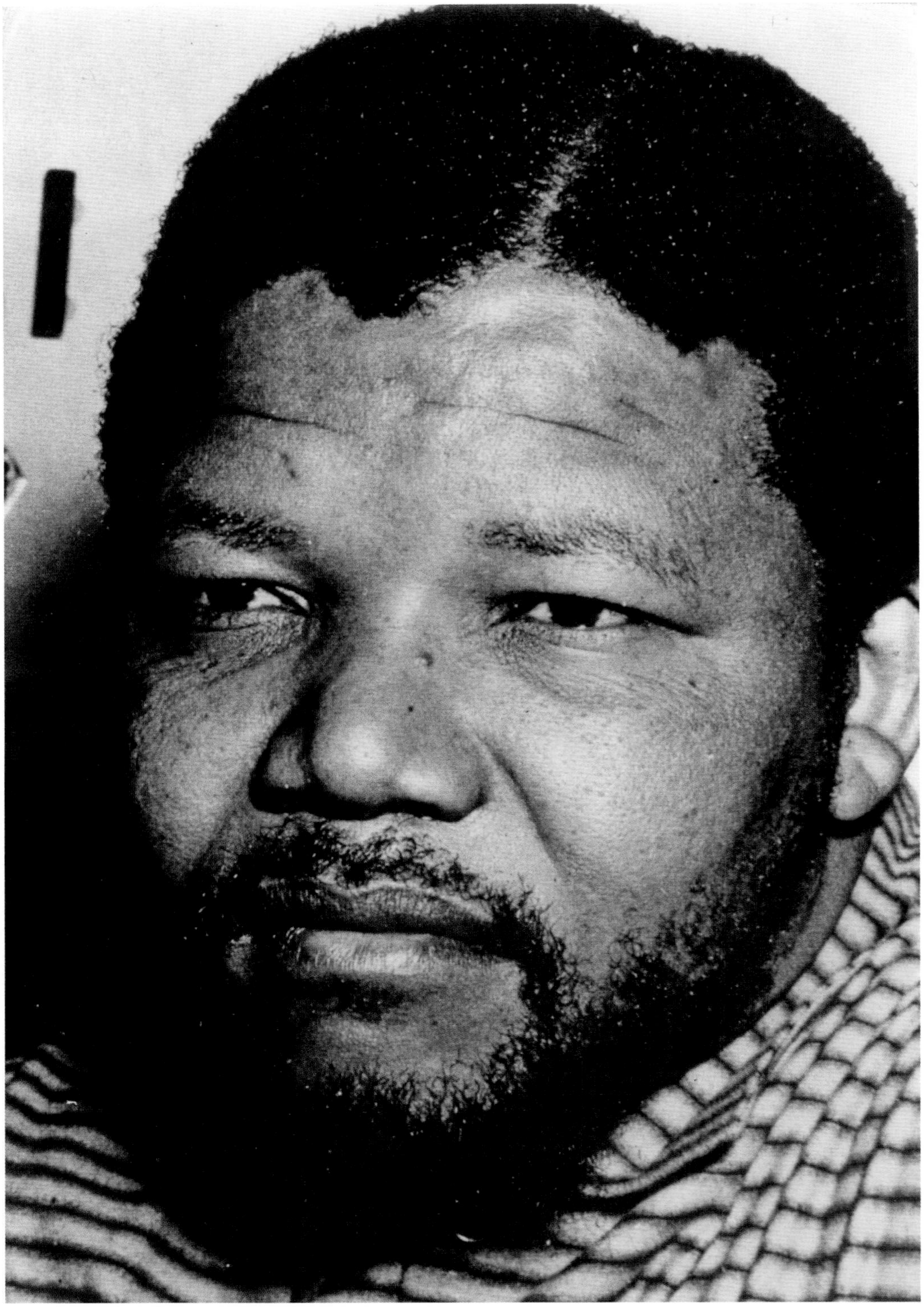

46

Nelson Mandela's Courtroom Speech

This is the final page of the statement Nelson Mandela, one of humanity's greatest heroes, read at his trial on 20 April 1964. Now known as the "I am prepared to die" speech, it was a pivotal moment in South African democracy. Mandela was found guilty of sabotage and sentenced to life imprisonment, but his courageous stand against apartheid resonated around the world and played a key part in its eventual collapse.

ABOVE Nelson Mandela in 1962, the year he was sentenced to five years in prison for leaving South Africa illegally and for inciting workers to strike. He was back in court in 1963-64.

OPPOSITE The final paragraph of Mandela's "I am prepared to die" speech. He added a handwritten message, his signature and the date to this copy, which he gave to a fellow political activist.

When 45-year-old Nelson Mandela rose to speak in a stately wood-panelled courtroom at Pretoria's Palace of Justice, he did not deny that he was guilty of acts of sabotage against the South African state. As he read slowly and deliberately from his 81-page statement, he eloquently explained why he had turned to violence: "I did not plan it in a spirit of recklessness, nor because I have any love of violence. I planned it as a result of a calm and sober assessment of the political situation that had arisen after many years of tyranny, exploitation, and oppression of my people by the Whites." A trained lawyer, Mandela made skilled use of the facts to put apartheid – South Africa's separation of different races – in the dock.

During my lifetime I have dedicated myself to this struggle of the African people. I have fought against White domination, and I have fought against Black domination. I have cherished the ideal of a democratic and free society in which all persons live together in harmony and with equal opportunities. It is an ideal which I hope to live for and to achieve. But if needs be, it is an ideal for which I am prepared to die.

The invincibility of our cause and the certainty of our final victory are the impenetrable armour of those who consistently uphold their faith in freedom and justice in spite of political persecution.

Amandla Ngawethu!

N Mandela April 1964

The trial started in October 1963, three months after security forces raided a farm in Rivonia, a suburb of Johannesburg. The farm had been used as a hideout by the military wing of the African National Congress (ANC), co-founded by Mandela, and police found a cache of weapons. At the time of the raid, Mandela was serving a five-year prison sentence for leaving South Africa without permission. He was ordered to stand trial with several men apprehended at the farm. All pleaded not guilty to 221 acts of sabotage designed to "ferment violent revolution". Mandela chose to make a statement rather than take the witness stand and he spent weeks working on his speech, receiving helpful advice from novelist Nadine Gordimer and British journalist Anthony Sampson. His lawyers urged him to leave out the last few words – "it is an ideal for which I am prepared to die" – fearing they might encourage the judge to impose the death penalty, but Mandela stood firm.

His statement to the court reflected half a century of struggle between the minority white government which ruled South Africa and the ANC, which opposed apartheid. Mandela spoke of the infamous shooting in the black township of Sharpeville on 21 March 1960, where 69 unarmed people were killed and 180 injured when police opened fire on a crowd demonstrating against pass laws which prevented freedom of movement. It was after Sharpeville, he said, that the South African government declared a state of emergency and banned the ANC: "the hard facts were that fifty years of non-violence had brought the African people nothing but more and more repressive legislation, and fewer and fewer rights." He admitted helping to set up the military arm of the ANC in autumn 1961 "because the Government had left us with no other choice". He acknowledged that he planned attacks on government buildings and other symbols of apartheid and that he gave advice on blowing up power plants and disrupting rail and telephone communications. He said he wanted to hurt the South African economy, "thus compelling the voters of the country to reconsider their position", but warned his foot soldiers, "on no

account were they to injure or kill people in planning or carrying out operations".

In his statement Mandela responded to prosecution charges that the Communist Party of South Africa had influenced the ANC by pointing out that the communists were the only political group "who were prepared to treat Africans as human beings and their equals; who were prepared to eat with us, talk with us, live with us, and work with us". But, in words clearly aimed at supporters abroad, he told the court that, unlike the communists, he was a great admirer of the parliamentary system: "The Magna Carta, the Petition of Rights, and the Bill of Rights are documents which are held in veneration by democrats throughout the world."

Mandela looked directly at the judge as he ended his statement with the words "I am prepared to die". The judge did not make eye contact again for the rest of the trial. He found all the men guilty but spared them the death penalty. Mandela was sentenced to life imprisonment and sent first to the notoriously brutal Robben Island off Cape Town.

The United Nations Security Council condemned the trial and led moves to impose sanctions on South Africa, but it took nearly three decades for the government to release Mandela. After he walked out of prison on 11 February 1990, he made a speech which ended with the famous last words from his 1964 trial statement.

When we visited Robben Island and were shown the tiny cell where Nelson Mandela spent so many years, we were inspired to reflect that his incarceration led to the dismantling of apartheid and to Mandela becoming president of South Africa. For us Mandela's experience and the racial harmony he and his government championed are testament to the power of the human spirit.

OPPOSITE Aftermath of the Sharpeville Massacre on 21 March 1960. Police opened fire on unarmed black protesters, killing 69 and injuring many more.

ABOVE The defiant fists of some of the eight men, Mandela among them, being transported from the Palace of Justice in Pretoria after being sentenced to life imprisonment on 12 June 1964.

47

Apollo 11 Mission Report

When we saw this entry in the Apollo 11 mission report which tracked the heart rate of the spacecraft's commander as he touched down, it reminded us of just how fast our hearts beat as we watched the first moon landing. On 20 July 1969, Neil Armstrong was one of two American astronauts who spent a day walking on the moon. No other single event in our lifetime has caught our imagination as spectacularly as this.

ABOVE Watched by more than a million spectators, Apollo 11's Saturn Five rocket is launched from Cape Kennedy, Florida, on 16 July 1969. Five days later, two of the three astronauts walked on the moon for the first time.

OPPOSITE ABOVE A readout of Neil Armstrong's heart rate as the lunar module landed on the moon. At the moment of touchdown, it reached 150 beats per minute.

OPPOSITE BELOW The three Apollo 11 astronauts: Mission Commander Neil Armstrong, Michael Collins and Buzz Aldrin. Collins remained in the command module as the other two landed on the moon's surface.

When the Soviets put the first man, Yuri Gagarin, into space in April 1961, they effectively dared the Americans to outdo them. We did not have to wait long. Only five weeks later, President Kennedy announced the ambitious goal, "before this decade is out, of landing a man on the moon and returning him safely to earth". Shortly before that pledge, the US National Aeronautics and Space Administration (NASA) sent Alan Shepard, the first US astronaut, into space. NASA then launched its Apollo moon programme, leaving the Russians lagging behind. The risks of space travel were tragically highlighted in 1967 when the first Apollo mission caught fire, killing its three astronauts. But NASA pressed on. By December 1968, Apollo 8 was tested in lunar orbit and five months later Apollo 10 staged a final trial of a lunar lander in orbit around the moon.

Apollo 11, the mission to land the first men on the moon, was set for July 1969. Three astronauts were chosen, all veterans of earlier missions: Neil Armstrong, commander; Buzz Aldrin, lunar module pilot; and Michael Collins, command module pilot. They named their lunar module "Eagle" and their command module "Columbia". Collins would orbit the moon in *Columbia* while Aldrin and Armstrong piloted *Eagle* to the surface for their moonwalk. The following day the moonwalkers would re-join Collins and return to Earth. Armstrong chose to take with him a fragment of one of the Wright brothers' propellers (see page 150) as a lucky keepsake.

At 04:00 on 16 July, the three astronauts awoke to the traditional pre-flight breakfast of steak and eggs. Armstrong was in his seat in the spacecraft by 07:00. Minutes later, he was joined by Aldrin and Collins in the tiny command module, perched on top of the Saturn V rocket

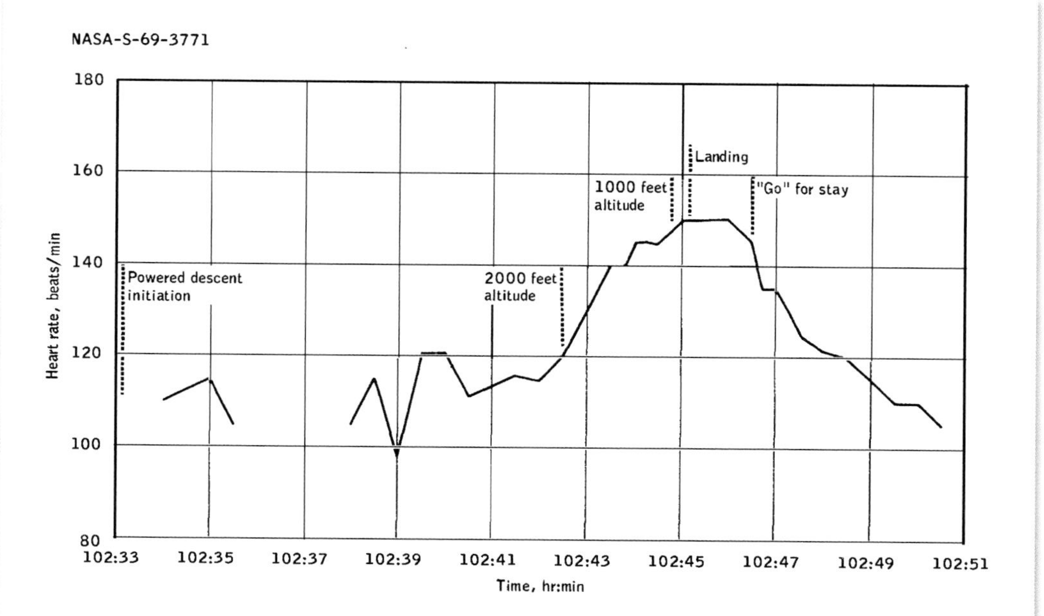

Figure 12-1.- Heart rates of the Commander during lunar descent.

more than 110 metres (360 feet) above the ground.

Just after 09:30, tens of millions of viewers in 33 countries heard these words from Cape Kennedy: "T minus 15 seconds. Guidance is internal. 12, 11, 10, 9. Ignition sequence starts. 6, 5, 4, 3, 2, 1, 0. All engines running. Lift-off. We have a lift-off, 32 minutes past the hour, lift-off on Apollo 11."

Twelve minutes later, the spacecraft was in earth orbit, and after 90 minutes Saturn's third-stage rocket pushed it into the correct trajectory for the moon. Three days later, right on target, it passed behind the moon and into lunar orbit. Aldrin and Armstrong climbed into the tiny lunar module and embarked on the most dangerous part of the mission – to land on the moon's Sea of Tranquillity, dodging any boulders and craters. They overshot their intended landing zone and Armstrong warned Aldrin to avoid a crater which they suddenly saw. Fuel was perilously low, so they had to land. They approached a flat spot and threw up a great cloud of dust. It is hardly surprising that Armstrong's heart was beating at such a rate at this moment. He was supposed to shut down the engine immediately in order

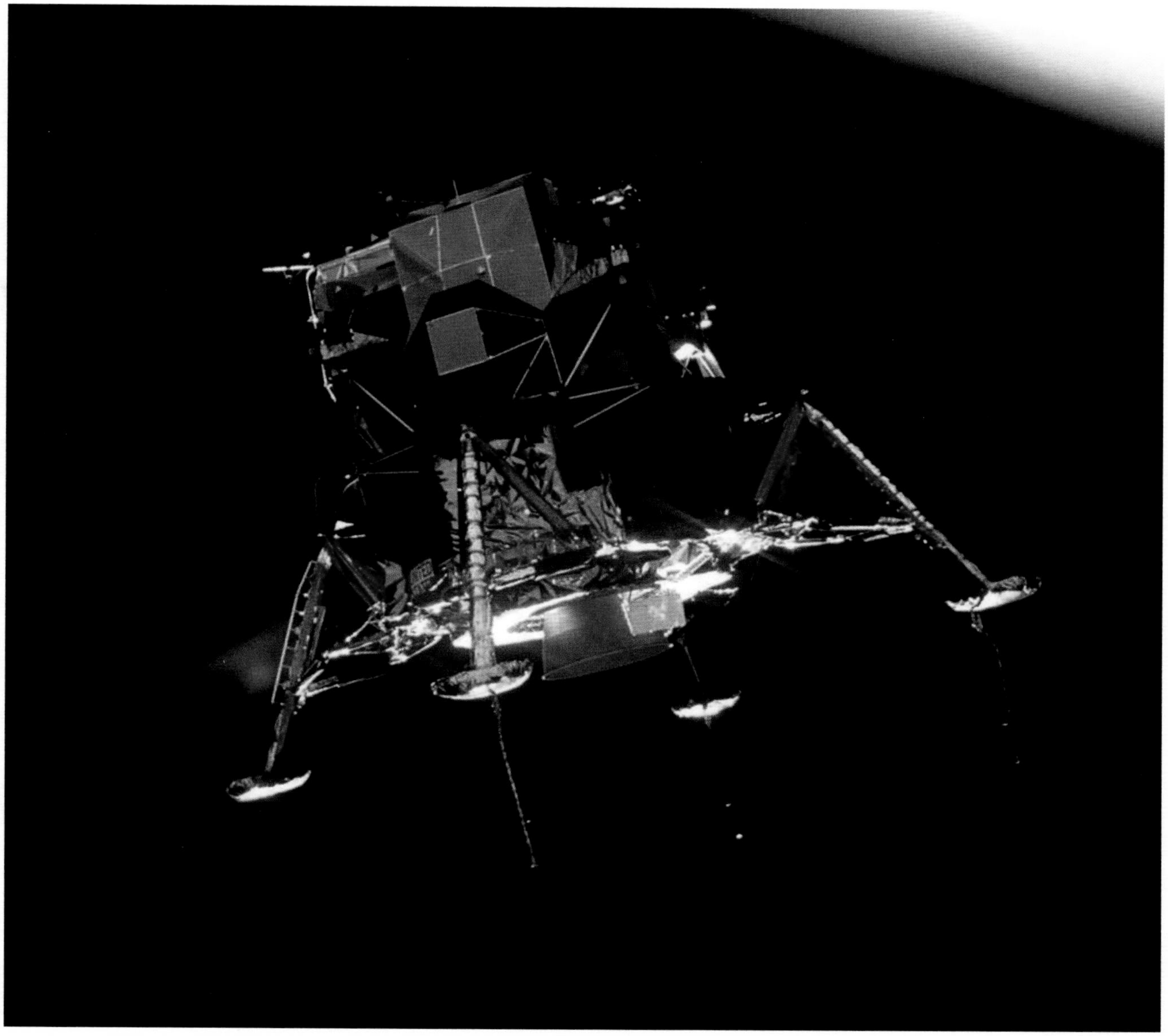

OPPOSITE Buzz Aldrin walks on the moon. In a chat with Armstrong he described the scenery as "magnificent desolation".

RIGHT The Lunar lander Eagle *preparing to descend to the surface of the moon. The thin, rod-like protrusions just visible under the landing pods are sensing probes to alert the crew to shut down the descent engine on touchdown.*

to avoid blowback from the exhaust, which could destroy the module, but he forgot. Seconds later, sure that *Eagle* was safely on the ground, he said, "OK. Engine stop." The descent stage's rocket would have run out of fuel less than a minute later.

At 16:17 on Sunday 20 July, the words rang out: "Houston, Tranquillity Base. The *Eagle* has landed." There was a huge sigh of relief from 450 console operators on the ground. "We're breathing again," said Mission Control. Too excited to sleep as planned, the astronauts emerged from their craft early. First came Armstrong and his unforgettable quote: "That's one small step for [a] man, one giant leap for mankind." People still debate whether he left out the "a".

The men spent two hours walking on the moon, talking to President Nixon and trying to push a US flagstaff into the surface. They only managed to force it in 5 centimetres (2 inches). They packed 21.5 kilograms (47.4 pounds) of moon surface material, including small rocks, into two boxes, left a plaque saying they had come "in peace for all mankind", and then climbed back into the module. As they lifted off using the separate rocket engine on their ascent stage after just twenty-two and a half hours on the moon, Armstrong said he saw the flag "fall over" in the exhaust blast.

From then on everything went like clockwork. They docked with the command module, jettisoned the lunar lander and set course for home. At dawn on 24 July, they splashed down in the Pacific Ocean 21 kilometres (13 miles) from the aircraft carrier *Hornet*, where President Nixon, security adviser Henry Kissinger and secretary of state William Rodgers awaited with congratulations. After three weeks' confinement being tested for possible contamination, the three astronauts were treated to a triumphant ticker-tape parade in New York.

Apollo 11 was an astonishing success for the United States and for the three brave men on board. At the time of writing, half a century after that mesmerizing flight, humans have still not landed on any other celestial body.

48

Woodstock Tickets

The Woodstock Festival occupies a well-deserved top spot in the history of pop culture. The "three days of peace and music" in August 1969 featured a kaleidoscope of well-known and up-and-coming performers ranging from Joan Baez to Jimi Hendrix. It was the world's most celebrated open-air musical event and became the symbol of an entire generation.

Afro-American folksinger Richie Havens walked on stage as the opening act of the Woodstock Festival just after 5 p.m. on Friday 15 August 1969. He was ill-prepared. He'd been booked to perform four songs much later that night but the headline groups which were supposed to be top of the bill had not yet arrived. They'd been held up by the traffic jams that became synonymous with Woodstock. Havens found himself performing for three solid hours: "I'd already played every song I knew and I was stalling, trying to think of something else to play." The song that came to him was "Freedom". He made up the words as he played his guitar, and this improvised encore made him a household name.

When organizers decided to hold a three-day summer music festival in upstate New York, they could not have imagined what they were getting into. Several towns turned down the festival – one because of the unacceptably large number of planned portable toilets. Just a month before the event, dairy farmer Max Yasgur finally agreed to rent the project some fields on his land near White Lake in Bethel, New York. More than 100,000 tickets were sold in advance, but a flurry of last-minute preparations meant there was not enough time to build ticket booths or put up proper enclosures. As more than 400,000 people descended on the venue and walked in through gaps in the fences, organizers were forced to make Woodstock a free event. Hippies, anti-Vietnam War protesters, civil rights activists and plain old music lovers came together to enjoy what promised to be a long weekend of sensational "sex, drugs and rock and roll".

The line-up of 32 acts was as varied as it was awe-inspiring: Janis Joplin, the Grateful Dead, Joan Baez, Ravi Shankar, Jefferson Airplane, Crosby, Stills, Nash and Young. It rained, but no one cared. "Make love not war" was the overriding theme. Peace and unity reigned supreme.

Logistical challenges were immense. Roads within an 8-kilometre (5-mile) radius of the area were so packed with cars that traffic came to a standstill. Frustrated concertgoers abandoned their vehicles and walked to the venue. Performers had to be airlifted in. Greg Rolie, keyboard-playing vocalist of Santana (which rose to fame at Woodstock), recalled: "We flew in and it was kind of like the film *Field of Dreams*, you know? 'If you build it, they will come'." Volunteer doctors and nurses dealt with minor injuries and food poisoning as well as tending to the many wounds on bare feet. Only a dozen police officers were on duty at the festival, but not a single incident of violence was reported. When Max Yasgur, the farmer who helped make Woodstock happen, addressed the crowd, he said: "Half a million young people can get together and have three days of fun ... if these kids are going to inherit the world, I don't fear for it."

The last act of the festival was delayed because of rain, so Jimi Hendrix's band Gypsy Sun and the Rainbows did not appear until 9 a.m. on Monday 18 August. Most people had gone home, but those who heard the performance never forgot it. Hendrix played for two hours non-stop, one of the longest performances of his career. He ended with a medley which included a chaotic version of the American national anthem. Hendrix's distorted solo guitar chords mimicked the "rockets" and "bombs" of the lyrics of "The Star Spangled Banner" (see page 108). His boldly irreverent treatment of a sacred song became a symbol of the age.

The importance of Woodstock was not immediately evident. After making it a free event, the organizers nearly went bankrupt. It was only when money from film and recording rights started pouring in that they made a profit. Even performers like Santana's Greg Rolie did not recognize its significance: "At the time we

OPPOSITE Tickets for each of the three days of Woodstock. They are now collectors' items and sell for many times their original $8 price.

BELOW Organizers expected 200,000 people to attend the three-day festival on this farm in upstate New York. More than double that number turned up.

thought of it as just another gig. It turned out to be the mother of them all."

Woodstock is now regarded as a defining moment in modern musical history. In the words of Joni Mitchell (who regretted turning down her invitation to perform at the festival and later wrote a song about it): "Woodstock was a spark of beauty" where half a million kids "saw they were part of the greater organism".

Today, Bethal Woods Center for the Arts stands on the hill where the Woodstock Festival happened, and outdoor concerts featuring music of all kinds take place in its stunning, shell-shaped pavilion.

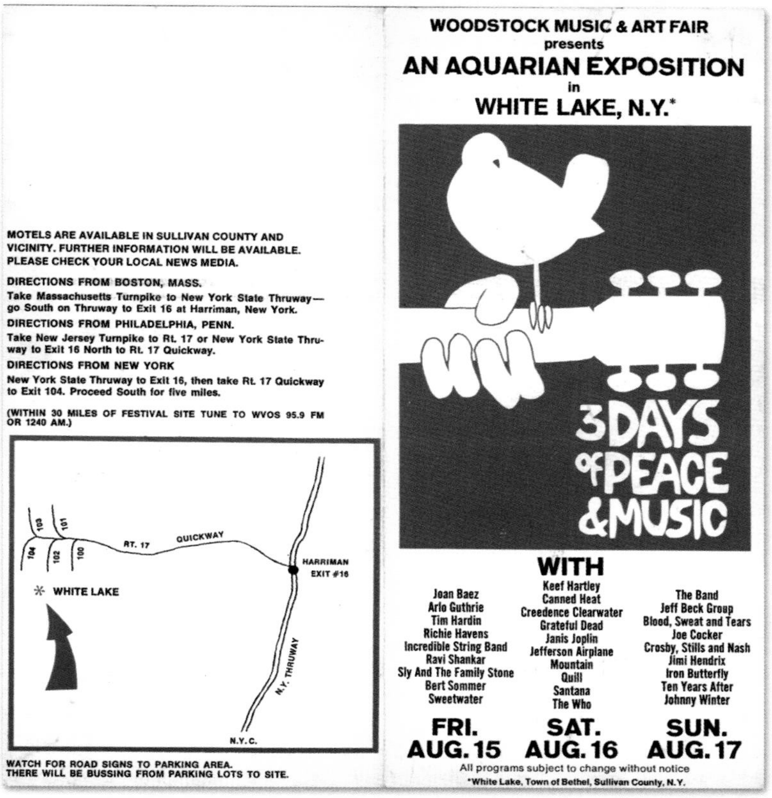
MOTELS ARE AVAILABLE IN SULLIVAN COUNTY AND VICINITY. FURTHER INFORMATION WILL BE AVAILABLE. PLEASE CHECK YOUR LOCAL NEWS MEDIA.

DIRECTIONS FROM BOSTON, MASS.
Take Massachusetts Turnpike to New York State Thruway—go South on Thruway to Exit 16 at Harriman, New York.

DIRECTIONS FROM PHILADELPHIA, PENN.
Take New Jersey Turnpike to Rt. 17 or New York State Thruway to Exit 16 North to Rt. 17 Quickway.

DIRECTIONS FROM NEW YORK
New York State Thruway to Exit 16, then take Rt. 17 Quickway to Exit 104. Proceed South for five miles.

(WITHIN 30 MILES OF FESTIVAL SITE TUNE TO WVOS 95.9 FM OR 1240 AM.)

WATCH FOR ROAD SIGNS TO PARKING AREA.
THERE WILL BE BUSSING FROM PARKING LOTS TO SITE.

WOODSTOCK MUSIC & ART FAIR
presents
AN AQUARIAN EXPOSITION
in
WHITE LAKE, N.Y.*

3 DAYS of PEACE & MUSIC

WITH

Joan Baez
Arlo Guthrie
Tim Hardin
Richie Havens
Incredible String Band
Ravi Shankar
Sly And The Family Stone
Bert Sommer
Sweetwater

FRI. AUG. 15

Keef Hartley
Canned Heat
Creedence Clearwater
Grateful Dead
Janis Joplin
Jefferson Airplane
Mountain
Quill
Santana
The Who

SAT. AUG. 16

The Band
Jeff Beck Group
Blood, Sweat and Tears
Joe Cocker
Crosby, Stills and Nash
Jimi Hendrix
Iron Butterfly
Ten Years After
Johnny Winter

SUN. AUG. 17

All programs subject to change without notice

*White Lake, Town of Bethel, Sullivan County, N.Y.

OPPOSITE Jimi Hendrix closing the Woodstock Festival on Monday morning, 19 August 1969. He was supposed to perform the night before, but rain and technical delays meant his show-closing performance was delayed.

LEFT Woodstock Concert Brochure. The front lists the performers. Its back offers accommodation information and travel directions.

BELOW Early arrivals managed to drive into the festival. By Woodstock's second day, authorities advised motorists to go home as roads around the venue were gridlocked.

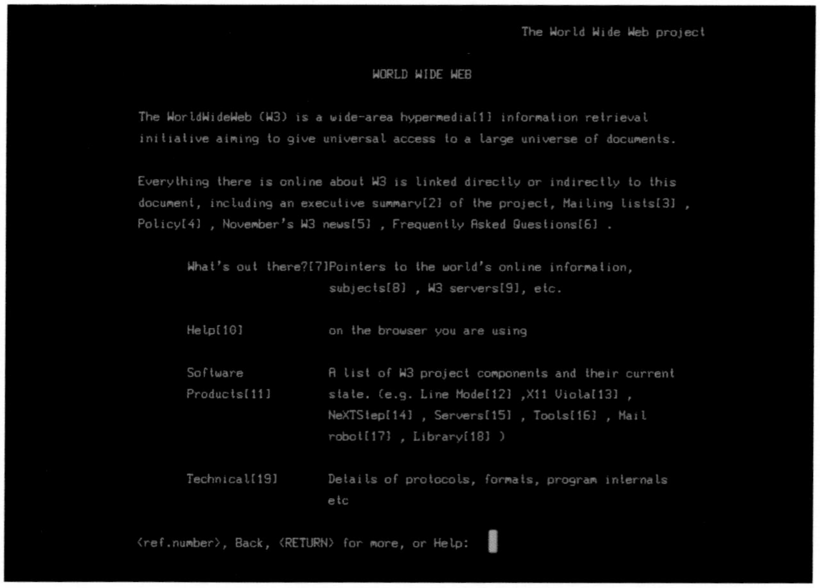

49

Tim Berners-Lee's World Wide Web Memo

Tim Berners-Lee's 1989 memo about information management was designed to help scientists share information. His World Wide Web has changed the world. Today more than half the population use the Web to browse, buy and blog, but, much to its founder's dismay, the Web has also become a vehicle for hatred, scams and surveillance.

ABOVE A screenshot of the world's first web page with instructions on how to use a browser, set up a web server and build a website. It went public in August 1991.

OPPOSITE Tim Berners-Lee's original proposal for what became the World Wide Web. The words "Vague but exciting" at the top of the document were written by Berners-Lee's boss, who advised him to spend more time on it.

Tim Berners-Lee's genius was obvious from an early age. He had a model railway in his bedroom at the family home in London, England, where he delighted in making electronic gadgets to control the trains. He admits: "I ended up getting more interested in electronics than in trains." Later on, while studying physics at Oxford University, he made a computer out of an old television set.

In the 1980s, Berners-Lee put his skills to use as a software engineer at CERN, the European Organization for Nuclear Research in Switzerland. He was struck by how difficult it was for the many scientists associated with the centre to share information about experiments and research. Material was stored on different computers and, to retrieve it, users had to log on and sometimes master a different program on each computer. He recalls: "Often it was just easier to go and ask people when they were having coffee."

Berners-Lee set out to create a system which could share data on a relatively unknown platform called "the internet", through which computers could communicate with each other. The internet was developed by the US Department of Defence in the late 1960s as a communication network which could survive a Cold War nuclear attack. Exchanging information on it, particularly documents, was difficult and time-consuming. Berners-Lee realized that by harnessing another emerging technology called hypertext, which linked related pieces of information, he could use the internet to share data. In March 1989, he laid out his vision of an easy-to-use global information system in the now famous document, "Information Management: A Proposal", but it was not immediately accepted. His boss wrote "Vague but exciting" on the cover. Undaunted, Berners-Lee persisted. Working on a NeXT computer, an early product of Apple co-founder Steve Jobs, he wrote the three building blocks of the World Wide Web: HyperText Markup Language (HTML), which formats and displays documents on the Web; Uniform Resource Identifier (URI – commonly called URL), a unique address identifying the name and location of a file; and Hypertext Transfer Protocol (the familiar "http" on web addresses), which allows the retrieval of data. Berners-Lee also designed and built the world's first web browser ("Worldwideweb.app") and its first web server ("httpd"). He published his epoch-making website on 20 December 1990.

At first the Web was limited to users at CERN and other research institutions, but in August 1991 members of the public were invited to join free of charge. Access to a free browser on a home computer made the internet easily accessible for the first time; however, the ground-breaking website was not a hit at first.

Vague but exciting ...

CERN DD/OC

Information Management: A Proposal

Tim Berners-Lee, CERN/DD

March 1989

Information Management: A Proposal

Abstract

This proposal concerns the management of general information about accelerators and experiments at CERN. It discusses the problems of loss of information about complex evolving systems and derives a solution based on a distributed hypertext sytstem.

Keywords: Hypertext, Computer conferencing, Document retrieval, Information management, Project control

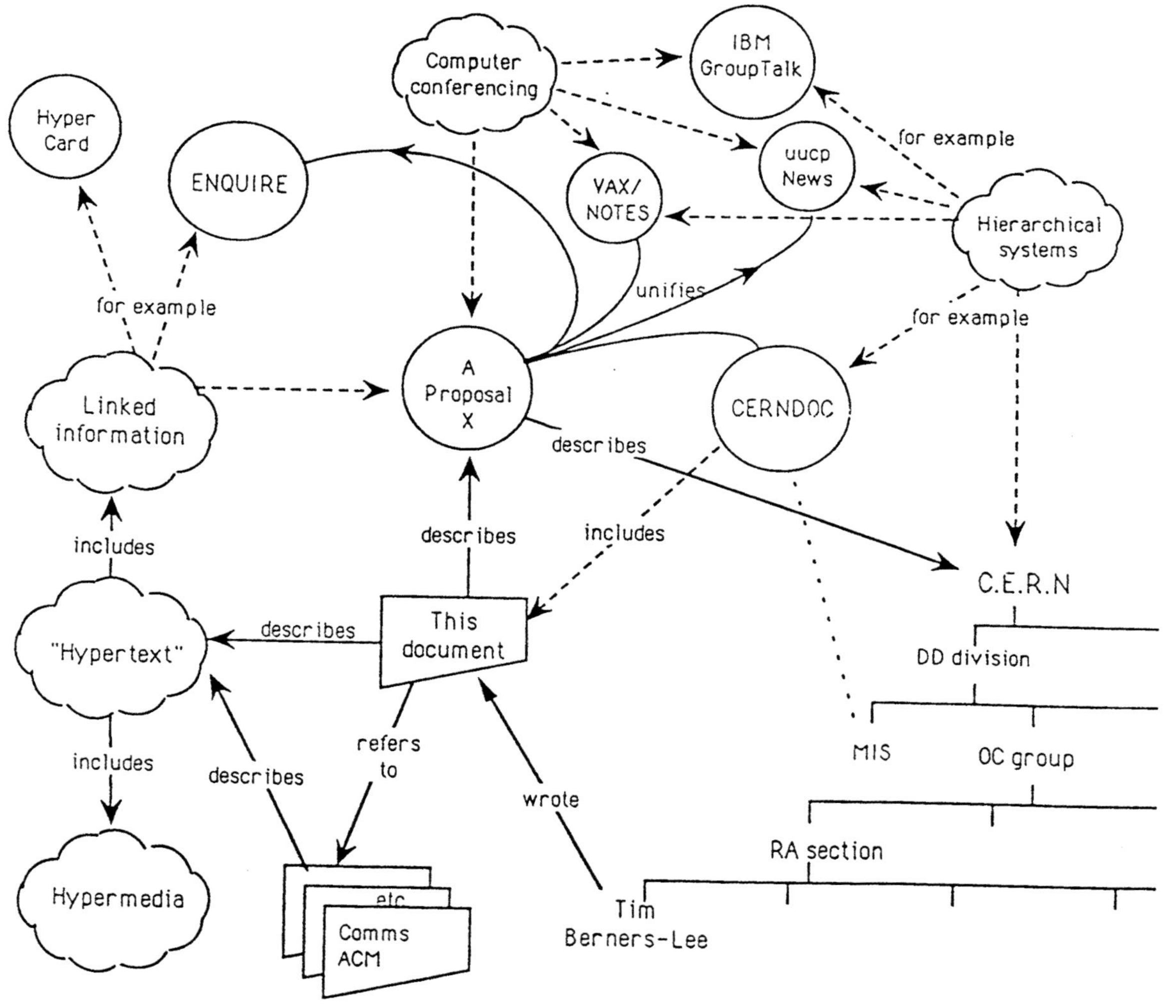

By 1993, there were only 130 sites connected to the Web. Two years later there were 23,500. By the year 2000, that number had jumped to 17 million and at the time of writing there are around two billion websites.

When he invented the Web, Berners-Lee predicted that it would radically transform the world in which we live, but he also worried about it becoming a disruptive force. He was right on both counts. The Web has changed the way we communicate, shop, learn and play, but it has also, in the words of its founder, "created opportunity for scammers, given a voice to those who spread hatred and made all kinds of crime easier to commit". Hate speech, the misuse of personal data and state-sponsored hackers are now part of Web life. And Berners-Lee's dream of a free Web open to everyone is threatened by tech giants like Google, Facebook and Twitter.

On the thirtieth anniversary of his invention, Berners-Lee acknowledged that "many people feel afraid and unsure if the Web is really a force for good". His World Wide Web foundation is developing new standards and guidelines aimed at stemming the abuse. Governments, companies and citizens are being urged to take a more proactive role in shaping a new "good Web". For its creator, "the fight for the Web is one of the most important causes of our time ... It won't be easy. But if we dream a little and work a lot, we can get the Web we want."

Berners-Lee has not gained financially from the Web, but he has been widely honoured. He received a knighthood from Britain's Queen Elizabeth and has modestly taken his place as one of the most significant inventors of the modern era. For us, no living person has shaped our lives more than the extraordinary Sir Tim Berners-Lee.

OPPOSITE Tim Berners-Lee. He is now dedicated to enhancing and protecting the World Wide Web's future.

ABOVE The world's first World Wide Web server on display at CERN visitors' centre near Geneva. The handwritten warning in red reads: "DO NOT POWER IT DOWN!!"

50

The Map of the Universe

This twenty-first-century map of the "Nearby Universe" shows the pattern of galaxies – each one a dot – within distance of Earth's own galaxy the Milky Way. It demonstrates the extraordinary size and complexity of the universe. Created by a team of astronomers from the USA, France and Israel, the colour of each galaxy denotes its distance from Earth – blue the closest, red the furthest away.

OPPOSITE ABOVE "The Map of the Universe". The dark shadow in the centre is our Milky Way galaxy, through which astronomers can see billions of other galaxies - each one a dot. The nearest are blue, the more distant red. The black dot circled top left is Andromeda, the galaxy closest to ours.

OPPOSITE BELOW Andromeda, our next-door galaxy, is visible to the naked eye but it is still an astonishing 2.5 million light years from Earth – that's 2.5 million x 10 trillion kilometres (2.5m x 6 trillion miles) away! Andromeda consists of around a trillion stars.

The scale of the universe is beyond comprehension, but this astonishing map is a useful stepping stone towards making sense of it. The astronomers who produced the map in 2013 presented it as a 3D video model. It describes only a tiny fragment of the whole universe, which contains hundreds of billions of galaxies and would need a map 160 times larger than this one.

This nearby universe of ours is gigantic enough. Distance in space is measured in light years. A light year is the distance light travels in a year – at its speed of neaarly 300,000 kilometres (186,000 miles) a second. Light from our sun, 150 million kilometres (93 million miles) from Earth, takes only eight minutes to reach us. So a light year is about 10 trillion kilometres (6 trillion miles). The sun and planets in our solar system are just a minute part of our Milky Way galaxy. The sun is our nearest star. Next comes Proxima Centauri, over 4 light years, 40 trillion kilometres (25 trillion miles) away. This map shows all the galaxies that are within 300 million light years of us. So the distance between us on Earth and each of these little coloured blobs – each one a galaxy – is unimaginably great. The nearest galaxy to our Milky Way is Andromeda. You can just spot it through binoculars on a clear night. It is a black dot circled on the extreme left of the map, and is 2.5 million light years away.

The man who brilliantly opened up the vast cosmos outside our own galaxy was Edwin Hubble, an American astronomer. In 1919 he took up a post at Mount Wilson Observatory in California, which owned the world's largest telescope at the time – the Hooker. It had a large reflective mirror 2.5 metres (8.2 feet) in diameter. Hubble established that the universe was expanding and that distant galaxies are moving away from us at breakneck speed. His discoveries helped later astronomers to build a more complete picture. One discovery is that our near neighbour Andromeda is actually moving towards us. The mutual gravity of Andromeda and the Milky Way is outdoing the expanding flow of much of the rest of the universe, meaning that our galaxy will collide with the Andromeda galaxy in four or five billion years' time!

It is now believed that the universe began with a great burst of energy – the Big Bang – 13.8 billion years ago. There are numerous versions of the theory, but perhaps the most widely accepted among astronomers is called "inflation". It argues that time, space and matter were created in two phases: a very brief period of "cold" expansion, when our universe grew from a singularity to about the size of a basketball at a rate much faster than the speed of light, followed by a "hot" Big Bang, when all the fundamental particles of the visible universe were created, along with mysterious dark matter and dark energy that comprise 95 per cent of the cosmos. Tiny quantum fluctuations prior to inflation caused a slight clumping of matter,

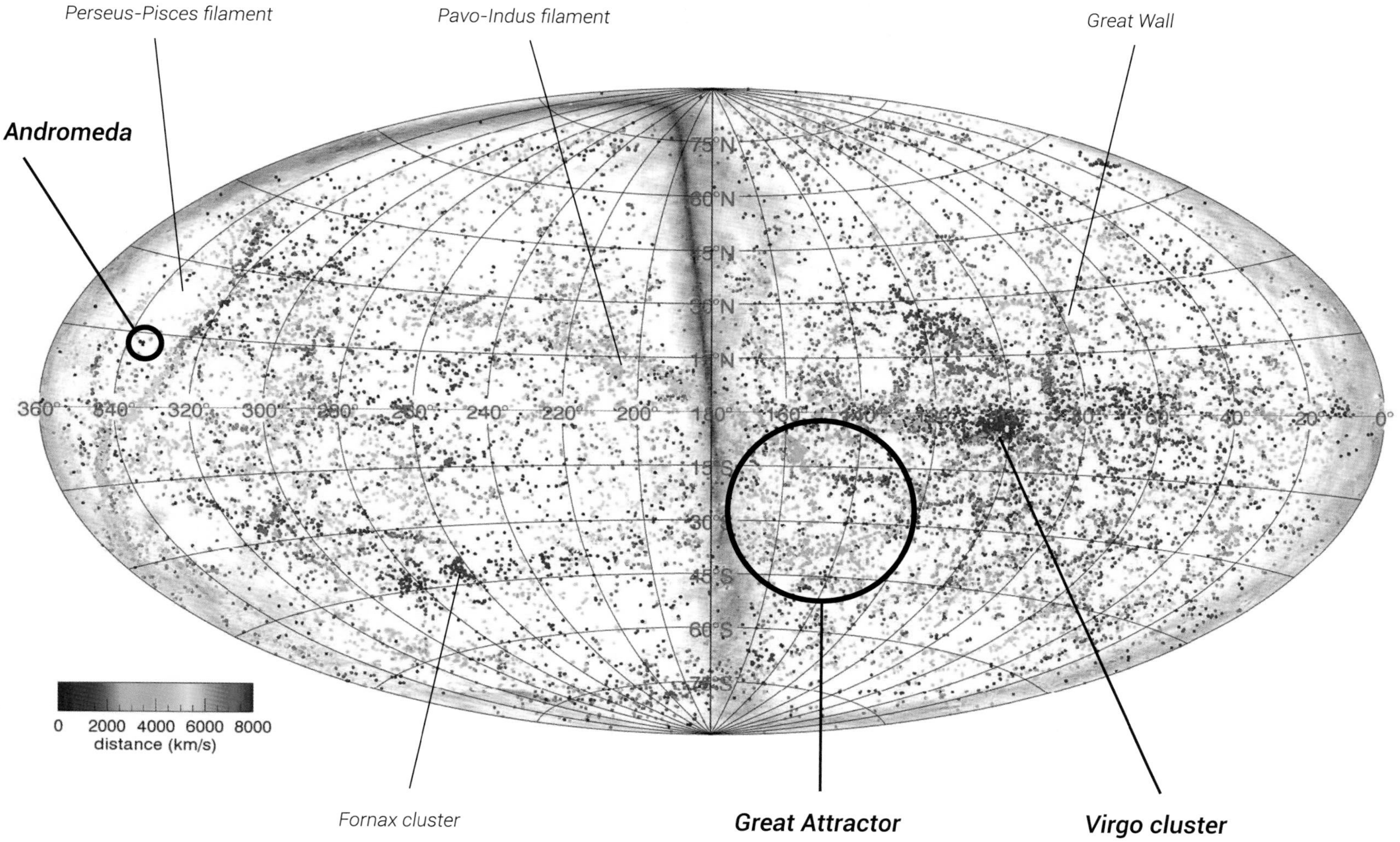
Perseus-Pisces filament
Pavo-Indus filament
Great Wall
Andromeda
Fornax cluster
Great Attractor
Virgo cluster
0 2000 4000 6000 8000
distance (km/s)

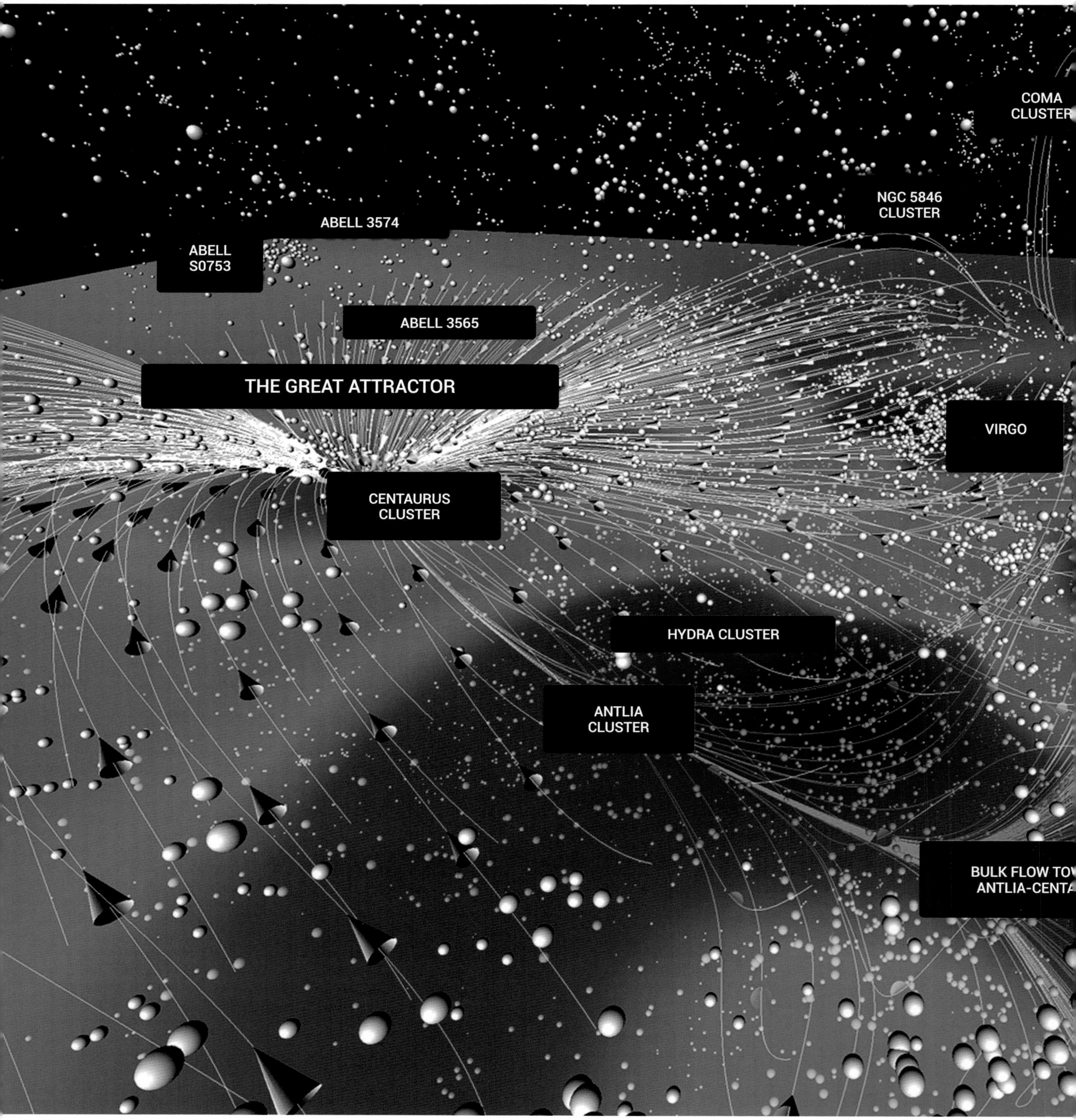
COMA CLUSTER
NGC 5846 CLUSTER
ABELL 3574
ABELL S0753
ABELL 3565
THE GREAT ATTRACTOR
VIRGO
CENTAURUS CLUSTER
HYDRA CLUSTER
ANTLIA CLUSTER
BULK FLOW TO
ANTLIA-CENTA

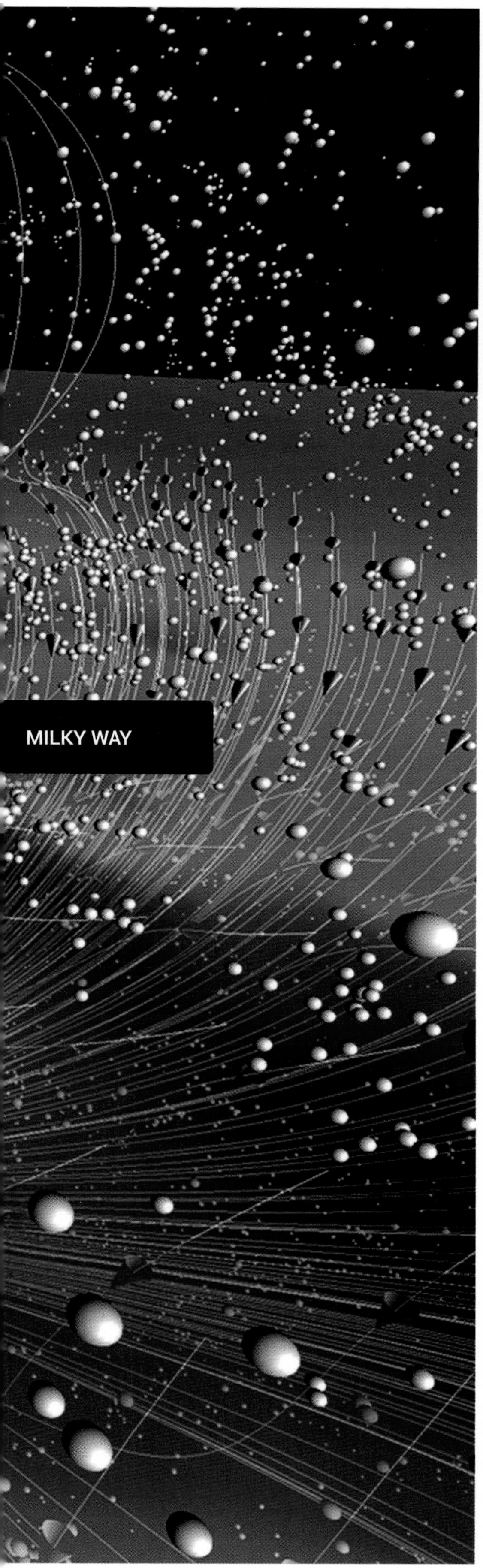

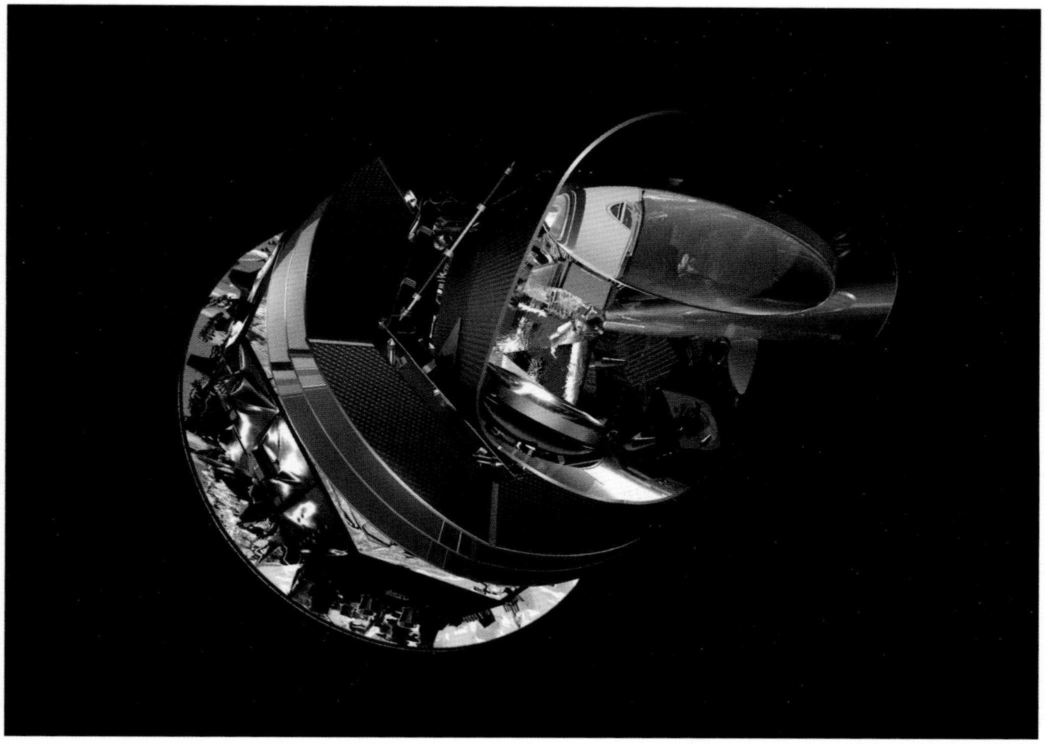

sowing the seeds for the stars, planets and galaxies we see in otherwise uniform space. The universe has been cooling and expanding ever since. One striking cluster of galaxies – coloured blue to the centre right of the map, is known as the Virgo cluster. It's the nearest cluster to us but still a mind-blowing 50 million light years away. The Great Attractor cluster – further away – is sucking in many of its neighbours.

Our knowledge is growing rapidly as telescopes improve. The larger the mirror, the more powerful the telescope. Interestingly, the type of astronomy that allows scientists to map the universe these days comes not from looking through a telescope with the naked eye, but by examining the data derived from a telescope's digital sensing technology. The 1960s American invention of the charge-coupled device (CCD) allows telescopes to probe far further into space than ever before. This remarkable breakthrough will take a new dramatic leap forward with the so-called Extremely Large Telescope – the ELT – being built at Cerro Amazonas in Chile. It will have a reflective mirror 39 metres (128 feet) in diameter, almost half the length of a football pitch.

Hubble's Hooker 2.5-metre (8.2-foot) mirror will be left far behind, but the great astronomer has been immortalized by the space telescope that bears his name. The Hubble telescope provides far clearer images than ground-based observatories, but it in turn will be outdone by the new James Webb space telescope that NASA will launch in 2021. This super-telescope will be stationed one million miles from Earth and promises to add massively to our knowledge of the universe.

The more we learn, the more astronomers are convinced that there is life somewhere out there. Tom Kerss of London's Greenwich Observatory told us: "Across all the galaxies there should be more potentially habitable planets than every heart beat in every human being that has ever lived."

LEFT A closer map of the near universe. Galaxies are white spheres. Virgo is the nearest cluster of galaxies to our Milky Way. The red and yellow Great Attractor is sucking in galaxies from the dark blue voids.

ABOVE The Planck space telescope launched by the European Space Agency in 2009. It has provided a mass of new detail about the scope and nature of the universe.

Index

Credits

The publishers would like to thank the following sources for their kind permission to reproduce the pictures in this book.

AKG-Images: 158, 183; /Album/Oronoz 69; /Bible Land Pictures 42, 43; /Liszt Collection 28; /North Wind Picture Archives 108

Alamy: 182; /Art Collection 22; /Ancient Art & Architecture 57; /Art Collection 73; / Chronicle 21, 142; /Granger Historical Picture Archive 96, 174b, 174t; /George Grassie/ Zuma Press 217; /Peter Horree 54; /Interfoto 194; /JV Photo: 23; /Erich Lessing 65; / The Picture Art Collection 32-33; /Scienicireland.com/Christopher Hill Photographic 58; /Tracksimages.com 199; /Fabrizio Troiani 46-47; /World History Archive 140

Alexander Turnbull Library, Wellington, New Zealand: 146-147

Archives New Zealand: 145

Australian War Memorial: 154, 155

Bridgeman Images: 12, 24-25, 36-37, 38t, 38b, 49, 64l, 67, 75b; /Archives Charmet 86; /Artothek 104; /Photo © Boltin Picture Library 18; /© British Library Board. All Rights Reserved 62-63, 81, 101, 103; /Brooklyn Museum Libraries, Special Collections 168; / Harry Burton/Hulton Archive 19; / Photo © Christie's Images 78r, 115; /Culture Club 77; /G. Dagli Orti /De Agostini Picture Library 13, 68t, 68bl, 68r, 100, 107; /De Agostini Picture Library 75b; /Godong 27b; /Granger 26, 61br, 76t; /Photo © GraphicaArtis 110; /Lebrecht Authors 33, 105, 106; /© Look and Learn 86; /PHAS/UIG 31; /Peter Newark American Pictures 111; /Pictures from History 35; /Luisa Ricciarini 17; /Tarker 102; /Universal History Archive/UIG 72

© British Library Board. All Rights Reserved: 82r, 141t, 141b

© Cern 214, 215

ESA/NASA: 221

Adam Evans via Wikimedia Commons: 219b

French National Archives: 97

Getty Images: 27t; /AFP 205; /Anne Frank Foundation, Basel 7, 171t, 172; / Anne Frank House, Amsterdam 171b; /Art Media/Print Collector 16, 40-41; /Bettmann 128, 162, 169; /Blank Archives 210, 213t; /Ron Bull/Toronto Star 139b; /Christophel Fine Art/Universal Images Group 86-87; /Condé Nast 166; /Corbis 165; /Culture Club 77; /Henry Diltz 212; /Daily Mirror/Mirrorpix 198; /DeAgostini 44, 88-89; /Peter Dejong/AP 173b; /John Dominis/The LIFE Picture Collection 213b; /Elliot & Fry/Royal Geographical Society 143; /Express 201t; /Christopher Furlong 82l; /Granger 74, 174t; /The Hebrew University of Jerusalem 159; /Heinrich Hoffmann/ullstein bild 179t, 179c; /Hulton Archive 39, 164; /Imagno 76c; /ITAR-TASS/Mark Redkin 184-185; /Keystone 179b, 204; /Keystone-France/Gamma-Keystone 120, 196; /Leemage/Corbis 98-99; /Barry Z. Levine 211; / William Lovelace/Express 201b; /Mansell/Mansell/The LIFE Picture Collection 50-51; / Thomas D. Mcavoy/The LIFE Picture Collection 188; /John D McHugh/AFP 83b; /Gjn Mili/The LIFE Picture Collection 186; /MPI 174; /Michael Nicholson/Corbis 122; /Werner Otto/ullstein bild 84t; /Popperfoto via Getty Images 127; /Rolls Press/Popperfoto 200; / Roger Viollet 167; /Uriel Sinai 45; /SSPL 131, 151b, 193; /Mario Tama 129; /Bob Thomas/ Popperfoto via Getty Images 126; /Ullstein bild/ullstein bild 79, 122-123; /Universal History Archive 30, 115, 130; / Eric Vandeville/Gamma-Rapho 195

SS Great Britain Trust: 116, 117, 119

Library of Congress: 133, 134, 135, 150, 151t, 152-153, 154

Maryland Historical Society: 109

Museum of London: 144

NASA: 148-149, 206, 207, 208, 209

National Archives, Kew: 61l

National Football Museum: 124t, 125

Nelson Mandela Foundation: 203

Parliamentary Archives: 137, 138

Private Collection: 34-35t, 53, 59, 60, 70-71, 156, 157, 160, 161, 178-179

Public Domain: 90l, 90r, 91, 92, 93, 94-95, 118, 121, 132, 176, 177, 178-179

Carole Raddato: 48

Service historique de la Défense, départment de L'Armee de Terre, Paris: 113

Shanghai Museum: 20

Science Photo Library: A.Barrington Brown. © Gonvillle & Caius College 190; /Sam Ogden 216

Shutterstock: 8; /Shevchenko Andrey: 78l; /Lance Bellers 83t; /The FA 125b; /Gianni Dagli Orti 10-11; /Design Pics Inc 99t; /Global Warming Images 56t; /Granger 29, 76t, 84b; / Kharbine-Tapabor 14; /James Kirkikis 61r; /SIPA 202; /Benjamin C. Tankersley/For The Washington Post 80; /Universal History Archive 30, 66, 99b,170

Topfoto: 139t

Courtois, Tully, et al: 219t, 220-221

United Nations: 187, 189

Wellcome Library: 191, 192r

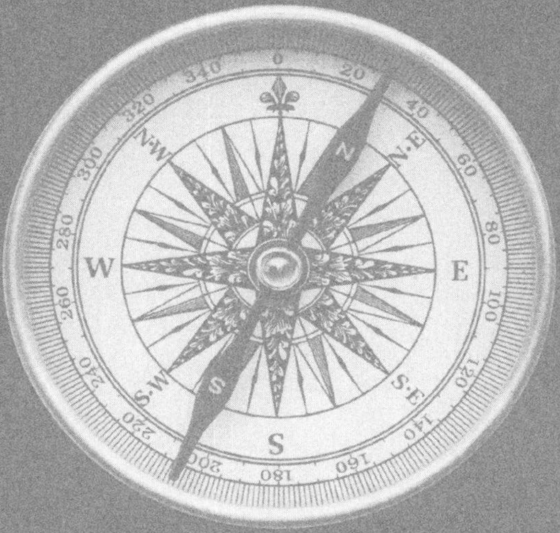
N·W
N·E
W
E
S·W
S·E
S
0
20
40
60
80
100
120
140
160
180
200
220
240
260
280
300
320
340

North Pole
ARCTIC OCEAN
Behring Strait
BEHRING SEA
Aleutian Islands
Alaska
RUSSIAN AMERICA
Arctic Circle
Hudson Bay
GREENLAND
Iceland
NORTH AMERICA
BRITISH AMERICA
Vancouver I.
Columbia R.
Missouri R.
Ohio R.
NEW YORK
UNITED STATES AMERICA
Gulf Stream
Bermuda Is.
Sargasso Sea
GULF OF MEXICO
Cuba
Hayti
Jamaica
CARIBBEAN SEA
Cape St. Lucas
Tropic of Cancer
SANDWICH ISLANDS
NORTH PACIFIC OCEAN
CENTRAL AMERICA
L. Nicaragua
R. Orinoco
VENEZUELA
GUIANA
COLOMBIA
Gilbert Is.
America Is.
Equator
Longitude West from Greenwich
Galapagos Is.
ECUADOR
PERU
Amazon R.
BOLIVIA
SOUTH AMERICA
BRAZIL
OCEANIA
Marquesas Is.
Navigators Is.
Society Is.
Feejee Is.
Friendly or Tonga Is.
Cooks Is.
New Hebrides
New Caledonia
Norfolk I.
Gambier Is.
Tropic of Capricorn
Pitcairn I.
Easter I.
SOUTH PACIFIC OCEAN
Juan Fernandez Is.
ARGENTINE CONFEDERATION
Rio de la Plata
NEW ZEALAND
Humboldt Current
Strait of Magellan
Falkland Is.
Terra del Fuego
C. Horn
South Shetland Is.
Antarctic Circle
Sandwich Land
Georgia I.
Graham Land
South Orkney
ANTARCTIC OCEAN
VICTORIA LAND
Mt. Erebus
South Pole
South Frigid Zone
ATLANTIC OCEAN